After You Say "I Do"

DEVOTIONAL

H. NORMAN WRIGHT

HARVEST HOUSE™ PUBLISHERS

EUGENE, OREGON

Cover by Terry Dugan Design, Minneapolis, Minnesota

AFTER YOU SAY "I DO" DEVOTIONAL

(formerly *Together for Good*)
Copyright © 2000 by H. Norman Wright
Published by Harvest House Publishers
Eugene, Oregon 97402

Library of Congress Cataloging-in-Publication Data
 Wright, H. Norman
   After you say "I do" devotional / H. Norman Wright
      p. cm.
    ISBN 0-7369-0981-8
    1. Marriage. 2. Marriage—Religious aspects—Christianity. I. Title.
 HQ734.W94973   2000
 306.81—dc21   00-024151

Printed in the United States of America.

02 03 04 05 06 07 08 / DP-MS / 10 9 8 7 6 5 4 3 2 1

Vows and Rings

So they are no longer two, but one.
Therefore what God has joined together,
let man not separate.
MATTHEW 19:6

What is your favorite part of a wedding ceremony? Is it the processional? The giving of the bride? The reading of the Scriptures? Saying the "I do's"? The exchange of vows? The pronouncement of "husband and wife"? Is it when the bride and groom kiss? What about the ring exchange?

> This ring I give you, as a symbol and pledge of my constant and abiding love.

> symbol *n.:* Something representing something else by association, especially a material object representing something abstract.

> pledge *n.:* A solemn promise to do or not do something.

Every part of the wedding ceremony has a purpose. The ring exchange tangibly symbolizes the vows we make. The next day, the rings provide the only visible evidence that a wedding ever took place. The rings say to the watching world that each person has taken a vow, that a pledge has been made:

> Will you have _____ to be your wedded (wife/husband) to live with (her/him) after God's commandments in the holy state of marriage, and will you love, honor, and cherish (her/him) so long as you both shall live?

Some people use rings for decoration. Some use rings to communicate status. Others to show wealth. Wedding rings speak of commitment. When a husband or wife wears a wedding ring, he or she tells the world, "I am committed to a person. I have given my life to this person. This person has pledged to love, honor, and cherish me for the rest of our lives together. This person has taken a vow to be faithful, and I, in return, have also vowed to be loving and faithful. This ring is a symbol of love and affection given and received."

Do you remember the vows, pledges, and professions you made on your wedding day? If not, find them and reread them. It will be a great time of renewal.[1]

1

Oneness

*For this reason a man will leave his father
and mother and be united to his wife,
and the two will become one flesh.*
EPHESIANS 5:31

oneness *n.:* 1. The state or quality of being one. 2. Uniqueness: singularity. 3. The condition of being undivided: wholeness. 4. Sameness of character. 5. Agreement: unison.

Oneness captures in a single, pregnant word the overarching goal of a Christian marriage. Oneness marks the summit of marital union. It is the peak toward which we climb. It summarizes scriptural teaching on marriage: "The two will become one."

Oneness is a state of harmony in which the husband and wife lovingly meet each other's needs and fulfill God's purpose for their marriage. Oneness is to make a third entity of two who forsake themselves for each other. It is symbolized by the formula engraved on my wedding band: "1 + 1 = 1." Oneness means that through everything we'll be one.

How can two distinct people from two distinct backgrounds with two different sets of needs, priorities, drives, and motivations make one life together? The difference between a great marriage and a poor marriage is the degree to which each partner is willing to meet the appropriate needs of the other. The secret of oneness lies in the biblical command to deny ourselves, take up our cross, and follow Jesus. To really love someone—anyone—requires denial of self and surrendering ourselves for another. Compromises must be made. Unless we have our cross in hand, these self-denials, sacrifices, and give-and-takes create resentment and bitterness.

When both the husband and wife are committed to sacrificially loving and serving the other, a fantastic oneness—becoming one flesh—occurs.[2]

Have you ever *really* said, "I will give up what I want to meet the needs of my life mate"?

2

50/50 or 100/100?

But God demonstrates His own love toward us,
in that while we were yet sinners, Christ died for us.
ROMANS 5:8 NASB

When two people get married, they have expectations of how the relationship should work. Often the unspoken assumption is that "my spouse will meet me halfway." Sometimes it's called the "50/50 Plan." When the husband and wife operate on this pattern, it's easy for it to spread to other members of the family.[3]

The 50/50 Plan says, "You do your part, and I'll do mine." It sounds logical, but couples who use it may be surprised.

A young man saw an elderly couple sitting down to lunch at McDonald's. He noticed that they had ordered one meal and an extra drink cup. As he watched, the gentleman carefully divided the hamburger in half, then counted out the fries, one for him, one for her, until each had half of them. Then he poured half of the soft drink into the extra cup and set that in front of his wife. The old man then began to eat, and his wife sat watching, with her hands folded in her lap. The young man decided to ask if they would allow him to purchase another meal for them so that they didn't have to split theirs.

The old gentleman said, "Oh, no. We've been married for 50 years, and everything has always been and will be shared 50/50."

The young man then asked the wife if she was going to eat, and she replied, "Not yet. It's his turn with the teeth."

Well, the problem with most 50/50 arrangements is that giving is based on merit and performance. There's a focus more on what the other person is giving than on what we are giving. And how do you ever know if your spouse has met you halfway?

Think about the type of love God gives you. No matter what we do, He gives us 100 percent. As Romans 5:8 shows, He gives us love even when we don't deserve it.

There's a better plan. It's called "The 100/100 Plan." Give 100 percent no matter what your spouse does. It really does work![4]

Communicate

The lips of the wise spread knowledge;
not so the hearts of fools.
PROVERBS 15:7

If you would like to be a couple whom others respect, admire, look to for advice, and consult for solutions, then read on. There is a way for all that to happen. The principle is summed up in one word: *communication*. Communicate according to the wisdom in the book of Proverbs, and others will want to connect with you. What does it mean to communicate this way?

Be someone who is able to give good advice and wisdom. "Plans fail for lack of counsel, but with many advisers they succeed" (Proverbs 15:22).

When you're on the receiving end of your partner's exhortation or reproof, then listen, accept, and evaluate. Don't react. "Wounds from a friend can be trusted, but an enemy multiplies kisses" (Proverbs 27:6). Your spouse is your friend.

If your partner needs guidance, don't run from it. Do it lovingly and sensitively. "He who rebukes a man will in the end gain more favor than he who has a flattering tongue" (Proverbs 28:23). But timing is everything. This is where discernment, patience, and prayer on your part is needed. "A word aptly spoken is like apples of gold in settings of silver" (Proverbs 25:11). You may want to ask one another when the best time is for a "deep" discussion.

Have a sense of humor. Laugh and help each other lighten up. "All the days of the oppressed are wretched, but the cheerful heart has a continual feast" (Proverbs 15:15).

One other guideline is essential. You need this—and so does your spouse. *Be an encourager*. Be a cheerleader. Show your sincere appreciation, and people will want to be around you. "An anxious heart weighs a man down, but a kind word cheers him up" (Proverbs 12:25).

Well, that's the plan. It's workable, and the best place to start putting it into practice is in your marriage.

Words Can
Change Your Life!

Pleasant words are as a honeycomb,
sweet to the mind and healing to the body.
PROVERBS 16:24 AMP

It's early. The alarm just went off. You both wake up, look at one another, and say...

What are the typical "first words" you say to one another in the morning? Is it a grunt, a command, a moan, a complaint, a blank stare? Or are your first words reflective of this proverb?

What do you say to one another as you go your separate ways for the day? Is it a list of tasks to do, a series of reminders, a "now don't forget this again" remark? Or do your departing words echo today's proverb?

> Let's consider a phone call during the day. Is it:
> "Did anything important come in the mail?"
> "I need _____ by dinner tonight."
> "Hi, I called to see how you're doing. I love you."

And what about the greeting you give to one another when you first meet at the end of the work day? Is it a check-up on tasks done or not done, a "where's the mail?" or "what's for dinner?" Or is it a gripe session about the unfairness of children, bosses, and freeways? Is it, "Hi. How are you? I hope you had a good day. I missed you"?

And what about the last words at night before you go to sleep. Or are there any?

Pleasant words set the tone for the day and evening. What you say the first thing in the morning, when you leave one another, when you see each other again, and when you go to bed has a definite life impact.

In *Kingdom of Love,* Hannah Hurnard reflects on the power of love: "Love always, and only, thinks lovely thoughts, so that the minds in which the Lord of Love makes His kingdom become kingdoms of light instead of darkness."[5] Hurnard says this lets people "enjoy a foretaste of the glory and joy of the creative life and work of heaven itself."[6]

Check out your thoughts and your words. Are they pleasant? Remember, the wisdom that is sweet to your soul includes building your marriage with positive, caring, and gentle communication.[7]

Accountability—
Does It Work?

And be subject to one another
in the fear of Christ.
EPHESIANS 5:21 NASB

Back in the 1800s, a husband in a village of Pennsylvania Quakers was beating his wife. The other men in the village decided to take action. One man wrote: "A bunch of us men went over there and took all of his clothes off and drug him through a field of thistles backwards. Then we told him, if he continued to deal unkindly with his wife, we were not going to take to it very lightly. We were going to get upset next time."

Extreme? Perhaps. But being accountable to other people does have many benefits.

Consider today's verse, Ephesians 5:21. Today people don't like the phrase "be subject to one another." The independent "give me my rights" spirit in America conflicts with the idea of being subject to other people.

Accountability helps us in many ways. For one thing, it helps protect us from isolation, from pride, from sin, from giving in to temptation and weakness. One of the best ways to protect ourselves from those weaknesses in our lives is to let people know about them—and ask them to keep us accountable.

Accountability also helps us avoid extremes. Without someone who can give us an objective evaluation of who we are and what we do, we will have a difficult time keeping balance in our lives.

A final benefit is that it helps us stay focused on our goals. It's easy to get so caught up in the details of life that we're not accomplishing what we feel like God called us to do!

Marriage is the best arena for accountability. As you and your spouse face the continuing pressures and stresses of life, it's best to handle life together, not solo. Two can always see more clearly than one. Your spouse can detect blind spots that you may not be able to see.[8]

Blame

You, my brothers, were called to be free.
But do not use your freedom to indulge the sinful nature;
rather, serve one another in love.
GALATIANS 5:13

"Who me?"
"I didn't do it."
"You asked for it."
"I didn't mean to."
"It was your fault. It would never have happened if you..."

Blame is the perpetual projection of responsibility on the other partner. One of the best lines I've heard was an accident report that said, "No one was to blame for the accident, but it never would have happened if the other driver had been alert."

People get away with a lot. An FBI agent embezzled $2,000 from the government, and he blew it all in one afternoon of gambling. He was fired, but then he was reinstated. Why? The court ruled that he had a gambling addiction and was protected under federal law because of his "handicap."

Or what about the man who applied for a job as a park attendant? The park ran a background check, and guess what they discovered? This man had been convicted more than 30 times for indecent exposure and flashing. Naturally, he was turned down. But he followed the new American pastime and sued the park service. After all, he had never flashed in a park—only in libraries and laundromats. You know the outcome. The officials hired him because he had been a victim of job discrimination. These funny but sad examples don't lessen the damage blame causes.

Blaming cripples the atmosphere in a marriage. It tears a couple apart. Too many couples follow the pattern of Adam and Eve and place the responsibility for problems onto the other spouse. Proverbs suggests a better way to live than blaming others: "A man who refuses to admit his mistakes can never be successful. But if he confesses and forsakes them, he gets another chance" (Proverbs 28:13 TLB).[9]

Encouragement
Is a Four-Eyed Fish

Encourage one another and build each other up,
just as in fact you are doing.
1 THESSALONIANS 5:11

Have you ever heard of the four-eyed fish? It's an odd-looking creature to say the least. Native to the equatorial waters of the Western Atlantic region, this fish's technical name is Anableps. (Just don't name one of your children Anableps!) It means "those that look upward" because of the unusual eye structure. This unique creature has two-tiered eyes. The upper and lower halves of each eyeball operate independently and have separate corneas and irises. So, if you were to confront one in its natural habitat, you would see him with his upper eyes protruding above the surface of the water. This helps him search for food as well as identify enemies in the air.

Now remember, this fish also has lower eyes. These stay focused in the water in the typical manner of most fish. On one hand, the fish navigates in the water like other fish. But they have the advantage of seeing what other fish can't see because of the upper eyes. They see in both worlds. If you were like this—having four eyes, two for seeing what actually is and two for seeing what might be—you'd be quite an interesting person.

What would it be like in terms of our marriage relationships? We'd be able to anticipate that our spouses would do their very best. And we would be able to help them along the way by encouraging them.

Encouragers are like prospectors or deep-sea divers looking for hidden treasure. Every person has pockets of underdeveloped resources within him or her. Your task is to search for these pockets in your spouse, discover them, and then expand them. At first what you discover may be rough and imperfect. Talent scouts and scouts for professional sports teams see undeveloped raw talent and ability, but they have the wisdom to see beyond that. They look into the future and see what can happen if all the potential were cultivated and developed. Is this what you do with your spouse?

An Alarm System

Be subject to one another in the fear of Christ.
EPHESIANS 5:21 NASB

One of the tallest skyscrapers in New England is the John Hancock Building in Boston. When this structure of more than 40 floors was built, there were all kinds of problems with the windows. During the stress of the freezing and thawing of the New England winter, the windows actually popped out of their frames and shattered. People walking on the sidewalk below were showered with glass. Businesspeople working at their desks suddenly found themselves seated a few inches from nothing, staring straight down at the street.

The architects and contractors got together and finally decided to install a small alarm system in each window. When the windows began to bulge and contract, the alarm system would let maintenance people know so they could make adjustments that would lessen the tension on the glass before it blew out and shattered.

Every person needs an alarm system that can help him or her relieve the tension before something shatters. One of the best alarm systems in marriage is accountability to each other.

Accountability is a scriptural principle that tells us to "be subject to one another." This means you choose to submit your life to the scrutiny of another person to gain spiritual strength, growth, and balance. Accountability means asking the other person for advice. It means giving the other person the freedom to make honest observations and evaluations about you. It means being teachable and approachable.

Accountability is not an option for those of us who know Christ. It is a crucial ingredient in Christian growth. Do you find the concept of being accountable to another person comfortable or uncomfortable? Why?[10]

The Phantom
of Your Marriage
(Not the Opera)

*Godliness actually is a means of great gain
when accompanied by contentment.*
1 Timothy 6:6 nasb

During World War II, the American forces in France had a phantom military outfit—a group called the Twenty-Third Headquarters Special Troops. With careful staging and show-business theatrics, they impersonated real troops and created an illusion of military strength to strategically fool the Germans. For example, to mask the true location of their real troops, they created fake tanks and other equipment that looked real from the air.

Were you aware that many husbands and wives have phantoms they bring with them into marriage? Their phantoms are mental images they think they need to battle. Their spouses can't see these phantoms; only the individuals who create them are aware of them—but they seem real nevertheless.

A phantom is an unattainable standard by which we measure our performances, abilities, looks, and characteristics. It's good to have a goal to aim for because it gives us motivation. But a phantom is an illusion, an apparition, or only a resemblance to reality.

What's the picture you have of how you should act as a husband or wife? Is this image so perfect, so idyllic that it's unattainable? It may be, but you might be judging your performance by a phantom. And since you cannot meet those standards, what's the result?

The greater the distance your phantom is from reality, the more frustrating it will be to you. You live in its shadow. It may be confusing for your spouse, who is unaware of your phantom. He or she is left wondering why you seem dissatisfied and unhappy. Phantoms can derail marriages.

Why not list the expectations you have for yourself as a husband or wife, then evaluate them? Where did they come from? Which are realistic? Which are not? Have the two of you ever discussed this?[11] Why not set a time to talk about them—and reevaluate them together?

What Did You Cost?

*The LORD your God has chosen you
out of all the peoples on the face of the earth
to be his people, his treasured possession.*
DEUTERONOMY 7:6

You are...a people for God's own possession.
1 PETER 2:9 NASB

What are your possessions worth? Go ahead, take a guess. You may be surprised. Many are amazed today when they itemize what they have. There's a show on television that has no action or violence or plot. "Antique Road Show" is held in a simple, large convention hall. People come to have a possession appraised. Some go away ecstatic; others are dejected.

Possessions of those who are famous or wealthy can grow in value to the point of being priceless. Would you pay $21,000 for Napoleon's toothbrush? I wouldn't. But a collector did—that much for a cruddy, old, used toothbrush. Someone else paid $150,000 for Hitler's car. At the auction of Jackie Kennedy Onassis' personal belongings, someone paid $211,500 for her *imitation* pearls. Were they worth it? No, not really. But they were to someone because they once belonged to someone significant.

If these items had human qualities, like a mind or emotions, they'd probably feel quite good to know that someone wanted them that badly. They would feel special because they were chosen to be special.

You were chosen to be special by your spouse. He or she said, "I want to be with you for the rest of my life. I'm willing to pay a price for you." It feels good to be a special possession, doesn't it?

All of us have been chosen. We are a people for God's own possession. What did we cost? It was a high price. In fact, the ultimate—the blood of Jesus. We were bought with a price, so the next time you look at your partner remember three things: 1) You don't own that person; 2) God does (He owns you, too); and 3) your partner was so valuable God sent His Son to die for him or her (and for you, too).

You're both valued possessions. Remember that and rejoice![12]

Thanking God
for Jesus

But clothe yourself with the Lord Jesus Christ.
ROMANS 13:14 AMP

Here is a prayer for you to read aloud today.

O God, our Father, we thank you that you sent your Son Jesus Christ into this world to be our Saviour and our Lord.

We thank you that he took our body and our flesh and blood upon himself, and so showed us that this body of ours is fit to be your dwelling place.

We thank you that he lived in an ordinary home, that he knew the problems of living together, that he experienced the rough and smooth of family life, and so showed us that any home, however humble, can be a place where in the ordinary routine of daily life we can make all life an act of worship to you.

Lord Jesus, come again to us this day.

Come into our hearts, and so cleanse them, that we, being pure in heart, may see God our Father.

Come into our minds, and so enlighten and illumine them that we may know you who are the way, the truth, and the life.

Touch our lips, that we may speak no word which would hurt another or grieve you.

Touch our eyes, that they may never linger on any forbidden thing.

Touch our hands, that they may become useful with service to the needs of others.

Come when we are sad, to comfort us; when we are tired, to refresh us; when we are lonely, to cheer us; when we are tempted, to strengthen us; when we are perplexed, to guide us; when we are happy, to make our joy doubly dear.

O God, our Father, help us so to live that, whenever your call comes for us, it may find us ready, so that we may enter at last with joy into your nearer presence and into life eternal; through Jesus Christ our Lord. Amen.[13]

The Building
of Trust

*Now faith is being sure of what we hope for
and certain of what we do not see.*
HEBREWS 11:1

Trust me." It's a phrase we either totally believe or totally distrust. Sometimes we say, "I wouldn't trust that person as far as I could throw him!" Trust is a bonding card of any relationship, but especially between husband and wife. It gives us a sense of predictability in our relationships. Abraham knew what trust was. He was "fully persuaded that God had power to do what he had promised" (Romans 4:20,21). But how would you define trust? What does it mean to your spouse? How do you build it?

Trusting someone means you choose to be vulnerable to him or her. Let's look at some of trust's characteristics.

First of all, trust can't be forced. As a couple, each of you has to make the choice to trust the other. It's also a judgment and an attitude. You have to be convinced that your partner is trustworthy. Trust involves risk. It's handing off the power to control something to someone else. If you say you trust your spouse, but then you check up on your mate or supervise what he or she does, that's not trust. If you really trust, you haven't made a back-up plan in case your spouse lets you down. If you do, you're sending a message to your spouse that you don't really trust him or her.

When you trust, there's a cost. It means choosing to step forward with a sign on that says, "Here I am. I'm vulnerable. Please handle me with care." Trust is fragile; it must be protected.

Trust is nothing to play with. It's serious business. As marriage partners, your individual reliability and faithfulness send the message, "I can be trusted." You are a promise keeper just as God is. In fact, if you want to see the ultimate trustworthy person, look at God. He's our model for marriage.[14]

The Heart
of Trust

*"Well done, my good servant!" his master replied.
"Because you have been trustworthy in a very small matter,
take charge of ten cities."*
LUKE 19:17

Couples who live their marital lives with trust have an unshakable faith in one another. Where does this confidence come from? It's simple. It starts with small matters, then intensifies each time an act of trust is honored. It means following through when you say yes to the requests of turning off the washing machine, bringing in papers before the rain hits, picking up the kids at a precise time, and praying for something.

Trust is reflected in another word—"loyalty." If someone is loyal, he or she doesn't bail out when the hard times hit. Loyalty was reflected in your wedding vows: "In sickness or in health." Loyalty survives the tough times. It's saying, "I will be here for you at the worst of times and when everybody else is dumping on you." Our loyalty as married people is to reflect the loyalty of God: "Never will I leave you; never will I forsake you" (Hebrews 13:5).

Trust in marriage grows by consistency. Consistence gives predictability; decisions are not made on impulse, but with careful thought—not based on how we feel at the moment.

Trust is also based upon kept promises. Conditional promises are not promises. It costs to keep a promise. When we give our word, we are duty bound to honor it even when it's hard or costly. Is this the pattern in your marriage?

Honesty is reflected in trust. This necessitates telling the whole truth instead of some of the truth, speaking directly so your spouse doesn't have to mind-read, fill in the blanks, or guess. It also means sharing not only information but also how you feel about it.

Is trust a bit more complicated than you thought? Probably. But the benefits are the best![15]

Love Is...

1 CORINTHIANS 13:1-7,11-13 MSG

If I speak with human eloquence and angelic ecstasy but don't love, I'm nothing but the creaking of a rusty gate.

If I speak God's Word with power, revealing all his mysteries and making everything plain as day, and if I have faith that says to a mountain, "Jump," and it jumps, but I don't love, I'm nothing.

If I give everything I own to the poor and even go to the stake to be burned as a martyr, but I don't love, I've gotten nowhere. So, no matter what I say, what I believe, and what I do, I'm bankrupt without love.

Love never gives up.
Love cares more for others than self.
Love doesn't want what it doesn't have.
Love doesn't strut,
Doesn't have a swelled head,
Doesn't force itself on others,
Isn't always "me first,"
Doesn't fly off the handle,
Doesn't keep score of the sins of others,
Doesn't revel when others grovel,
Takes pleasure in the flowering of truth,
Puts up with anything,
Trusts God always,
Always looks for the best,
Never looks back,
But keeps going to the end....

We don't yet see things clearly. We're squinting in a fog, peering through a mist. But it won't be long before the weather clears and the sun shines bright! We'll see it all then, see it all as clearly as God sees us, knowing him directly just as he knows us!

But for right now, until that completeness, we have three things to do to lead us toward that consummation: Trust steadily in God, hope unswervingly, love extravagantly. And the best of the three is love.

The Silent Marriage

Blessed are you when men hate you,
when they exclude you and insult you
and reject your name as evil, because of the Son of Man.
Rejoice in that day and leap for joy,
because great is your reward in heaven.
For that is how their fathers treated the prophets.
LUKE 6:22,23

Who's the third person in your marriage? The answer is simple. It's Jesus. When two Christians marry, there is someone else present at all times. Yes, *all* times—and there's nothing to be embarrassed about. Who created us the way we are? Nothing is ever a surprise to the Lord.

So...who are the people who know you're a Christian couple? Those at church? That's a given. But what about outside the church? Nowhere does the Word of God tell us to be silent witnesses. Make a list of everyone you know at work, at your kids' activities, and in your neighborhood who might not know about your involvement with Jesus. Did you know the word "witness" comes from the concept of martyr? Martyrs never kept their mouths closed.

Many people today live as silent witnesses. They say, "We don't talk about our faith all that much. We live it. It's a bit uncomfortable saying, 'I'm a Christian.' So we just live it out." Part of that is great—living it out. But some are so silent no one knows they are witnesses!

Can you think of anyone you need to tell this week about your faith in Christ? There's someone around you who's in need of knowing. Why not take that list you made and use it as a prayer list? Ask the Lord to give you an opportunity to share Jesus with them. And when you do, be sure you let them know what He's done for you in your marriage. Tell them and let them see it.

Be a vocal witness!

What Do You Remember About Your Parents?

*Grace and peace to you from God our Father
and the Lord Jesus Christ. I thank my God
every time I remember you.*
PHILIPPIANS 1:2,3

What do you remember most about your parents? Have you thanked God for what you remember about them?

We all have some negative memories of our childhoods. Some have good cause to remember their childhood pain, but sometimes it seems there's an epidemic of parent blaming these days. Here's a way to balance the difficult times with positive memories of hope. Use these questions as a sharing springboard for you and your mate:

- Where did you go on vacation? What did you do?
- What did you enjoy doing with your dad most? With your mom?
- What smells remind you of dad and mom?
- What was your favorite room in your house?
- What was your favorite family tradition?
- What were the family jokes?
- What special phrases or nicknames did your family invent?
- What was your favorite Christmas? Why?
- What was your favorite birthday? Why?
- What problems did your parents help you through as a teenager?
- What did other people think about your parents?
- What values from your childhood are you trying to pass along to your children?
- What did you learn from your parents about God?

As you think about these questions, thank God for the good memories and the power they have to influence your own home's strengths and stability. You may want to write some of your positive thoughts down and consider sending them to your parents. It's a practical and tangible way to let them know how much you appreciate them.[16]

What's Working in Your Marriage?

If anything is excellent or praiseworthy—
think about such things.
PHILIPPIANS 4:8

If I held a marriage seminar with 100 couples and asked everyone: "What are the problems and difficulties in your marriage?" what do you think would be the outcome after everyone shared? There would be a dark cloud of doom and despair over all of us. Everyone would probably leave discouraged and without hope. I also doubt if many would benefit from the time together. I'm not suggesting that we overlook or ignore the problems—but there are better ways to solve them.

If I were to ask every couple to share what is working for them, what a different atmosphere and outcome we would have following the meeting! Couples would be encouraged and challenged by what they heard. They would have discovered new ways of revitalizing their own marriages.

Attitude and approach makes a huge difference. In baseball, for example, even the best hitters fall into hitting slumps. They try and try to break out of it. Many will get videos of themselves batting to see what they can learn. The videos they select will make a major difference. Some will look at videos taken when they're in the slump. They watch their worst performances, thinking that if they focus on this they can learn what they're doing wrong and correct it. Unfortunately, this doesn't work very well. Others select older videos that show them in a hitting streak, doing fantastically. They watch and observe what they were doing that worked. Soon, they're able to get back to that level because they concentrated on what was working.

Marriage isn't all that different. The best step any couple can take to solve problems is to focus on what is working. I'm sure there are many times when you and your spouse get along. Can you describe specifically what you and your spouse do differently during the good times? Think about it. Identify it. Use it to keep on track.

Romance—Yes!

[Love] always protects, always trusts,
always hopes, always perseveres.
1 CORINTHIANS 13:7

Bill and Pam Farrel share the following insights about romance.

Just what is romance? Is it flowers and candlelight? Unhurried time together? Cozy snuggling? Maybe. Is it a quiet walk on the beach or a leisurely stroll through the forest? Is it an adventurous date spent parasailing and scuba diving? Maybe. Is it a cup of espresso by the fire or sparkling cider on the dance floor? Is it red-and-black satin lingerie—or pristine white lace and cotton? Maybe. Romance is personal. Romance is all about each other's loves, likes, and preferences. That is why romance is unique to each couple....

Good connections. That's what love is all about. A connection between two hearts. And we can strengthen that by strengthening it strand by strand. When we built our home, I helped prepare the wiring for the electrical outlets and switches. In each electrical cable were strands of different colors. Each had to be prepared for a strong connection. In the same way, we need to carefully maintain each strand of our love for a strong connection between hearts....

In the blockbuster movie hit *Twister,* there is a thrilling scene where the main characters go on the ride of their lives. The two scientists are chasing a tornado when the tornado suddenly turns toward them. Seeking lifesaving shelter the two dart into a water shed. There, the man spots pipes that go at least 30 feet into the ground. He frantically suggests they strap themselves together, then strap themselves to the pipes. They do this just in time for the tornado to settle upon the shed. The shed gets pulverized around them as the two are lifted off the ground. They stare right into the eye of the tornado—yet they survive. They were strapped to the anchor—the pipes that held them safely in the midst of the twister. That is a picture of what knowing God personally can do for a couple in love. God can be a sure anchor, a protection for your love—no matter what twister life may send your way God can and will hold you heart to heart.[17]

What's Your
View of God?

[Moses replied,] "May it be according to your word,
that you may know that there is no one like the LORD our God."
EXODUS 8:10 NASB

If you were asked to describe God, what would you say about Him? Where did you learn about who He is and how He operates this world that He created and sovereignly rules over?

Children are the best to give us glimpses of how we used to think or, for some of us, how we still think. Here are some sayings attributed to children writing to pastors:

"Dear Pastor, I know God loves everybody, but he never met my sister."

"Dear Minister, I would like to bring my dog to church on Sunday. She is only a mutt, but she is a good Christian."

"I would like to read the Bible, but I would read it more if they would put it on TV."

"Dear Pastor, I would like to go to heaven someday because I know my big brother will not be there."

A father overheard his young daughters talking during a thunderstorm one day. The older daughter said matter-of-factly, "That thunder you just heard is God moving His furniture."

The younger daughter nodded her head like she understood and looked out the window at the pouring rain for a minute before she replied: "Yes, He just moved His waterbed, too."

What are your notions about God? Some of us view Him as a giant policeman up there with a club, while others see Him as a loving grandfather figure. But God is so much more than these. He's infinite. He's sovereign. He is to be feared and worshiped and loved.

Once again, what's your view of God, and where did you get it?[18] What's your partner's view? What have you learned about God since you've been married?

Pray As a Couple

And when He arrived at the place, He said to them,
"Pray that you may not enter into temptation."
And He withdrew from them about a stone's throw, and He knelt
down and began to pray, saying, "Father, if Thou art willing, re-
move this cup from Me; yet not My will, but Thine be done."
LUKE 22:40-42 NASB

Have you ever prayed "Not my will, but Yours"? It goes counter to what our society teaches. It goes against "me first" and "I'm in control of my life." But as Christians we are people who pray. Think about these words from George Burrick:

> Imagine life to be like a woven rug. Science sees the patterned threads from the earthbound side of the frame, not in their weaving but only when they have been woven, and traces their regularities. Great art in music and drama stands likewise, and glories in the color and imagination of the design. But prayer stands with the Weaver as He works. The Weaver says in graciousness: "You shall help me in prayer and thought and labor, though for your own good I still must guide. Some of your wishes shall be granted, for through the granting you shall more surely learn: and I will still guide. Some of your wishes cannot be granted. When the design is complete, and you can see it from the other side of time, you will understand. And your best prayer is still the prayer of Christ, 'Not my will, but...' "

As a couple pray this prayer together:

> I surrender to you my hopes,
> my dreams,
> my ambitions.
> Do with them what you will, when you will, as you will.
> I place into your loving care
> my family,
> my friends,
> my future.
> Care for them with a care that I can never give.
> I release into your hands
> my need to control,
> my craving for status,
> my fear of obscurity....
> For Jesus' sake, amen.[19]

—Richard Foster

The Friendship
of Marriage

Love (God's love in us) does not insist on its own rights.
1 CORINTHIANS 13:5 AMP

What love helps a marriage last? You may be surprised because I'm not going to begin with *agape*, which is what most people expect. I'm starting with another kind of love—friendship love. In a national study of hundreds of couples who had fulfilling marriages, couples were given 39 factors that would best explain the success of their marriages and why they were successful. Both husbands and wives were asked to put these factors in order of importance for their marriages. The fascinating fact was that the top 7 selected by both husbands and wives were the same. The first and second choices reflect the type of love we're considering here. They were: "My spouse is my best friend" and "I like my spouse as a person."[20]

This love is called *phileo*. In the Bible, *philos* means friendship love. Romantic love cannot sustain a relationship, but companion or friendship love can. A friend is someone you like to be with. You enjoy his or her company; you like his or her personality; you can play and work together well. You have shared interests. It's not that you are loved only because of what you share, but by sharing you develop a different kind of love that means companionship, communication, and cooperation. One writer describes it as "companionate love":

> This may be defined as a strong bond, including a tender attachment, enjoyment of the other's company and friendship. It is not characterized by wild passion and constant excitement, although these feelings may be experienced from time to time. The main difference between passionate and companionate love is that the former thrives on deprivation, frustration, a high arousal level, and absence. The latter thrives on contact and requires time to develop and mature.[21]

How is the friendship factor in your marriage?

Nicknames from
the Past

He who mocks the poor shows contempt for their Maker.
PROVERBS 17:5

Dennis Rainey shares the effect of rejection in a person's life:

When I was in first grade, a few friends and I began to choose who would be "in" and who would be "out." One of the first "outs" was Lois. She came from a poor family and couldn't dress as well as the others. She was also slow in class, which didn't help. So we quickly excluded her.

The "in" group rejected Lois as a person—slowly at first, but ruthlessly as the years passed. By the time we reached high school, she was the butt of countless jokes. When we were seniors, she had such an inferiority complex that I don't recall seeing her look up from the floor that entire year.

Years later I recognized my false values and my haughty, foolish evaluation of Lois. I wept when I thought about my cruelty to her. I asked God to forgive me for my arrogant, childish behavior. She was made in the image of God every bit as much as I was.

Peers can have poisoning tongues. William Hazlitt wrote, "A nickname is the hardest stone the devil can throw at a man." Some never forget the names they have been called.

Here are a few nicknames we've come across: Dummy, Pit-i-ful Paul, Messy, Fatso, Peewee, Runt, Brick-Brain, Ornery, Grasshopper Brain, Yo-Yo, Troublemaker, Slow Learner, Bones, Motor-Mouth, Sloppy, Sleepy, Devil's Daughter, Nerd, Turkey, Lardo, Bird Legs, Space Cadet, Rebellious, Simple Sally, Buzzard-Beak, Metal-Mouth, Freckle-Face, Weirdo, and Geek. Names like these can really hurt.

The way your mate views himself today was heavily influenced by his peers as he grew up. Even today, your mate may be very peer-dependent. He may self-consciously wonder if he's wearing "just the right" outfit or using "just the right" lingo. He may doubt his ability to relate to your friends.

Remember, you are a mirror to your mate. You can still stop those condemning voices from his or her past by replacing them with positive words in the present.[22]

Someone Is Watching You

Keep your behavior excellent among the Gentiles,
so that in the thing in which they slander you as evildoers,
they may on account of your good deeds, as they observe them,
glorify God in the day of visitation.
1 PETER 2:12 NASB

You're being watched. It's true. People are watching your life. Others are checking you out. They want to see if what you say matches up with what you do. They want to see if being a Christian makes any difference in what happens in your marriage.

Peter has four suggestions for you as individuals and as married couples. First, he says to live a clean life. Don't get involved in "fleshly lusts." If you do this, you'll get negative attention. You'll stand out.

Second, don't do anything that gives other people the opportunity to slander you. As Christians, we need to live in such a way that when others say something bad about us it won't be believed. Silent integrity does more than deny charges.

Third, do some good deeds for non-Christians. They need your help, and they need your Jesus. The story of the Good Samaritan sticks with us since it involves helping a stranger. Remember, others are noticing your good deeds—not just your words.

Fourth, never forget you're being observed. Warren Wiersbe tells a story that illustrates this:

> In the summer of 1805, a number of Indian chiefs and warriors met in council at Buffalo Creek, New York, to hear a presentation of the Christian message by a Mr. Cram from the Boston Missionary Society. After the sermon, a response was given by Red Jacket, one of the leading chiefs. Among other things, the chief said...

> Brother, we are told that you have been preaching to the white people in this place. These people are our neighbors. We are acquainted with them. We will wait a little while and see what effect your preaching has upon them. If we find it does them good, makes them honest and less disposed to cheat Indians, we will then consider again what you have said.[23]

Watch the Tongue

Death and life are in the power of the tongue,
and those who love it will eat its fruit.
PROVERBS 18:21 NASB

If you've ever been to a major league baseball game or watched one on TV, you've probably seen the following:

The major league baseball pitcher takes his warm-up throws. When the first batter steps up to the plate, the first pitch sails over the catcher's head and slams into the screen. The next one hits the dirt and bounces up, almost hitting the batter in the back.

Now the batter is shaken, and he finally steps up to the plate. After three swings at the missile burning across the plate at 90 miles an hour, he's glad he's out of there. This pitcher was a loose cannon.

Ryne Duren, former pitcher for the New York Yankees, liked to intimidate batters like that. He was known as the patron saint of the "psych out." He knew how to mentally harass opposing batters, "dusting them off" with an assortment of wildly launched pitches that left them terrified.

Unfortunately, words are sometimes hurled like that in the home. Instead of a baseball, we launch hurtful, intimidating words at each other, inflicting fear, pain, and guilt. We learn what the wise man meant when he said death is in the power of the tongue.

Winston Churchill was a master with the power of the tongue. Once, after he had too much to drink, his spiteful opponent, Lady Astor, said to him, "Mr. Prime Minister, I perceive you are drunk." Churchill smiled and replied, "Yes, Lady Astor, and you are ugly. But tomorrow I shall be sober."

Even though you may be this skillful with a sharp remark, what do you gain when you make such statements? Scripture warns that those who love to use the power of the tongue destructively will "eat its fruits." Often, those fruits are resentment, discord and revenge. It's true they hurt others; but they also poison relationships.[24]

How's the communication in your marriage? Your tongues could be used to build up one another. It's a much better way.

Marriage Thoughts

As for me, far be it from me that I should sin against
the LORD by failing to pray for you. And I will teach you
the way that is good and right.
1 SAMUEL 12:23

Read these out loud to each other meditatively. One of you read a point and the other make a comment. Then reverse roles. Continue until you have read and commented on each idea. Conclude in prayer.

- God has given couples no greater gift than the ability to laugh at life together. The joy of sharing humorous secrets and private jokes breathes energy into a marriage.

- Some walls are visible, most are not. Most walls are constructed in the mind. When walls go up in marriage, someone is hurting.

- You and I have no greater need than the need to feel wanted. Each of us longs to be significant. We yearn for a sense of being valuable to our mates for who we are.

- If simple chores are left undone, it may also be that important matters—like time spent with the children—are being left undone. To succeed at work but fail at home is to fail.

- Nothing our spouses can do for us can touch us so deeply as faithfully praying for us day after day—long after another person would have moved on to something new.

- When we pray for each other, our hearts become softer and more forgiving toward our mates. It is impossible to hate others when we're earnestly praying for them.

- It is easier to pray *for* each other than to pray *with* each other. To pray with each other is a brave step toward intimacy.

- When a husband and wife wear wedding rings, they tell the world, "I am committed to a person. This person has taken a vow to be faithful and I, in return, have also vowed to be loving and faithful."

- Without maintenance, the estate of marriage can crumble.

- Happy couples don't feel they have to perform to be loved.[25]

Are You Mature?

To sum up, all of you be harmonious, sympathetic, brotherly,
kindhearted, and humble in spirit; not returning evil for evil,
or insult for insult, but giving a blessing instead; for you were
called for the very purpose that you might inherit a blessing.
1 PETER 3:8,9 NASB

Would you say you're a mature person? Most of us would. Peter, in today's passage, gives us some checkpoints for maturity. Only he's talking about spiritual maturity.

Let's consider these as they apply to marriage.

The first one is unity or "let all be harmonious." Is there a oneness of heart, a similarity of purpose and harmony in your relationship? We're called to live this way with other believers, even those to whom we're married.

Mutual interest is the next checkpoint. "Sympathetic" means when your spouse is weeping, you weep. When he or she rejoices, you rejoice. There is no competition, envy, or jealousy between you. When your spouse gets the attention or the raise or the promotion, you rejoice with him or her.

Friendship and affection are found in the admonition "let all be brotherly." Friends give comfort during a time of need. They reach out rather than wait to be called.

"Kindhearted" is another checkpoint for spiritual maturity. How could you demonstrate kindness toward one another this week?

The next one is humility. You let others give you the praise rather than giving it to yourself. Humility means no self-promotion or spotlighting yourself.

Now the last one, "don't return evil for evil," translates into "be willing to forgive." How do you know if forgiveness has occurred? Well, if you've forgiven your partner, you won't try to strike back or get even. You'll restrain from saying anything ugly in return. You'll do something good for your spouse, whether you think they deserve it or not. Remember that you've been called to endure harsh treatment.

It may be easier to reflect these traits of spiritual maturity with others you don't know as well, but the real test comes in marriage.[26]

You Can
Get Along

Get rid of all bitterness, rage and anger, brawling and slander, along with every form of malice. Be kind and compassionate to one another, forgiving each other, just as in Christ God forgave you.
EPHESIANS 4:31,32

Getting along with others is not always the easiest task. It not only takes work, it requires the absence of four different spirits.

The *competitive spirit*. Whenever there are several people involved in any task, it's important to work together. You get much more accomplished when you function as partners rather than competitors. This is difficult for some because many of us were raised to be competitors, and we live in a competitive society. When you're competitive you look out for yourself, disparage the successes of others, and focus on winning rather than on serving others. It's possible, however, to do your best and live a life of excellence without it being at the expense of others, especially your partner.

The *critical spirit* destroys not only others but the person possessing it. Often it comes from either being overly critical of ourselves or from being a perfectionist. No matter the reason, it's not a good way to live. God's Word says, "Therefore let us stop passing judgment on one another. Instead, make up your mind not to put any stumbling block or obstacle in your brother's way" (Romans 14:13).

Some people struggle with a *vain spirit*. We're enamored with ourselves; our calling in life seems to be to impress others. We love to look in the mirror. Our goal is to capture people's attention and live off their applause. When this spirit overtakes us, it's difficult to reflect the presence of Jesus in our lives. The two can't live together.

The last spirit is very destructive. It's the *adversarial spirit*. When we're at odds with another person and feelings linger, bitterness and resentment come into play. Perhaps resentment has seeped into your marriage. In marriage we're called to be allies. God's Word tells us there's a better way to live. Go back and read today's Scripture again. Let the spirit of these two verses indwell your heart and run your life.[27]

You're a Gap-Filler

It is not good for the man to be alone.
I will make a helper suitable for him.
GENESIS 2:18

The first time God said something was not good, it had to do with man being alone. God created Adam isolated in the garden; he had no human counterpart. So God created a woman to meet his need for intimacy. In the original text, the Hebrew word for "suitable helper" means "one matching him." Adam needed someone who could complement him because he was incomplete by himself. This is one of the purposes of marriage: *to complete one another.*

Remember the original *Rocky* film? Sylvester Stallone was the main character. In this film he had a love relationship with a woman named Adrian. She was a little wallflower who worked in the pet shop. She was the sister of Pauly, an insensitive guy who worked at the meat house. His goal in life was to become a debt collector for a loan shark. He was a real winner!

Pauly couldn't understand why Rocky was attracted to Adrian. "I don't see it," he said. "What's the attraction?"

Do you remember Rocky's answer? The scriptwriters came up with not only a great response, but one that reflects Genesis 2. Rocky said, "I don't know, fills gaps I guess."

"What gaps?"

"She's got gaps; I got gaps. Together we fill gaps."

In his simple but profound way, Rocky expressed it well. He said that he and Adrian each had empty places in their lives. But when the two of them got together, they filled those blank spots in one another. And that's exactly what God did when He fashioned a helpmate suitable for Adam. She filled his empty places, and he filled hers.

What are the gaps the two of you are filling in your marriage? Thank God for what your partner is filling up.[28]

Are You Sleeping
with the Enemy?

For our struggle is not against flesh and blood.
EPHESIANS 6:12

A lot of jokes picture marriage as a battlefield. *MS* magazine once advised: "Marriage is the only war where you sleep with the enemy." I would rather picture the entire world as the true battlefield and your marriage as being God's smallest battle formation for winning the war. In truth, your marriage is taking place on a spiritual battlefield, not a romantic balcony. Every married couple needs to understand the following biblical principle:

Your mate is not your enemy.

Picture your marriage as two people joined together in a foxhole, cooperating in a battle against a common enemy. Take a good look at your own foxhole. Are you fighting the enemy or each other? As a friend of ours told me, "I was so busy standing up in the foxhole duking it out with my husband that I had no time to be involved in fighting against the real enemy."

Keep in mind that whenever you declare war on your mate, ultimately you are opposing God Himself. You are rejecting the person He provided to complete you, to meet your needs.

Here's a practical test to discover if you view your mate as an enemy or as a fellow soldier. Do you focus on the negative in your mate or on the positive? When you marry, you're so caught up in your new spouse that he or she can seem to do no wrong. But within 12,000 miles or 12 months, whichever comes first, you reverse the process. You are now so focused on what your mate does wrong that you are oblivious to what he or she does right!

I love Robert Louis Stevenson's exhortation for us as we look at our spouses. He says, "Make the most of the best and the least of the worst."[29]

A Morning Person

In the morning, O LORD, you hear my voice.
PSALM 5:3

Are you a morning person, or are you married to one? You know what they're like. They wake up bright-eyed and bushy-tailed at 6:00 A.M. (or earlier). They're ready to face the day and can't wait to start talking—even before coffee!

Some of us are just not wired that well for morning. You may feel the day should begin at 10:00, not 6:00! Sometimes people that are early-morning "alerts" are insensitive to their partners and need to heed the admonition of Proverbs: "If you shout a pleasant greeting to a friend too early in the morning, he will count it as a curse!" (27:14 TLB).

Whether you fit the 6:00 crew or the 10:00, keep in mind there is something good that can come out of the morning: time alone with God. That's what David did in today's psalm, and it's mentioned other times in the Scripture as well.

> Evening, morning, and noon I cry out in distress, and he hears my voice (Psalm 55:17).

> But I cry to you for help, O LORD; in the morning my prayer comes before you (Psalm 88:13).

> Because of the LORD's great love we are not consumed, for his compassions never fail. They are new every morning; great is your faithfulness (Lamentations 3:22,23).

Is there a better way to begin your day? Not really. If you're feeling down and the day looks dim and dreary, make a choice to look *up*. You'll be amazed at what you'll see!

Me? Irritated?
Frustrated?

But he who has a glad heart has a continual feast
[regardless of circumstances].
PROVERBS 15:15 AMP

*I*rritation. It's like a splinter that makes your finger hurt every time you touch it. It's like a rock with a jagged edge inside your shoe cutting into the bottom of your foot every time you take a step. It comes out in the expressions on our faces and the tones of our voices. It sounds like a cat yowling because it can't get to its food or go outside.

Irritation often happens when we're frustrated because we can't get our way, which happens often when we're married! Let's face it. We won't always be able to do what we want when we want, when we're married. We won't always be able to watch the TV program we want or make love as often as we want. Welcome to Life 101.

Here's a formula to keep in mind: *The higher the level of our desire to be perfect and/or be in control, the higher the potential to be frustrated and irritated.* It's not a good way to live life—or experience marriage for that matter.

Irritation and frustration don't come from the outside. They come from the inside. They're windows into our inner emotional lives. It's not our circumstances or what others do that's the problem. All these things do is trigger what's already residing inside of us. If we're frustrated and irritated much of the time (and especially with our loved ones), it could be there's something we haven't dealt with in our past, something we're afraid to face (and we're running from), something we haven't yet identified or won't admit. Whatever it is, some questions to consider are: "Do irritation and frustration give a person what he or she wants in life? Do they convey Christ's love to others?" If not, then why keep responding this way? God has freed us to learn to accept, adjust, relax, and enjoy Him. If we do, we can enjoy others—especially our spouses.

Satisfying Sex

I am my beloved's, and his desire is for me.
SONG OF SOLOMON 7:10 NASB

Joyce and Cliff Penner have written numerous books about sex, worked with thousands of couples, and conducted seminars on sex for 25 years. Dr. Neil Clark Warren asked them for their recommendations to help couples have mutually satisfying sexual relationships. Here are some of them as well as their suggestions. Discuss these (but not in front of the kids!).

- Since the man is never truly satisfied unless the woman is, he has to shift his results orientation to her process orientation; he has to learn to soak in and enjoy the music.
- Since a man's need for connection is not felt like a woman's, we recommend you go her way.
- A woman needs to learn how to take.
- Each of you is responsible for the pleasure you are able to give and receive in any sexual experience.
- The woman must be free to lead in the sexual experience.
- For the greater pleasure and sexual satisfaction, the man learns to listen to and follow the lead of his wife during sex.
- The formula: The husband adores his wife; his affirmation ignites her passion and she invites him sexually.
- Here is the positive feedback system for married life. As you adore her and she invites you, mutual affirmation will flow.
- Each of you has the responsibility to allow the other to find sexual fulfillment.
- Anticipation, not spontaneity, is the key to passion.
- You cannot be expected to fulfill your biblical responsibilities for sex in marriage until you have healed from your past.[1]

These are just a few of their suggestions. There are many more in their book *Men and Sex*. Why not get a copy and read it together?

The Rhythm
of Your Marriage

Wives, submit to your husbands as to the Lord....
Husbands, love your wives, just as Christ loved
the church and gave himself up for her.
EPHESIANS 5:22,25

Marriage is more than a set of rules and roles. It's true that you need to work out who does what and when. It's also true that there must be some division of labor. It's true that you need to discover who has the capability and giftedness in certain areas. There are many couples who have all of the above worked out, but the way they function is still awkward. They don't work together as a team, but as two disjointed individuals.

Headship and submission are two areas that create tension for many couples. Dr. Larry Crabb says:

> A really good marriage has the feel of a man and woman blending together into natural movement where individuality is obviously present but really isn't the point, something perhaps like dance partners of many years who anticipate each other's steps with practiced ease.
>
> The rhythm of the music and the dancers' movements are two separate ingredients, and although it's clear that one directs the other, you don't sense that the dancers are working hard to keep in step with the music. The rhythm is *in* them; they move with it naturally, effortlessly, with every movement fitting the music because the music is part of them.
>
> Learning how headship and submission actually work in a marriage is sometimes as clumsy as an inexperienced teenager learning to dance. There are rules to follow, there are roles that lay out the steps to take, but neither rules nor roles creates the awareness of rhythm that makes for good dancing.
>
> There is a rhythm in relationship, a rhythm that can only be heard as the great truths about God are played over and over again.[2]

How's the rhythm of your marriage?

The Great Pursuit

My dove in the clefts of the rock, in the hiding places
on the mountainside, show me your face, let me hear your voice;
for your voice is sweet, and your face is lovely.
SONG OF SONGS 2:14

Have you noticed that the lovers in Songs are rarely depicted together? Their drama is less about the consummation of love than the zigzagging journey toward it. In one scene, they're in hot pursuit, inviting the other to "come away with me." In the next, they're coy, reluctant to answer the door.

In chapter 3, the beloved can't find her lover even though she desperately searches. You can probably remember a similar experience: "Why isn't she answering the phone?" "Have I lost him?" Later you realized this was exactly what your spouse had in mind.

Silly love games? Yes—and no. "That's the way we are made," explains Dr. James Dobson. "Most of us want what we have to stretch for—what we can only dream about achieving. We are excited by a challenge, by that which is mysterious and elusive."

So how do we keep the pursuit alive?

This is one of the places where marriages often break down. One or both partners decide their spouse is now a known commodity, no longer a mystery to discover or a prize to win. Maybe one of us has made matters worse by smothering the other, giving him or her little incentive or room to pursue.

The longer we've been married, the more proficient we need to become at the art of pursuit and invitation. Ask: "How long has it been since I stepped back and noticed some new tender shoot trying to surface in my partner's soul?" We'll nearly always find those new shoots if we look for them, and it's crucial that *we* be the one to explore it and delight in it with our partners.

The point is not to play games or to make one another insecure. We need not always be either in pursuit mode or in retreat. But each marriage needs to find a romantic rhythm that works, one where each person feels wanted and has the chance to want.[3]

Honor Each Other

Show proper respect to everyone: Love the brotherhood
of believers, fear God, honor the king.
1 PETER 2:17

How do you respond to the following questions:

- Do you honor one another?
- What is your honor based upon?
- What does it mean to honor one another?

These three questions ought to keep you talking for a while. Perhaps we need to begin with honor. We use the word, but what are we saying? The word "honor" in Greek means "to highly value, to prize, to not take lightly, to esteem, to give weight to, and to ascribe worth." When you look at the Scripture, you find that the word "glory" in the Old and New Testament often has the same definition as honor.

Scripture gives three levels of honor that are used with people. One level is based on performance, another is based on character, but the top level is intrinsic honor. What's that? It's the honor possessed by God Himself. And He gives it to each one of us. It's actually an attribute of God, but He passed it on to us by creating us in His image. Isn't that something?

Perhaps you've prayed, "Lord, we honor You" or "We give honor to You." And we are to honor God. But we're also to honor one another. It's nothing our spouses earn—it's to be a free gift.

Now, if you thought the first three questions were hard, wait until you hear these:

- Can you describe how you are "highly valuing" your partner?
- Can you describe how you "prize" your partner?
- What is one way that you don't take your partner lightly?
- How are you ascribing worth to one another?[4]

What About
Tomorrow?

Why, you do not even know what will happen tomorrow.
What is your life? You are a mist that appears for a little while
and then vanishes. Instead, you ought to say, "If it is the Lord's
will, we will live and do this or that."
JAMES 4:14,15

What happened in the yesterdays of your life that are significant? Think about it for a minute. In the past 20 years, what are the three most significant events of your life? Of your marriage? How did they impact you? How did they affect you spiritually? Often we get caught up in remembering the past a bit too much, and get we stuck there. We spend too much time experiencing the past good times, especially if the present is kind of ho-hum. But sometimes it pays to stop and take stock of the past in order to set a course in the present.

James has an unnerving message for each of us: Life in the future is uncertain. What we have to look forward to is not the certainty of the events of the past, but the inevitability of the unexpected occurring in the future. In fact, the best-case scenario that you could imagine could occur as easily as the worst-case scenario. Life is uncertain. That's nothing new. It has always been that way.

Life is also short and challenging. We're not to live in fear of the future or to constantly ask, "What if?" Facing the future with our spouses makes it less threatening. The way Chuck Swindoll puts James 4:14,15 in perspective is great.

> *Life is challenging.* Because it is short, life is packed with challenging possibilities. Because it is uncertain it's filled with challenging adjustments. I'm convinced that's much of what Jesus meant when He promised us an abundant life. Abundant with challenges, running over with possibilities, filled with opportunities to adapt, shift, alter, and change. Come to think of it, that's the secret of staying young. It is also the path that leads to optimism and motivation.[5]

You as a couple have challenges awaiting you in the future. Face them and rejoice.

The Ministry
of Marriage

You are the light of the world....Let your light so shine before men.
MATTHEW 5:14,16 AMP

In marriage, two people accept a ministry. The first ministry of marriage is to each other—to help each other grow emotionally, socially, intellectually, and spiritually in a journey to become what God has gifted each person to be. Marriage partners grow emotionally by learning to give and receive care and nurture. They grow socially by learning all the little skills—listening, compromise, communication, conflict resolution—that make it possible to live with someone else, skills that readily translate into relationships in the larger world. They learn intellectually by sharing and testing ideas. They learn spiritually by praying for and with each other, by participating in a community of faith together, by working together in service.

If they are faithful to their first ministry, couples are ready for a second ministry of marriage—ministry to children. The arrival of children almost always puts a strain on a marriage, so only if partners have learned what it means to love unselfishly can they support each other as parents.

The third ministry of marriage is to the community of faith. It takes a lot of work for two people to get a marriage to the point where they have something to offer as a couple to others. Two people who haven't worked on the first ministries of their marriage, ministering to each other and to their children, are like an empty cup offered to a thirsty world. They have nothing to offer others.

How does this relate to you? If you and your spouse have worked on your first ministries, it's likely you'll have something to offer to your church, your community, and your world.

The fourth ministry of marriage is to the world. Sometimes this ministry takes the form of organized, formal outreach projects to serve a broken world. This is an important part of the path to spiritual connectedness, part of the journey to becoming soul mates.[6]

Praying Together

Be unceasing in prayer.
1 Thessalonians 5:17 AMP

Charles and Martha Shedd shared their experience in learning to pray together.

> We would sit on our rocking loveseat. We would take turns telling each other things we'd like to pray about. Then holding hands we would pray each in our own way, silently.
>
> This was the beginning of prayer together that lasted. Naturally, through the years we've learned to pray in every possible way, including aloud. Anytime, anywhere, every position, every setting, in everyday language. Seldom with "thee" or "thou." Plain talk. Ordinary conversation. We interrupt, we laugh, we argue, we enjoy. We hurt together, cry together, wonder together. Together we tune our friendship to the Friend of friends.
>
> Do we still pray silently together? Often. Some groanings of the spirit go better in the silence.
>
> > "I've been feeling anxious lately and I don't know why. Will you listen while I tell you what I can? Then let's pray about the known and unknown in silence."
> >
> > "This is one of my super days. So good. Yet somehow I can't find words to tell you. Let's thank the Lord together in the quiet."
>
> Negatives, positives, woes, celebrations, shadowy things—all these, all kinds of things we share in prayer. Aloud we share what we can. Without the vocals we share those things not ready yet for words.
>
> Why would this approach have the feel of the real? Almost from the first we knew we'd discovered an authentic new dimension.
>
> In becoming best friends with each other, we were becoming best friends with the Lord.
>
> And the more we sought his friendship, the more we were becoming best friends with each other.[7]

Integrity

If you must choose, take a good name rather than great riches;
for to be held in loving esteem is better than silver and gold.
PROVERBS 22:1 TLB

Imagine for a moment that you're on a major TV quiz show, and you're on a winning streak. One question to go and you make it to the top. The question is asked; you give the answer. It's correct! You've done it! But all of a sudden the announcer says, "We have one more question for you." You're shocked. It shows on your face. But the announcer goes on. "You've won, but now you've got a choice of prizes. You can have all this wealth—the money, the boat, the new car, the European trip—or you can have integrity. Which do you want?" Silence. Dead silence. You may even look at your spouse. But he or she can't help. Perhaps you're wondering now which you would take. You may even ask, "Why not both?" But if you had to choose, which one would it be?

That may be a tough decision for you, especially as you look at the bills, the house, what the kids need, and so on. We all have a need for money. Much of it is justified. But sometimes we place too high a value on wealth and moving up.

Think for a moment: Does wealth bring us closer to God? Or might we tend to drift away? Does it cause us to move closer together as a couple or create distance? It's easier to become enamored with our own ability when we're financially comfortable unless we remember that whatever we have belongs to God. Yes—even in community property states. What you own as a couple is God's. It's not wrong to have money; God never condemns wealth.

Proverbs leaves us with a thought about this issue: "Better to be poor and honest than rich and a cheater" (Proverbs 28:6 TLB). "Better be poor and honest than rich and dishonest" (Proverbs 19:1 TLB).

Think about it as a couple.

What's a
Soul Mate?

Having gifts...that differ according to the
grace given us, let us use them.
ROMANS 12:6 AMP

When you got married, you probably did so in the hope
that you had found a "soul mate"—someone who would understand you, someone with whom you could be connected in
a deep and spiritual way, someone whose innermost being fit
with yours.

Whether or not you have a soul mate for a spouse depends
less on whom you chose to marry than it does on the journey
you've taken in your marriage. Soul mates don't find each other
in the choice to get married. Instead, they *create* a bond between
themselves in the many seemingly insignificant choices of daily
living. But becoming soul mates involves more. Because marriage is a union of two people in a covenant before God, marriage is partially a spiritual journey. So becoming real soul mates
involves working together on a relationship with God.

What are you as a couple working toward in incorporating
spiritual disciplines into your lives and marriage? A closer relationship to God, certainly. But most likely you are also working toward a marriage that has meaning. Soul work is
relationship work. Because we have been created in the image
of a God who seeks relationship, the desire for relationship is
deeply imbedded in us. We become soul mates with someone
by working together on the multiple relationships of life—relationship with God, relationship with each other, relationship
with children, relationship with extended family, relationship
with the community of faith, and relationship with the larger
community.

Soul mates intentionally help each other work on the many
relationships that make up a meaningful life. Soul mates recognize each other's natural resources—gifts, interests, and
motivations. They help each other define, develop, and value
these resources. They support each other in the pursuit of their
shared and individual ministries.

If you choose to do the work required for you and your
spouse to connect at the deepest levels, the likelihood that you
will bond together as soul mates is greatly increased.[8]

Get It Right...
Sometimes

My dear children, I write this to you so that you will not sin.
But if anybody does sin, we have one who speaks to the Father in
our defense—Jesus Christ, the Righteous One.
1 JOHN 2:1

Do you expect your spouse to get it right *all* the time? Come on, be honest. Do you? Do you want him or her to walk, talk, act, and work perfectly according to your standards? Some people live this way. Their expectations allow no margin for error.

Standards are good to work toward, but your partner won't get it right all the time. Neither will you. You'll both fail.

God may be easier on you than you are on your spouse or yourself. Notice how God addresses us in today's passage. He calls us "dear children." Children have a lot to learn. And when a child is in a learning mode he or she makes mistakes, such as falling down every now and then and skinning a knee. God wants us to be obedient and follow Him. But He's also saying to us, "Little children, I don't want you to sin. I want you to live a Christian life. To help you do this I've given you My Word so that you can grow and mature and keep from sinning. But if you do sin, I've taken care of that for you as well." Charles Stanley said:

> We can't be perfect and we won't ever be perfect, but we can enjoy the perfection of Christ Jesus. We can accept His lovingkindness. We can acknowledge that He doesn't expect us to be perfect, but He does expect us to keep growing in Him, and to keep trusting Him day by day. He says that as we do that, He will work out His perfection in us. We won't have to struggle to do it, strive to do it, or knock ourselves out to do it. He'll do the work. He'll bring about His perfection in us in His timing, using His methods, and all for His purposes![9]

Saint Valentine

This is my beloved and this is my friend.
SONG OF SOLOMON 5:16 NASB

The legend of Saint Valentine dates back to early Rome. Each year, the Romans celebrated a holiday in honor of their god Lupercus. It became a festival for lovers. On February 15, they also worshiped Juno, the goddess of marriage. On this festival day, the young women would drop their names into a jar so young men could draw them out. They would then be partners for the holiday.

But not everyone in Rome worshiped the legendary gods. Some Christians, who worshiped their one true God, also lived in the city under heavy persecution.

In 496, Pope Gelasius wished to communicate the Christian view of true love. He looked for a martyr who had exhibited a life of loving others. He came across the story of St. Valentine. There are two legends of St. Valentine. One is that St. Valentine was a Christian doctor who lived to help other people get well. He would even pray for his patients after he had given them medicine. St. Valentine was also a local Christian leader.

In those days it was illegal for Roman soldiers to marry. Claudius "The Cruel" wanted all men to go to war, so he did not allow them to marry. St. Valentine felt for these young people in love and would perform secret wedding ceremonies. When Claudius discovered what St. Valentine was doing, he had him jailed. While in jail, St. Valentine met the jailer's daughter, a young blind girl. In Rome during this era, the blind were seen as cursed, as unlovable, but St. Valentine befriended her and treated her blindness. (In the second legend about St. Valentine and the blind girl, some accounts say that he may have known her previously and treated her blindness with salve, hoping it would help her regain her sight—and this, too, angered the Roman authorities.)

St. Valentine was sentenced to die on February 14. It was said that he wrote a note of encouragement to the jailer's daughter and signed it "from your Valentine." Legend says that when the jailer's daughter unrolled the papyrus note from Valentine, for the first time in her life she could see.[10]

43

To Love or Perish

We should love one another.
1 JOHN 3:11

There is one extra special day a year devoted to love—Valentine's Day. Hearts 'n' flowers. Sweetheart banquets. A needed reminder that there is still a heart-shaped vacuum in the human breast that only the three most wonderful words in the English language can fill—I love you.

Don't think for a moment that such stuff is mere sentimentality. As a fellow named Smiley Blanton wrote in his book many years ago, life really does boil down to love or perish:

Without love, hopes perish.
Without love, dreams and creativity perish.
Without love, families and churches perish.
Without love, friendships perish.
Without love, the intimacies of romance perish.
Without love, the desire to go on living can perish.
To love and to be loved is the bedrock of our existence.

But love must also flex and adapt. Rigid love is not true love. It is veiled manipulation, a conditional time bomb that explodes when frustrated. Genuine love willingly waits. It isn't pushy or demanding. While it has its limits, its boundaries are far-reaching. It neither clutches nor clings. Real love is not shortsighted, selfish, or insensitive. It detects needs and does what is best for the other person without being told.

Does your mate know how greatly you treasure her or him? Do you tell—and show—your love how you feel? Why not give your spouse a love note? How about a candlelight dinner? Remember when you said "I do"? Add two more words: I *do* love you!

Those simple little words—we so easily forget to say them. We assume others know how we feel, so we hold back. Strangely, as we grow older and realize more than ever the value of those three powerful words, we say them even less.

I love you. Simple, single-syllable words, yet they cannot be improved upon. Nothing even comes close. They are better than "You're great." Much better than "Happy birthday!" or "Congratulations!" or "You're special." And because we don't have any guarantee we'll have each other forever, it's a good idea to say them as often as possible.[11]

Love Is...

First Corinthians 13:1-7,11-13
Wuest's Expanded Translation

If in the languages of men I speak and the languages of the angels but do not have love... I have already become and at present am sounding brass or a clanging cymbal. And if I have the gift of uttering divine revelations and know all the mysteries and all the knowledge, and if I have all the faith so that I am able to keep on removing mountain after mountain, but am not possessing love, I am nothing. And if I use all my possessions to feed the poor, and if I deliver up my body [as a martyr] in order that I may glory, but do not have love, I am being profited in not even one thing.

Love meekly and patiently bears ill treatment from others. Love is kind, gentle, benign, pervading and penetrating the whole nature, mellowing all which would have been harsh and austere; is not envious. Love does not brag, nor does it show itself off, is not ostentatious, does not have an inflated ego, does not act unbecomingly, does not seek after the things which are its own, is not irritated, provoked, exasperated, aroused to anger, does not take into account the evil [which it suffers], does not rejoice at the iniquity but rejoices with the truth, endures all things, believes all things, hopes all things, bears up under all things, not losing heart nor courage. Love never fails....

When I was a child I was accustomed to speak as a child. I used to understand as a child. I was accustomed to reason as a child. When I have become a man and have the status of an adult, I have permanently put away the things of a child, for we are seeing now by means of a mirror obscurely, but then, face to face. Now I know only in a fragmentary fashion, but then I shall fully know even as also I was known. But now there remains faith, hope, love; these three. But the greatest of these is this previously mentioned love.[12]

What Would You Do Differently?

[Realizing that you] are joint heirs
of the grace (God's unmerited favor) of life.
1 PETER 3:7 AMP

A couple married for 47 years said:

> If we were starting our marriage over again now, as a wife I would not attempt to keep our home in such immaculate condition as to neglect my family's wifely and motherly needs. I would put Christ first, and spend more time with my children and husband. I also would surrender my all to the Lord at the beginning of our marriage, and pay much more attention to my husband....
>
> As a husband, I would exercise more self-control in openly expressing my temper, spend even more time with my children in helping them at school and teaching them the essentials of leading a holy and God-fearing life. I would try to be more sensitive to my wife's fears of spending too much money on cars and boats. I failed to clarify to her satisfaction that such transactions had hobby benefits to me....

A couple married 58 years said:

> [*The husband said,*] If I were starting my marriage over, I couldn't really think of anything I would do differently. I was in love with her when I married her and have been every minute since then. But I think I would try communicating [better], sharing what I was doing better.... Also, rather than making a decision, I would talk it over with her before I make it. I think [those are] the only things I would change.
>
> [*His wife said,*] And I think [in] our earlier years, and up 'til the recent years, in our disagreements I had the very ugly habit of bringing up past things. Not just disagreeing on what we were disagreeing about, but bringing up, "Well, if you hadn't done that." I think I would say sooner, "I'm sorry."

What will you say in 58 years? Now is the time to set the tone for your future years together.

Knowing
God's Will

Trust in the LORD *with all your heart*
and lean not on your own understanding.
PROVERBS 3:5

How do I know God's will?" has been asked by many people. But before this question can be answered, another question should be asked: "Am I willing—and am I ready—to do God's will?" If the answer is yes, then the other question follows.

Remember that what God has in mind for you may take you by surprise. Perhaps this is best expressed by Isaiah 55:8: "'For my thoughts are not your thoughts, neither are your ways my ways,' declares the LORD." In order to discover and do God's will there are three words to keep in mind. The first is "initiative." "Jesus gave them this answer, 'I tell you the truth, the Son can do nothing by himself; he can do only what he sees his Father doing, because whatever the Father does the Son also does'" (John 5:19).

The second word is "timing." "There is a time for everything, and a season for every activity under heaven" (Ecclesiastes 3:1). God's timing is perfect; He is never too early or too late. Waiting may be the best step you can take until all the indications say, "Yes, this is the time." Praying for wisdom in timing is essential. Sometimes in marriage one person influences the other to act ahead of God's will. It takes *both* partners to pray for wisdom *and* patience.

The last word is "submit." "Trust in the LORD with all your heart and lean not on your own understanding; in all your ways acknowledge him, and he will make your paths straight" (Proverbs 3:5,6). To know and do God's will there can't be any power struggle between the two of you or God. He wants our wills to be submissive to Him. The more we value control and power, the greater struggle we will have. But along with God's will being dependent on His initiative and His timing, He also needs to be in charge, and this means He's in charge of your marriage as well.[13]

How to Handle Problems

For though we live in the world, we do not wage war as the world does. The weapons we fight with are not the weapons of the world. On the contrary, they have divine power to demolish strongholds.
2 CORINTHIANS 10:3,4

Problems—we've all got them. How we solve them is based not so much on what we do with them but how we think about them. Here are five possible ways of thinking about our problems.

Curse the problem. This, in essence, means adding a negative opinion to the negative facts of the situation—in other words, compounding the negativity.

Nurse the problem. Focusing time and attention on the problem itself rather than on its solution.

Rehearse the problem. Replaying the problem until the person is actually thinking about very little other than the problem.

Disperse it. A technique used in tackling scientific problems is to break a problem down into its component parts and then to work at each part until an answer is reached. As the component problems are solved, the big problem is also solved. This principle holds true for all of life. One of the most effective things a person can do about what seems to be an overwhelming problem is to attempt to break it down into its smaller component problems and then deal with the smaller issues one at a time.

Reverse it. Seek out the positive. No situation or circumstance is 100 percent bad. There is always some glimmer of hope, some ray of light. Recognize negativity for what it is—a distraction from a positive solution. Dismiss the negativity. Of course, you do not ignore the problem in hopes that it will go away. To the contrary! Disposing of the negative thought means facing the problem *and* facing your negative response, making a conscious decision that the negative response is going to do nothing to solve the problem, and in that light, refusing to dwell on the negative and turning instead to the positive. Only you can reverse the way you feel about a problem.

Which of these approaches reflects your marriage?[14]

Led by God

In all your ways acknowledge him,
and he will make your paths straight.
PROVERBS 3:6

Have you ever wondered what God is leading you to do as a couple to serve Him? Do you know God is going to do something wonderful in your life? Can you feel Him working, but you don't know what He wants for you yet? If so, consider these words by Dr. Charles Stanley:

> If you experience a deep restlessness in your spirit—and you know that you are right with God—you, too, can trust God to be at work leading you into His next lesson, His next place of service, His next opportunity for you. He doesn't ask that you make those next moves happen. He asks only that you be obedient to His leading. You can trust Him to bring the right people and circumstances to pass.
>
> In many ways, living within God's will is like riding a raft on a stream. There are rocks to avoid. There are times when you must put your oar in the water to help guide the raft into the current or away from danger. There are places to stop along the journey. But overall, there is no striving in floating downstream. The stream is one of God's creation; it flows according to God's principles. You must simply be willing to put yourself in God's raft and trust Him to give you the strength and wisdom to make a successful journey in the way that He has ordained for you to travel.
>
> "Will it get me where I want to go—which is to a deeper and more intimate relationship with God, or to the accomplishment of something God has told me to do?"
>
> "Will it help me make somebody else successful?"
>
> "Do I have to violate a spiritual principle to get there?"
>
> "Will it fulfill God's purpose for my life?"[15]

If you are feeling led by the Lord to do something, ask yourself these questions.

Labels

Whoever claims to live in him must walk as Jesus did.
1 John 2:6

Some men and women walk through life burdened by a load of baggage. Sometimes it's in the form of a label slapped on them such as "slow," "inept," "stupid," "irresponsible," and "loser." It's as if someone wrote this word on a tag, attached it to their chests, and now it determines what happens to them for the rest of their lives. Some people continue to live this out in their marriages. Others acquire new labels once they're married.

During the Vietnam War, a mobile army surgical hospital (MASH) would prepare for the incoming helicopters with their load of wounded and dying soldiers. A system of triage was used to categorize the wounded by the severity of their injuries. One color tag was placed on the dying to indicate they could not be saved. They were hopeless; they would not recover. A second color tag was used for those with superficial wounds. They would receive medical attention and recover. The last color tag was placed on those who were critical but could make it with medical care. They might recover.

A critically wounded man was brought to one mobile hospital, and after examination he was tagged with "critical—will not recover." He was given a painkiller and left to die. But a nurse came by, saw he was conscious, and began to talk with him. After a while she felt he could probably make it. So she reached down, took off the tag, and replaced it with one that read "salvageable." Because she changed the tag, he's alive today.

Are you walking through your life with the wrong tag? How do you see yourself—critical and unsalvageable? Or do you have hope for your recovery? What about your partner?

If you have a tag on you, who placed it there? Could you have been the one to put the tag there?

The tag God puts on you has just one word—"salvageable." Let Him work on any wounds you have and give you full recovery. And let your partner help you as well.[16]

Elevators
and Isolation

The LORD God said, "It is not good for the man to be alone.
I will make a helper suitable for him."
GENESIS 2:18

Listen to the words of Chuck Swindoll.

Elevators are weird places. You're crammed in with folks you've never met, so you try really hard not to touch them. And nobody talks, except for an occasional "Out, please" or "Oh, I'm sorry" as somebody clumsily steps on someone's toe. You don't look at anyone; in fact, you don't look anywhere but up, watching those dumb floor numbers go on and off.

It's...as if there's an official sign that reads: No Talking, No Smiling, No Touching, and No Eye Contact Allowed Without Consent of the Management, No Exceptions!

In a strange sort of way, an elevator is a microcosm of our world today: a crowded impersonal place where anonymity, isolation, and independence are the norm. In fact, our lives are being diluted, distorted, and demeaned by this "elevator mentality."

Dr. Philip Zimbardo, author of one of the most widely used psychology textbooks, addressed this issue in a *Psychology Today* article entitled "The Age of Indifference."

> I know of no more potent killer than isolation. There is no more destructive influence on physical and mental health than the isolation of you from me and of us from them. It has been shown to be a central agent in the etiology of depression, paranoia, schizophrenia, rape, suicide, mass murder....The Devil's strategy for our times is to trivialize human existence in a number of ways: by isolating from one another while creating the delusion that the reasons are time pressures, work demands, or anxieties created by economic uncertainty; by fostering narcissi and the fierce competition to be No. 1....

Sometimes isolation enters into a marriage relationship. It has no right to ever be there. Wasn't it God who said, "It's not good for man to be alone"? He knows what's best. Talk, smile, touch, and look at one another.[17]

A Constructive Suggestion?

He who listens to a life-giving rebuke
will be at home among the wise.
PROVERBS 15:31

How do you handle it when someone takes you to task, especially when that someone is your spouse? He or she criticizes you or makes "constructive suggestions." Do you enjoy it? Probably not. Does it make you feel better? Probably not. Do you usually say, "You're right. Thanks for telling me"? Probably not. But you know what? Even though we need all the help we can get, most of the time we resist correction.

The Bible talks about the word "reproof." In Hebrew, it means "to correct or to convince." It's not always other people who correct us. It could be God's Word. A slight course correction now may prevent disaster later on.

But too often we do what Solomon talks about in Proverbs 1:23,24: "If you had responded to my rebuke, I would have poured out my heart to you and made my thoughts known to you. But since you rejected me when I called and no one gave heed when I stretched out my hand..." In verse 24 the word "rejected" means a direct digging in of the heels and saying, "Don't confuse me with the facts. My mind is made up." We call this stubbornness. It's ironic that so often when someone else says we're stubborn, we respond with, "No, I'm not!"

When Solomon says, "No one gave heed," it's as though others are ignoring what is said or, worse yet, are totally insensitive.

Verse 25 says, "Since you ignored all my advice and would not accept my rebuke..." Two problems jump out here. Neglecting counsel implies indifference, which is like saying, "Hey, don't bother me. I don't care!" This attitude certainly doesn't build a close and loving relationship in marriage.

And when it says, "not accept my rebuke" what word comes to mind? You're right—defensiveness. The defensive person says, "You're wrong. I'm right and I won't consider it anymore."

So, when you hear a rebuke, what's your response going to be? You have a choice. So reread today's verse. It offers some pretty good advice.

Control— Give It Up!

*There is no fear in love. But perfect love drives out fear,
because fear has to do with punishment. The one who fears is not
made perfect in love. We love because he first loved us.*
1 JOHN 4:18,19

Some individuals never seem to get the message about control. They know they can't control everything, but they keep trying. Why? Because they feel compelled to be in control of every aspect of their lives. They push, pull, persuade, manipulate, and withdraw. Yes, withdraw. Silence and withdrawal are great ways to control others. What is it that prompts this lifestyle?

Control is a camouflage for fear. Who wants to be afraid or even admit they are? Not me. Not you. Fear makes us feel vulnerable. We believe that if others knew we were afraid, they would take advantage of us. So we do the opposite and hide our fears by going on the offensive.

Control is a cover-up for insecurity. A secure husband or wife doesn't always need to be in control. He or she can defer to others, ask their advice, be comfortable when someone else leads. But when we are insecure, we go overboard by trying to control everything and everyone. There's an emptiness within us when we're insecure; we're like a bucket with a hole in it. We can never get filled up enough, but we keep trying through control.

Control covers low self-esteem. When we feel down on ourselves, worthless, lacking in something, we don't want our partners to know about it. And we may even blame them for helping to create the problem. So we overcome this self-esteem problem by making them pay through control. But we're fooling ourselves. Control never fulfills; it never solves the basic problem. Control perpetuates it. It never draws others closer; rather, it pushes them away.

Give God the reins of your life. Let him control you. When God is in control you'll be amazed at how much better your relationship with your partner will be.

Insults

Finally, all of you, live in harmony with one another;
be sympathetic, love as brothers, be compassionate and humble.
Do not repay evil with evil or insult with insult, but with blessing,
because to this you were called so that you may inherit a blessing.
1 PETER 3:8,9

Some have a real gift when it comes to the fine art of insults. Men seem especially adept at this. Why? Because men's style of humor is different from women's. Men use gentle insults, poke fun at one another, emphasize each other's goofs and mistakes, and throw in some sarcasm from time to time. They enjoy putting each other down. There's nothing wrong with any of this—when it's in fun, when it's mutual, and when it's between men. Often it occurs because of caring for these other men. They're friends. Some women also fall into this pattern.

Sometimes, the tendency to use insults and put-downs seeps into marriage. Then it becomes destructive. It's easy to fall into this trap because we know our partners better than anyone else. Within a marriage, insults and sarcasm hurt. A husband may make a wisecrack to his wife that seems funny to him. He laughs and so do the kids, but she runs off crying to her room. He wonders, *Now, what did I say?* Keep this question in mind: Will my insult or sarcastic comment fit in with today's passage? Use that as your guide. It will help.

Often we learn sarcasm from the sitcoms and comedy shows we watch. Put-downs and comments seem to be an accepted part of our culture. But as Christians, this culture is not to be ours. If sarcasm and insults seem to be the norm, the most powerful way to change that is to memorize today's Scripture. Make it a project, then note the changes that take place when these verses are put into practice.

Look Around

I keep asking that the God of our Lord Jesus Christ,
the glorious Father, may give you the Spirit of
wisdom and revelation, so that you may know him better.
EPHESIANS 1:17

It's right in front of your nose. Are you blind? Can't you see it?" Most kids hear this from their parents at some time or another—and it's true. You can be looking at something and not see it. It happens to us as adults, too. Unfortunately, it seems that men have more vision problems than women. A man can open the refrigerator looking for an item and say, "Honey, where's the mustard? Are we out of it again?" And his wife walks over, reaches in and picks it up where it's been staring him right in the face. Husbands also tend to walk by the overflowing trash container for days as well.

William Randolph Hearst, the renowned newspaper publisher, invested a fortune in collecting great works of art. You can still see some of them at Hearst Castle in California. One day he heard about a piece of artwork that was very valuable. He wanted to find it and add it to his collection. His art agent searched all over the world in the various art galleries and couldn't locate it. Months later he did find it—in one of Hearst's own warehouses. It had been stored right under his nose, but he couldn't see it!

It happens to us, too. Some Christians are continually searching for something more in life. They're not fulfilled because they just don't understand who they are and what they have in Christ. Paul knew about this. That's why he prayed what he did in today's verse. He wanted us to understand the fullness of our inheritance. It is difficult for us to imagine or fully comprehend all that God has done for us. There will always be some part of what we have been given that will remain a mystery. We need to stop and think about all that we have. Then we can say, "It's there right in front of me."[18]

Four Gifts

*I know that there is nothing better for men than to be happy
and do good while they live. That everyone may eat and drink,
and find satisfaction in all his toil—this is the gift of God.*
ECCLESIASTES 3:12,13

These interesting verses from the book of Ecclesiastes talk
about four gifts God has given to us.

The first gift is the ability to rejoice and enjoy life. To what
extent are you enjoying your life right now? Is there something to rejoice in that you are overlooking? What would your
spouse say about this? Being a Christian means we have the
capability of enjoying life regardless. That's an important
word. "Regardless" of what is or isn't happening, we can rejoice and be happy. The writer of Proverbs said, "All the days
of the desponding and afflicted are made evil [by anxious
thoughts and forebodings], but he who has a glad heart has a
continual feast [regardless of circumstances]" (15:15 AMP).

The second gift is the ability to do good independently from
what others do for us. God helps us develop a heart of generosity and helpfulness toward others—*regardless!* If you wait
for your partner to do good before you act, you're letting that
person control what you do. Does that put a new light on it?
You bet!

The third gift is the appetite to eat and drink. *Yes!* The ability to enjoy our food. If that sounds basic and mundane, just
remember it's one of God's gifts. Who enjoys eating the most
in your marriage?

The fourth gift is the ability to see good in all our labor. Do
you see it that way? Some of our work is boring and routine,
but do you look for the purpose in all that you do? Your partner may need some help with this, too.

As you live through today, reflect on the four gifts. It could
make a big difference in how you view life.

Do You Know
How to Fly?

Let all bitterness and indignation and wrath...
and quarreling...be banished from you.
EPHESIANS 4:31 AMP

Have you flown much? If you have, you probably have a few experiences to relate, some of which you could have done without. Like the time lightning struck next to the plane and the thunderclap made you think you'd just lost an engine. Or the times the air was rough—really rough with the 747 bouncing all over the sky, trays spilling, and people throwing up. Or it may have been a continuous bumping for two hours that kept you in your seat without being able to take that needed trip to the bathroom. That rough air has a name—turbulence. Building a marriage is similar to flying a plane.

Bad weather and turbulence are just part of flying. It's possible to avoid some of it, but there are times where you can't get around it or over it. You've just got to go through it until you get to the calm air on the other side. This sounds a bit like the journey of marriage, doesn't it? There are four degrees of turbulence—light, moderate, severe, and extreme. When your coffee jiggles, you're in light turbulence; when it spills you're in moderate. Pilots make every attempt to avoid severe and extreme.

In every marriage there will be some turbulence. If you want to totally avoid it do what a pilot does—stay on the ground and go nowhere. As you go through light and moderate turbulence you have an opportunity to grow and become different, more Christlike, because of this experience. This turbulence can refine your marriage. But just as severe and extreme turbulence can cause structural damage to the plane or injure the passengers, it can do the same to a marriage and its passengers. So what does a pilot do when encountering extreme turbulence? The pilot slows down. There will be a rough ride, but slowing down eliminates some of the risk.

What can you do to slow down the escalation that happens in marital turbulence? It's something to think about.[19]

What's It Like
for You to Pray Together?

Be unceasing in prayer.
1 Thessalonians 5:17 amp

One of the reasons for praying silently together has to do with the unique way God has created us in both our gender and personality differences. Most men prefer to put things on the back burner and think about them for awhile. If a man has the opportunity to reflect on what he wants to pray about, he will eventually be more open to praying together. Extroverts find it easier to pray aloud because they think out loud, whereas introverts need to think things through silently before sharing. Silent prayer is less threatening. Some prefer reflecting for awhile first, then writing out their prayers. There is nothing wrong with this.

There are numerous reasons for praying together. When a man and woman marry, they no longer think and act as single people. It is no longer "I" but "we." Life is now lived connected to another person. Everything you do affects this significant person. You're a team of two; when both partners participate, they function better. When you confront problems and crises in your life (and you will), it's a tremendous source of support and comfort to know that here is another person who will pray for you and with you. When you're struggling financially, have problems at work, must make tough decisions, or face a medical crisis, it's wonderful to be able to share the burden with your spouse.

Couples need to pray together for the health of their marriage, too. When you married, you entered into a high-risk adventure. The vows you took at your wedding will be attacked on all sides. Praying together makes your marriage stronger as well as helping to protect you from reacting sinfully toward your spouse.

Scripture's promise about the effectiveness of prayer includes the prayers of married couples. Jesus said, "Again, I tell you that if two of you on earth agree about anything you ask for, it will be done for you by my Father in heaven. For where two or three come together in my name, there am I with them" (Matthew 18:19,20).

The Wall of Tenderness

*Therefore, as God's chosen people, holy and
dearly loved, clothe yourselves with compassion,
kindness, humility, gentleness and patience.*
Colossians 3:12

Here's a story from the book *Becoming Soul Mates*:

We realized early in our marriage that a prerequisite to
intimacy of any kind was a foundation of respect for each
other....As a result, we've tried to build and maintain
what I've since referred to as a "Wall of Tenderness" designed to keep out destructive attitudes while keeping us
close to each other. This wall entails:

- Not discussing problems in harsh, angry tones, but in
  attentive conversation, while working toward solutions that genuinely satisfy both of us.
- Not joking cuttingly about each other....
- Never kidding about divorce.
- Saving constructive criticism for when we're alone and
  in a receptive frame of mind.
- Being willing to give in to each other's preferences,
  and developing a language for conveying when that is
  really needed. Some friends encouraged us to reserve
  the simple phrase "this is really important to me" for
  those times when we most need to be heard....
- Regularly giving verbal and nonverbal encouragement to each other for who we are as well as for what
  we do. This includes doing things that make the other
  person feel treasured, including dinner dates, gifts,
  massages, prayers, and time alone together without
  distractions.
- Fostering an attitude that says, in effect, "I'd rather die
  than hurt or bring shame on you. You're the one precious person to whom I've committed my love for the
  rest of my life."

These actions and attitudes have helped us to build a
strong foundation for our marriage.[1]

Which of these principles are in place in your marriage?
Which of the principles mentioned would help you?

Purity

A husband must not divorce his wife.
1 CORINTHIANS 7:11

Many look at holiness as a bunch of rules. Believing that holiness is out of reach, the very idea gets dismissed quickly. But the true believer has to take personal holiness seriously. God demanded it, and it is the seed of the reality of God inside us. We are called to walk in holiness. Righteousness is the outward working of holiness, and in that context we walk in purity.

Christian men are no greater than they are pure. The most significant description a man can have said about him is that he is a man of God. He is righteous and honest.

In no way do we live in a gray-colored world. Our yeas are to be yeas and our nays should be nays. When Jesus becomes our standard, we do not commit sins of the body because it is no longer in our nature. There is no sex outside of marriage because we are determined not to break the covenant we made when we married. Why does God hate divorce? Because He has established marriage as a physical manifestation of an invisible reality. Marriage models our relationship to Christ. Jesus married the church and will never divorce it. When we defy God and divorce, we are incorrectly modeling the church's relationship to Christ.

We learn to keep our word even if it hurts, even if we are not getting along in our relationships. When we become willing to be changed by constructive observations, we develop an awareness that opposites attract and likes often repel. Our differences may be used to make us one. In reality, our purity is proof of our differences, not our agreements. We keep our covenants because we are people of integrity, not because we have to or are forced to by law. We want to keep our promises. Proverbs warns us to guard our hearts—our integrity—because out of them are the issues of life.[2]

Are You Listening?

He who answers before listening—that is his folly and his shame.
PROVERBS 18:13

In marriage you've been called to listen. Do you know what listening means?

Lord, I am certainly a fool. How many times a day I answer before I listen! Instead of being quick to hear, I race to speak (see James 1:19).

Lord, Your ears are never too dull to hear (see Isaiah 59:1). But mine are often so dull that I miss most of what is being said. And if I can't hear the audible and sometimes loud voice of my partner, how will I hear the still, small voice of the Lord?

How can I change, Lord? Today this is my prayer: Give me ears to hear (see Matthew 11:15). Give me a heart that waits (see 1 Corinthians 13:4). Give me a tongue that hesitates (see Proverbs 10:19).

Please help me listen—even to words I don't really want to hear. Behind my partner's complaints, let me hear his or her disappointments. Behind long stories that seem to derail the issue at hand, let me hear the memories and dreams that mean the most to my spouse. Behind seemingly unfair reproaches, let me hear a valid hurt.

And behind our companionable silences, help me hear love.

Amen.[3]

Who is the one in your marriage who can really listen?

When are the times you really need to be listened to? How can your spouse tell when you really need a listening ear?

Talk this over for a while. When you do, be sure to listen—even if the words make you uncomfortable.

Tired?
- Just Wait (Part 1)

But those who hope in the Lord will renew their strength.
They will soar on wings like eagles; they will run and not
grow weary, they will walk and not be faint.
ISAIAH 40:31

The word *walk* is used again and again in our conversations. "It's an easy walk." It's used in songs "Walk right in." The hostess in the restaurant tells you as she leads you to your table "Walk this way." We ask "How's your walk with the Lord?"

Those who play in high school and college bands know what it means to walk. They walk for miles in parades. Others call it marching, but it all comes down to the same thing— wearisome walking.

You can get tired walking. You can get to the place where you're so weary you don't think you can raise your foot for one more step. Have you experienced that yet? If not, you will.

Take a look at this passage again. Have you ever felt as though you were flying like an eagle, just soaring above the crowd? When you do, you feel as though you could take on the entire world. You've got energy and interest. We'd all like to soar above it all and feel those updrafts. But most of us are just walking along one step at a time. Escape isn't available.

Isaiah used the word walk in a different way. It wasn't the aimless walking around or walking outside to the garage. The Hebrew word here means "setting out on a journey with a goal in mind." The children of Israel were in Babylon as prisoners of war. They prayed. God answered. He said they could have freedom rather than slavery. The door was open. All they had to do was walk home. They couldn't ride, they had to walk. Fifty thousand did. Two hundred fifty thousand stayed behind. You have to walk to get where you're going. It may be tiring, but look at the alternative.[4]

Tired?
Just Wait (Part 2)

Though youths grow weary and tired,
and vigorous young men stumble badly,
yet those who wait for the LORD will gain new strength.
ISAIAH 40:30 NASB

Have you ever waited for your spouse? You hear "I'll be there in just a second," and you know what that means! Wait—wait—wait. We don't really like to wait all that much. This is the age of instant everything—breakfast, service, attention, even responses from God. But there is a waiting that can change your life. Joe Brown tells this personal story:

My dad had told me that the parade was scheduled to start at nine o'clock that morning. It was already nine-thirty, and I still did not see a parade. People kept saying, "Just be patient, in about fifteen minutes..." When you are five years old, fifteen minutes is an eternity.

Moments later, I saw the crowd beginning to stir and then cheer, and I heard a band playing. It was not long before I saw the twirling majorette and the high-stepping drum major.

Wait a minute! Had I not been told that the parade was to start at nine o'clock? But it was almost ten o'clock before I saw the first band. What happened?

"Son," my father explained, "the parade started right on time, at nine, just as you were told. But it took the parade an hour to get to where you were."

Before I could experience the sights and hear the sounds, I had to wait for the parade to get to me.

The parade has already started. Oh, it might not be in front of you yet. You might not be able to see the festivities at this point, but if you are ever to see it—if you are ever to experience God and His parade of power and strength and victory in your life—you have to get on the route, adjust your clock to God's time schedule, watch, listen, and wait.

You can wait by placing God first in your life, first in your marriage. Talk with Him together.[5]

Wait Some More

Though youths grow weary and tired, and vigorous
young men stumble badly; yet those who wait
for the Lord will gain new strength.
Isaiah 40:30 NASB

Yesterday we talked about waiting. And parades. God will equip you to deal with every surprise, every upset, every burden, every overload, and every conflict with your life. You may be discouraged, you may not see any hope, you may not see any answer. Listen. You may hear something in the distance coming down the road. He does it by you walking with and waiting on Him. Joe Brown describes it for us:

> God promises that if we will patiently but actively wait on Him, we will once more hear a song in our hearts. If we wait upon the Lord, we will smile again and hear the sound of our own laughter. If we wait on the Lord, we will walk and not become weary—and His parade will never pass us by.
>
> We must wait on God—wait until we see Him, until the parade comes to the place where God has planted us. We have to become like a rope, intertwined with God Himself.
>
> When we wait on God and walk with God, we will not worry about controlling Him; He will control us. We become entwined with God as He moves into our lives and takes over. When God is in control and directs our lives, life itself becomes an adventure. Life becomes the parade. It becomes an exhilarating experience with God because He is everywhere we go and in everything we do—walking across a desert, getting up and going to work, brushing out the toilet bowl, waiting for a child to finish baseball practice, or playing a game of golf.
>
> This kind of life is not out of reach. It is not something reserved for preachers and teachers and missionaries. No, walking in God's abundant strength is attainable for everyone who is willing to listen and grasp hold of God.

What is that I hear? Listen! Listen closely with your spirit. Is that not a trumpet tuning up? Wait right there—where He has placed you. The parade is on its way.[5]

Do You Have
a "Rubber" Marriage?

Be kind and compassionate to one another,
forgiving each other, just as in Christ God forgave you.
EPHESIANS 4:32

He who covers over an offense promotes love,
but whoever repeats the matter separates close friends.
PROVERBS 17:9

All marriages need to have the qualities of rubber. First of all, rubber is *resilient* and *elastic*. It bounces back when stress bends it out of shape, and it expands to fit irregular surfaces. Spouses need to do that with each other. Sometimes our partners seem to be strangely inconsiderate and irrational. We need to bounce back from the hurts and disappointments inevitable in any close relationship, realizing that no one is perfect. The love that underlies a marital commitment can stretch around bumps in the road.

Rubber also *erases* mistakes. In marriages, the partners stand ready to forgive the mistakes and hurts inflicted by their mates. (In this process, the flexible quality of rubber also comes into play.) But forgiveness must not be a mere whitewash based on the pretense that either the wrong did not happen or that it did not matter to the injured one. Here we draw a distinction between "forgiveness" and "reconciliation." We can forgive someone without that person's participation if we conduct a transaction between ourselves and God, letting go of our bitterness or hurt toward the person who wronged us. Reconciliation requires the participation of both parties. You resume normal relations only after the one who has inflicted the hurt acknowledges his or her wrong and repents of it. That means saying "I was wrong" in one way or another, implying that the offense will not be repeated.

For reconciliation to occur, the offenders must indicate what they would do differently if they had the situation to live over again. (The injured party must also be willing to acknowledge that he or she is not entirely blameless.) Without this kind of rethinking, a couple leaves open the likelihood of repetition.[6]

Your Words Matter

For then will I turn to the people a pure language, that they may all call on the name of the LORD, to serve him with one consent.
ZEPHANIAH 3:9 KJV

Professor Higgins only had a few months to win a wild, seemingly impossible bet. In the play *My Fair Lady*, the professor wagers a significant sum that he can take a shrill flower-selling commoner off the streets of London and pass her off at an upcoming royal ball as a poised, aristocratic lady. He intends to do this amazing feat by simply changing how she talks. The professor surpasses his own enormous expectations. Not only does he turn Liza into the talk of the royal ball, but she is also mistaken for royalty herself. In the process of all this, Professor Higgins falls in love with her.

That is exactly what the Holy Spirit is bent on doing with us. He is already in love with us, but He wants to change the way we talk. God has big dreams for us (marriage to His Son, for one), and He is going to pull it off. The truth, though, is that we are in much worse shape than Liza. We are shrill and uncouth. We are not yet ready for the marriage supper of the Lamb. We talk like the world talks. We've forgotten that words matter. In a culture loud with verbalized confusion, we've become deaf to the death rattle of our own language.

If language is the litmus test of our souls, we are in dire need of a doctor. We force our words into tightly caged definitions that keep us from taking responsibility and acknowledging our sin. We did not sin; we were indiscreet or our behavior was inappropriate. We do not gossip; we simply give all the facts so people can pray intelligently. Our speech is shot through with self-protection and accusation. We use language to hide our own sin and point out another's. We say things we don't mean and mean things we don't say.[7]

What are your thoughts about this subject?

One of These Days

There is a time for every event.
ECCLESIASTES 3:1 NASB

Have you ever said, "Not right now...but maybe someday"? It's good at times to wait for conditions to be just right, but sometimes waiting can lead to regrets. Many couples have said, "We'll wait until the children are grown" or "We could afford this now, but we'll wait a bit."

Some wait to say "I love you" or "You look great today" until a special occasion. For some people, someday will never come. Then all you have are regrets. Ann Wells wrote:

> My brother-in-law opened the bottom drawer of my sister's bureau and lifted out a tissue-wrapped package....[The item inside] was exquisite: silk, handmade and trimmed with a cobweb of lace. The price tag with an astronomical figure on it was still attached.
>
> "Jan bought this the first time we went to New York, at least eight or nine years ago. She never wore it. She was saving it for a special occasion. Well, I guess this is the occasion."
>
> He took the slip from me and put it on the bed with the other clothes we were taking to the mortician. His hands lingered on the soft material for a moment, then he slammed the drawer shut and turned to me.
>
> "Don't ever save anything for a special occasion. Every day you are alive is a special occasion."
>
> I remembered those words through the funeral and the days that followed when I helped him and my niece attend to all the sad chores that follow an unexpected death....
>
> I'm still thinking about his words, and they've changed my life....I'm not "saving" anything; we use our good china and crystal for every special event—such as losing a pound, getting the sink unstopped, the first camellia blossom....
>
> "Someday" and "one of these days" are losing their grip on my vocabulary. If it's worth seeing or hearing or doing, I want to see and hear and do it now....I'm trying very hard not to put off, hold back, or save anything that would add laughter and luster to our lives. And every morning when I open my eyes I tell myself that it is special.[8]

What in your life or in your marriage have you put on hold?

Affection—A Different Way

Be kind and compassionate to one another,
forgiving each other, just as in Christ God forgave you.
EPHESIANS 4:32

What makes a marriage work today? Affection is a key component. Being consistently affectionate—and not just at those times when one is interested in sex—is a must in marriage. Sometimes nothing is shared verbally. It can be sitting side by side and touching gently or moving close enough that you barely touch while you watch the sun dipping over a mountain with reddish clouds capturing your attention. It could be reaching out and holding hands in public. It could be doing something thoughtful, unrequested and noticed only by your spouse.

Affection is demonstrated in many ways and displays.

Here's a delightful story that reveals loving affection. A couple had been invited to a potluck dinner. The wife was not known for her cooking ability, but she decided to make a custard pie. As they drove to the dinner, they knew they were in trouble because they smelled the scorched crust. Then when they turned the corner, the contents of the pie shifted dramatically from one side of the pie shell to the other. He could see her anxiety rising by the moment.

When they arrived, they placed the pie on the dessert table. The guests were serving themselves salad and then went back for the main course. Just before they could move on to the desserts, the husband marched up to the table, looked over the number of homemade desserts and snatched his wife's pie. As others looked at him, he announced, "There are so many desserts here and my wife so rarely makes my favorite dessert that I'm claiming this for myself. I ate light on all the other courses so now I can be a glutton."

And a glutton he was. Later his wife said, "He sat by the door eating what he could, mushing up the rest so no one else would bug him for a piece, and slipping chunks to the hosts' Rottweiler when no one was looking. He saw me looking at him and gave me a big wink. What he did made my evening. My husband, who doesn't always say much, communicated more love with what he did than with what any words could ever say."

Are you this kind of person?

How to Have
a Nervous Breakdown

The fruit of the Spirit is...peace.
GALATIANS 5:22

*And the peace of God...will guard your hearts
and your minds in Christ Jesus.*
PHILIPPIANS 4:7

Here is a slightly different way to look at peace. Perhaps you can relate to it. J.L. Glass has written a humorous article titled "Five Ways to Have a Nervous Breakdown." He lists the ways as follows:

1. Try to figure out the answer before the problem arises. "Most of the bridges we cross are never built because they are unnecessary." We carry tomorrow's load along with today's. Matthew 6:34 says: "Do not worry about tomorrow, for tomorrow will worry about itself."

2. Try to relive the past. As we trust him (God) for the future, we must trust him with the past. And he can use the most checkered past imaginable for his good. See Romans 8:28.

3. Try to avoid making decisions. Doing this is like deciding whether to allow weeds to grow in our gardens. While we're deciding, they're growing. Decisions will be made in our delay....Choice "is a man's most godlike characteristic."

4. Demand more of yourself than you can produce. Unrealistic demands result in "beating our heads against stone walls. We don't change the walls. We just damage ourselves." Romans 12:3 says, "Do not think of yourself more highly than you ought, but rather think of yourself with sober judgment."

5. Believe everything Satan tells you....Jesus described Satan as the "father of lies" (John 8:44). He's a master of disguise, masquerading as an angel of light. But our Lord declared that his sheep follow him because they "know his voice" (John 10:4). They have listened to it in his Word.[9]

Not only do these five lead to a breakdown, they don't do much for a marriage either. How could you apply Matthew 6:34 and Romans 12:3 to your marriage?

A Faithful Friend

A man of many companions may come to ruin,
but there is a friend who sticks closer than a brother.
PROVERBS 18:24

You just can't depend on anyone. They let you down when you need them the most." Sound familiar? Whether it happens to us in business or with a friend, it's disappointing. We look for predictability in other people, and when they let us down, it's irritating. The best description of this dilemma is found in Proverbs: "Trust in a faithless man in time of trouble is like a bad tooth or a foot that slips" (25:19 RSV).

When we encounter unfaithfulness in a friend, it feels like the rug was pulled out from under us. And it often happens when we're the most vulnerable. Scripture is filled with examples of this problem. For instance, look at David. He was wounded more emotionally by friends than by his enemies. He shared this hurt in one of the psalms: "If an enemy were insulting me, I could endure it; if a foe were raising himself against me, I could hide from him. But it is you, a man like myself, my companion, my close friend, with whom I once enjoyed sweet fellowship as we walked with the throng at the house of God" (55:12-14).

We expect friends to keep their word as well as our confidences. Faithful friends do that. When this is violated, relationships are often severed. Proverbs also states, "A perverse man stirs up dissension, and a gossip separates close friends" (16:28).

Friendship is part of the marriage relationship. We're called to be friends to each other, not just lovers. The security of marriage is enhanced when we know we can depend on our partners to be faithful as well as keep their word. What a great place to practice friendship!

The Lies We Tell

You shall not give false testimony against your neighbor.
EXODUS 20:16

We're a country of proficient liars. We cultivate and practice telling lies. We're good at it no matter how young or how old we are. Two out of three people in our country see nothing wrong with lying.[10]

We can destroy another's reputation and cripple the ministry of a person or a church by our lies. But worst of all, we destroy ourselves before God: "The LORD detests lying lips, but he delights in men who are truthful" (Proverbs 12:22). "There are six things the LORD hates, seven that are detestable to him: ...a false witness who pours out lies and a man who stirs up dissension among brothers" (Proverbs 6:16,19).

We lie by embellishing stories we tell. We lie by leaving out portions to create another impression. We can speak the truth in such a way that it destroys—especially in marriage. God's Word says to speak the truth in such a way that it better cements our relationships. "Speaking the truth in love, we will in all things grow up into him who is the Head, that is, Christ" (Ephesians 4:15).

We make insinuations about other people and situations, then back out of it by saying we didn't mean it. "Like a madman shooting firebrands or deadly arrows is a man who deceives his neighbor and says, 'I was only joking!'" (Proverbs 26:18,19). Has this ever happened in your marriage?

We also lie by spreading gossip. You know, information that may be true—or may not be. Sometimes we're like walking supermarket tabloids. God's Word says: "The words of a gossip are like choice morsels" (Proverbs 18:8).

When lies occur in marriage, trust vanishes. Pray that God will help you be a person of truth. And remember, "an honest answer is like a kiss on the lips" (Proverbs 24:26) and pray: "Set a guard over my mouth, O LORD; keep watch over the door of my lips" (Psalm 141:3).

Love Is. . .

1 Corinthians 13
Paraphrase by Angela McCord

If I go to language school and learn to speak a hundred different languages, preach to thousands all over the world, and lead all to Christ, but have hate in my heart in a silent war with my neighbor who's built his privacy fence on my side of the boundary line, my words are nothing except the screaming of a heavy metal rock band.

If I have a doctorate in theology, science, language arts, and literature and can raise mountains out of the dust of the plains, but am only concerned with the size of my paycheck, wardrobe, and house, it is as if I don't exist...have never existed.

If I give up a good salary opportunity to work in compassionate ministries, tithe ten percent, give the rest to the poor and eventually die for them, but only do it to get my name in the paper, and I lose sight of lost hungry souls, I certainly don't gain anything but lose my own soul.

Love walks the floor all night with a crying baby, smiles as she greets new visitors in Sunday school. She doesn't want what she doesn't have. She doesn't say, "Look how wonderful I am" but "Look how great you are." She doesn't snub anyone, isn't always looking in a mirror, and doesn't make a mental list for retribution when things don't go her way. She doesn't close herself in but opens her heart and makes herself vulnerable to others.

Love remains while the world crumbles around her.

The only things that are really important are faith in God, hope for the future, and love from God for every man. But you cannot have faith or hope until you first understand and demonstrate love.

I can work with the poor like Mother Teresa, write literature like C.S. Lewis, sing like Sandi Patty, move people like Gloria Gaither, preach like Billy Graham, have spiritual insight like James Dobson, be a great leader like Martin Luther King, Jr., and a martyr like Ghandi, but until I love like Jesus my soul is lost.[11]

Character

And endurance (fortitude) develops maturity of character.
ROMANS 5:4 AMP

If you were going to mentor a young couple or share some marital advice with them, what would you say? Perhaps it would be words such as these:

> Of all the strengths you bring into a marriage, none is more valuable than your character. That may not sound as exotic as romance, wit, or charm, but character is the beam that holds the structure together. Without it marriage is little more than cotton candy or shifting winds.
>
> Good character is never fickle. People who have it stand like rocks when the going gets tough. They aren't dependable one day and flaky tomorrow. They don't run like scared rabbits when the relationship starts to rattle. Character means we stay....
>
> Character takes its vows seriously. Very seriously. It still believes that a promise is a promise, a commitment a commitment, and that two people in love dedicate themselves to each other for life.
>
> "In sickness and in health, for richer and for poorer" means what it suggests. Character doesn't believe marriage is a turnstile, a stop on the road, or a phase in life. Marriage isn't an experiment to dabble at to see if it works out.
>
> Love isn't for irresponsible people. It isn't for the immature. Marriage wasn't created for those who can't tell time, keep appointments, call home, leave notes, or keep in touch. Love is too good to be wasted on independent souls. Only the truly interdependent know how to share meaningful affection. Only those who learn to blend reach true intimacy.
>
> Character means you give everything double effort when you need to. Character means if need be you will stand tall in the wind and the rain and the darkness, determined that you will see the light again.[12]

Did these ideas cause you to remember your first months of marriage? What are your thoughts now?

Our Work Is a Gift

We all live off his generous bounty, gift after gift after gift.
JOHN 1:16 MSG

Most of what we have we've worked for by the sweat of our brows and the labor of our hands. But who gave us those hands, along with the strength to use them and the mind to coordinate them? Were they not all gifts?

Or maybe our work is mental, not manual, and we are where we are in life because of years of education. But who gave us the mind to utilize that education? Who integrated the circuitry for the storage and retrieval of our thoughts? Who provided the neurological current that makes thoughts possible?

Or maybe our work revolves around certain issues burning in our hearts, and that's why we're social workers or judges or why we volunteer at homeless shelters. We live and work by the dictates of our consciences. But who did the dictation for our attitudes of truth and justice, our sense of right and wrong, our compassion? Where did these grand notions originate? Were they not engraved on our hearts the way the commandments were etched on stone? Were they not also gifts?

The love we give; the love given to us. Are they not gifts? And faith, that most primal of spiritual responses, did it not also come to us as a gift?

The air we breathe. A gift. The lungs to breathe it. A gift. The involuntary muscles that keep us breathing. A gift. Our waking to a new day. A gift.

Whatever we start with, if we follow it far enough back, the source is God and His generosity in sharing it. It's all a gift. *Everything.* We live, quite literally, off His generous bounty.

So great is God's generosity; so little is our gratitude. Yet still He gives "gift after gift after gift."

Have you identified all the gifts He's given to you? Your marriage is one of them! Preserve it. Protect it. Let it reflect Jesus' presence.[13]

Smile—
It's a Choice

*The fruit of the Spirit is love, joy, peace, patience, kindness,
goodness, faithfulness, gentleness and self-control.*
GALATIANS 5:22

Perspective can make a big difference in how you deal with what happens to you in life. For example, take the case of Fred, a landscape contractor. His first job was to remove a huge oak stump from a field. Fred had to use dynamite, but the only problem was that he had never used any before. He was kind of nervous about it, especially with the old farmer watching every move he made. So he tried to hide his jitters by carefully determining the size of the stump, the precise amount of dynamite, and where it should be placed to get the maximum effect. He didn't want to use too small an amount and have to do it over, nor did he want to use too much. He went about it scientifically.

When he was ready to detonate the charge, Fred and the farmer went behind the pickup truck where a wire was running to the detonator. He looked at the farmer, said a prayer, and plunged the detonator. It worked...all too well. The stump broke loose from the ground, rose through the air in a curving arc, and then plummeted down right on the cab of the truck. Fred's heart sank, and all he could think of was the ruined cab. Not the farmer. He was full of amazement and admiration. Slapping Fred on the back he said, "Not bad. With a little more practice you'll get it in the bed of the truck every time!"

Some of us are like Fred and some of us are like the farmer. We hit hard times and give in to discouragement, or we see how close we came to making it work and say, "Next time I'll get it right!" Who's the "Fred" in your marriage? Who's most like the "farmer"?

Remember, the fruit of the Spirit is joy. It's a realistic optimism, not the absence of hardship. It's the choice we make when we smile as the tree stump lands on our truck and say, "It could be worse. I'll learn how to make it better." Which perspective do you live by?[14]

Monthly Celebrations

We will rejoice in you and be glad.
SONG OF SOLOMON 1:4 NASB

Celebrate your marriage promise at least once a month. It isn't necessary to spend a lot of money on these mini-celebrations, but they are powerful acts in bonding couples together when they've been invested with thought and planning—and observed faithfully.

Here are some suggested ground rules for establishing and making the most of regular celebrations.

Plan an outing at least once a month for just the two of you.... *Gatherings with other people don't count!* For some reason, couples have a hard time with this concept. They recite all the things they do in each other's company—attending church potluck suppers, visiting friends and relatives, going to parties and dinners, cheering their kids at athletic events—and think they've offered proof of their attempts at togetherness. But think about it: how much do you actually talk to your spouse at these kinds of events? ...How much do you actually *see* your partner? ...Let's not even talk about any expressions of affection in group settings. Again: *gatherings with other people don't count for these once-a-month outings!*

Take turns planning the event. One month it's your responsibility, the next month it's your spouse's. Realize that planning and implementing the outing is an important part of expressing your appreciation for your partner.

When it's your turn to plan the celebration, make the arrangements to do something that you know your spouse would particularly enjoy. This is critically important. The idea behind monthly celebrations is to provide an opportunity for self-giving. So when it's your turn to plan, try to take the attitude, "I am willingly doing this for you to show you I care." Participate in the chosen activity cheerfully, not grudgingly. There is joy in seeing another person's joy. If you plan a celebration with the express purpose of delighting your mate, you may well experience a delight of your own.

Keep your celebrations as simple as your time and budget require. The critical component...is spending time together.

Be creative. Never repeat an activity more than once a year.[15]

Life Is a Process

By the seventh day God had finished the work he had been doing;
so on the seventh day he rested from all his work.
GENESIS 2:2

Read the words of Richard Swenson:

> The driven notion that we must relentlessly pursue activity every waking minute is fatally flawed—both practically and theologically. If we insist that we must be "all things to all people all of the time all by ourselves"; that God requires no less than total, all-out, burnout effort; that it would insult Christ's sacrifice for us to rest; that there are too many opportunities for us to slow down—then we will find ourselves backed up against a logical juggernaut. If these arguments hold, then how could we defend ever ceasing our efforts?
>
> Whenever we quit for a day, it is always arbitrary. The world is not yet perfect—but we cease our efforts? There is still more to be done—and yet we are going to sleep? The fact is, whenever we quit we are abandoning the job unfinished. Because *the job can never be finished.*
>
> Life is always a process, and it is the *process* that God is concerned with more than *productivity.* He knows perfectibility is not possible and that all our labors are feeble against the brokenness of the world. When we overly emphasize *productivity* (a typically American thing to do), we often pervert the *process:* instead of faith, we substitute work; instead of depth, we substitute speed; instead of love, we substitute money; instead of prayer, we substitute busyness.
>
> God does not give out monthly productivity sheets. All He asks is, "Do you love me?" Such love is not measured by units per hour (productivity), but rather by consistently loving the person standing in front of you at the moment (process). It does not have to do with the past nor the future, but the present. Right now. Are you bringing the kingdom of God to bear on whatever you are doing—right now?[16]

What are your thoughts about unfinished work, productivity, and the process? How do these relate to your marriage?

Flawed Thinking

God had finished the work he had
been doing; so...he rested.
GENESIS 2:2

God does not have to depend on human exhaustion to get His work done. He is not so desperate for resources to accomplish His purposes that we have to abandon the raising of our own children in order to accommodate Him. God is not so despairing of where to turn next that He has to ask us to go without sleep five nights in a row. Chronic overloading is not a spiritual prerequisite for authentic Christianity. Quite the contrary, overloading is often what we do when we forget who God is.

Our contemporary drivenness assumes that God never reaches down and says, "Enough, my child. Well done. Now go home and love your children. Encourage your spouse. Rest. Pray. Meditate. Sleep. Recharge your batteries. I'll have more for you to do tomorrow. And by the way, don't worry." Remember who you are dealing with. Since God is the author and creator of my limits, then it is probably okay with Him that I have limits. He probably does not expect me to be infinite and is a little surprised when I try. It is okay with Him if I am not all things to all people all the time all by myself. As a matter of fact, it is probably *not* okay with Him if I assume otherwise.

You see, it is okay for me to have limits—God doesn't.

It is okay to get a good night's sleep—God doesn't sleep.

It is okay for me to rest—God doesn't need to.

It is probably even okay to be depressed—because God isn't.

We do not know a lot about what heaven looks like, but this much we know: God is not pacing the throne room anxious and depressed because of the condition of the world. He knows, He is not surprised, and He is sovereign.

It is okay if we have limits. He is able.[17]

Slow Down

Seek ye first the kingdom of God.
MATTHEW 6:33 KJV

What steps can a couple take to bring balance to their hyperactive and overly committed lives?

Inherent in the understanding about overload is the need to prioritize. If we have more to do than we can possibly do, then we must choose.

Many people do not consciously realize what their priorities are.

Get priorities from the Word of God.

Look through God's eyes, and then act on what is seen.

Seek *first* the kingdom of God, and everything else *later*.

People are more important than things.

Once we clearly understand our priorities, the next step is learning how to say *no*. It is only a two-letter word and yet one of the most difficult to speak.

If most of us are already too busy, then we have some cutting back to do. Determine to do less, not more. But also determine to do the *right things*—another decision that requires a clear understanding of priorities. All activities need to be assessed for their spiritual authenticity.

Don't saturate your schedule. There is no need to feel guilty if your calendar has empty dates and open spaces.

Listen to God's advice. Take control of each area in your life where He has given explicit instructions.

God is a multiplying coefficient for our labors. We might only do 50 percent of all that we had planned tomorrow and yet *accomplish* 500 percent more in terms of eternal significance—if our efforts are sensitive to the promptings and empowerment of the Holy Spirit.

Someone has said, "God can do in 20 minutes what it takes us 20 years to do." Let's trust more and do less.

Is it busyness that moves mountains...or faith?[18]

The Right Time

There is a time for everything,
and a season for every activity under heaven.
ECCLESIASTES 3:1

Solomon had a lot to say about time, and he said it simply. His famous comparison of opposites, perhaps one of the most profound descriptions of life, says there's an appointed time for everything.

For example, consider this comparison: There is a time to be born, a time to die. That's obvious, but what we sometimes forget is that those times are out of our hands. Have you ever thought about when you might die? How old you'll be or want to be? We avoid thinking about it, but it's already set in God's timetable. Have you as a couple talked about this? There are two questions to ask ourselves: "Will I be ready to die?" and "What do we want to accomplish for Him before that time comes?"

There's also "a time to plant and a time to uproot." If you put seeds in the ground at the wrong time, you're throwing away your money. If you don't uproot, or harvest, at the right time you've lost it. We have our own timetables for making changes and achieving goals, but sometimes things don't work out. It could be that God's timetable differs from ours. Ask Him about changes in your life as a couple. When your ideas match His timing, things happen for the best.

There's also "a time to weep and a time to laugh." We look forward to times of laughter and fun. We need them for our very health. But we also need times to weep. C.S. Lewis said, "Pain is God's megaphone. He whispers to us in our pleasure (when we laugh), but He shouts to us in our pain (when we weep)."[19]

Has this been your experience? If not, it will. Fortunately, when we experience affliction we're not alone because God is there with us. It's all part of His timing.

The Deformity

Do not conform any longer to the pattern of this world,
but be transformed by the renewing of your mind.
Then you will be able to test and approve what God's will is—
his good, pleasing and perfect will.
ROMANS 12:2

Do you remember the movie *The Elephant Man*? It's the story of a deformed man who eventually achieves dignity. Although his body continued to thicken and deform, he changed by gaining a sense of personal worthiness and purpose.

There are many people today who aren't deformed in the physical sense, but they are in other ways. Some have deformed attitudes that are basically negative and pessimistic. This impacts a marriage. Fortunately, this deformation is curable. Some have habits that have been deformed into addictions. This can destroy a marriage. Fortunately, this deformation is also curable.

There is one deformity that mars every person alive. It's called sin. It's a spiritual deformation distorting our values and our minds. It can even cripple our abilities. You may not be able to see it from the outside, but it's there. The worst part is that the image of God, in which we were created, has been marred. Look around, read the paper, watch the news: the results of sin's deformity are everywhere.

But, praise God, He intervened to change this deformity. It wasn't an external patch-up job either. It's called "regeneration"—being born again—and gives us a brand-new life in Christ.

The word that is used to describe this change is "transformation," which means "changing." This is not anything we can bring about, it's the Holy Spirit bringing about a major renovation.

So, here are the key words for today:

Deformation: In what area do you still feel deformed?

Regeneration: When did you experience this step in your life?

Transformation: What area of your life needs this?

Renovation: In what way would you like to be renovated?[20]

Talk about these words as a couple.

Be a Peacemaker

Now when he saw the crowds, he went up on a mountainside
and sat down. His disciples came to him, and he began
to teach them, saying:…"Blessed are the peacemakers,
for they will be called sons of God."
MATTHEW 5:1,2,9

There are a number of misconceptions about who a peacemaker is. Some think that to be peacemakers we should:

- avoid all arguments and conflict
- be passive and nonconfrontational
- be easygoing and let others always have their way

What kind of marriage would this be?

The peace Jesus is talking about doesn't happen because of avoidance tactics. In fact, it's just the opposite. A peacemaker forces problems and settles them. In the last century, one of the old weapons used in the West was a revolver called "The Peacemaker." It served its purpose, but the peacemaking this passage talks about doesn't blow people away!

Look at God's Word and the emphasis on living in peace:

> If it is possible, as far as it depends on you, live at peace with everyone (Romans 12:18). Let us therefore make every effort to do what leads to peace and to mutual edification (Romans 14:19).

To be peacemakers, we've got to be at peace with ourselves. Peacemakers don't add fuel to the fire when there are conflicts. Peacemakers look for the positive and bring it out. They look for solution-oriented alternatives. Peacemakers don't bait others to lure them into arguments. A peacemaker knows how to arbitrate in order to settle disputes. A peacemaker watches what he or she says: "Pleasant words are a honeycomb, sweet to the soul and healing to the bones" (Proverbs 16:24).

Would your partner call you a peacemaker? Where are your peacemaking skills? What skills do you need to develop to make you a more effective peacemaker?

Reintroduction

*Better one handful with tranquillity than two handfuls
with toil and chasing after the wind.*
ECCLESIASTES 4:6

In the book *Becoming Soul Mates*, Les and Leslie Parrott have compiled over 50 stories of how couples have developed spiritual intimacy in their marriages. Here's a story to encourage you to nurture this dimension of your relationship.

A couple we knew gave us some advice several months before we married twenty-three years ago. That advice has served us well and upon reflection is one of the main ways we have cultivated spiritual intimacy in our relationship.

Our friends introduced us to the "principle of reintroduction." Simply put, this principle acknowledges that every day we change as individuals based on our experiences that day. In order to build a growing relationship as a couple, then, we must make time to "daily reintroduce" ourselves to each other. We share the mundane and the profound. We disclose what's going on in our lives and genuinely inquire about each other's life.

Frankly, this was fairly easy to do when we were first married and had few distractions. We had lots of time for meaningful dialogue, cups of coffee, and sharing activities together. But as children came and other adult responsibilities began to crowd our schedules, we were grateful we had established the habit early on and that it still prevails. For no amount of reading the Bible and praying together genuinely builds our relationship if we haven't bared our lives with each other on a regular basis and feel convinced that we are "naked and unashamed" with each other in the fullest sense of that biblical definition of intimacy.

Now our daily reintroduction habit usually takes the form of a long walk, an extended cup of coffee (decaf now), or a long phone call if I'm out of town. But we keep very short accounts, and we can testify that we depend on this habit to keep us growing, both as individuals and as a couple.[21]

Romance
Versus Infatuation

Love endures long.
1 CORINTHIANS 13:4 AMP

Love and infatuation are quite different. What some call love is really infatuation. And if that is the case, then both it and the relationship will die. There is a blindness to infatuation that makes people see what they want to see. Later they discover that what they thought they saw is not what they got. When their infatuation dies, it's like stepping out of a plane without a parachute. The trip down is long and painful.

The longer we are married, the more we understand (hopefully!) the kind of love that binds us together when we are at our best and at our worst. As a friend put it, "There are many times when we look at each other and there is no physical or passionate response. That's okay. It's been there before and it will be there again. We're not threatened when it's not because we know that we love each other. That's permanent, lasting. And we think it's also a gift from God. And for that we rejoice."

When couples begin their lives together there is usually a sense of romantic or passionate love. That's good. For many people that's how it begins. It can be the overture that comes before the main event—lasting love. Romance and passion are easy; love is work. The difference? "Romance is based on sexual attraction, the enjoyment of affection and imagination. Love is based on decisions, promises, and commitments."[22]

There is a benefit to romantic or passionate love:

> Passionate love performs a powerful service as long as it lasts. It focuses the total attention of two people on each other long enough for them to build an enduring structure for their relationship. The passion to love experience will never hold the two of them together forever. But building "enduring structures" for a relationship takes a lot of time and effort, and if two people are not attracted to one another physically, the hard work might never get done. That's another function of passionate love—the life-changing experience of being accepted and valued. Passionate love focuses a bright, positive light on each of the persons involved, and both of them fall in love not only with each other, but also with themselves.[23]

Stress and Attitude

For as [a man] thinks in his heart, so is he.
PROVERBS 23:7 NKJV

Let not your heart be troubled.
JOHN 14:27 NASB

Have you experienced stress in your marriage? Did you know that most stress comes from ourselves—our thoughts and our attitudes? That's right, our inner responses are the culprits. What we put into our minds and what we think about affects our bodies. Consider one way in which your thought life is affected daily: the media. What you listen to on the radio or what you watch on TV, especially if it's the news, impacts your life.

What is the first thing you listen to on the radio in the morning? What is the last TV program you watch at night before you go to sleep? There may be a correlation to the stress you feel.

What you think about when you're driving can stress you out, too. If you are stuck on the freeway and have an appointment in 20 minutes, do you say "I can't be late! Who's holding us up? Those clowns! I've got to get out of this lane"? Do you lean on the horn and glare at other drivers? Getting upset is caused by your thoughts and the way you are responding to a situation over which you have no control.

In this type of situation quit fighting it. Go with it. Give yourself permission to be stuck in traffic. Give yourself permission to be late. Tell yourself, "All right, I would rather not be stuck here and would rather not be late. But I can handle it." Instead of fussing you could pray, read a book, put in a tape or CD, smile at the other drivers, or sit back and relax. By doing this, you take control of the situation—and your stress drains away. You may not be able to take this attitude into every situation, but in many you can. Why not try it today? It may keep your heart from being troubled.

How does stress affect your marriage? Which partner is the most stressed? What can be done to help that partner?

The Love
of Money

*The love of money is a root of all kinds of evil. Some people,
eager for money, have wandered from the faith
and pierced themselves with many griefs.*
1 TIMOTHY 6:10

We all need money. Prices climb and paychecks shrink. The battle gets especially rough for a couple if they have children. How do you save for a college education when tuition at many schools can cost as much as $12,000 to $20,000 a year? Then there's the cost of room and board and books!

Some people have a different kind of problem with money—they love it. It becomes the reason for their existence, the source of their ambition, their goal in life, their god.

What part does money play in your life?

- [How much] time do you spend worrying about money?

- Do you spend more time thinking or worrying about money than you spend praying each day?

- When you're feeling down, discouraged, or hurt, do you jump in the car to go off on a shopping spree to make you feel better?

- Does your value as a person fluctuate in accordance with the ups and downs of your net worth?

- To what extent is money the source of arguments between you and your partner?

- If you listed all of your canceled checks, what message would they tell about the place money has in your life?

- To what extent do you operate on a well-defined budget that you both are aware of and each has a voice in creating?

- How do you plan to handle extra money that comes in unexpectedly? (That does happen, you know.)

- To what extent do you and your spouse pray about money and the direction God wants you to take in using it for His kingdom and glory?

Think about these issues together and talk over your answers.[24]

Who Is Your
Source of Advice?

Declare what is to be, present it—let them take counsel together.
Who foretold this long ago, who declared it from the distant past?
Was it not I, the LORD? And there is no God apart from me,
a righteous God and a Savior; there is none but me.
ISAIAH 45:21

We're a generation and culture of advice givers and advice gatherers. Everyone has an opinion, and he or she is ready to give it—solicited or not. And the advice about marriage abounds. Click on the internet, input the word "marriage" in the search window, and watch what you find. Or you could go an old fashioned way and look at the "Dear Abby" advice columns in newspapers. You'll find these in Christian magazines as well, which, incidentally, are other sources of advice.

Today there are multitudes of books on marriage. The problem is what to select and which ones have anything new. Many marriage books are just a rehash and repackaging of something that's been said before.

And then there are the radio and TV talk show hosts who allow anyone to voice their opinion. Too often advice and opinion are not based on truth.

And then there are your friends—some are advice givers whether you want it or not.

We all could use some help in our marriages. But when it's given freely, do you ask about the advice giver's credentials? Sometimes we go to other sources first, rather than going straight to the one who wants us to talk to Him. God says to us, "Talk to Me about your concerns." God's credentials are impeccable. "It is I who made the earth and created mankind upon it. My own hands stretched out the heavens; I marshaled their starry hosts" (Isaiah 45:12).

Talk to God first and then ask Him to guide you to the many valuable sources available to help your marriage grow. God's not against books, columns, or counselors. He just doesn't want to be left out of the picture.

Ten Helpful Suggestions

*Husbands, love your wives, just as Christ loved
the church and gave himself up for her.*
EPHESIANS 5:25

Here are today's ten commandments for loving your partner. They should bring a smile to his or her face.

1. *Silence is not always golden,* especially between husband and wife. Ask your partner when a good time just to talk would be.

2. *When you love your partner, you take his or her feelings and viewpoints seriously* even when they differ from your own. When you disagree, say, "I see things differently, but maybe I can learn from you." Believe it!

3. *Tell your partner how much you value him or her.* Perhaps you could use a creative word picture.

4. *Don't stop at complimenting your partner once.* Look for something else nice to say. If he or she is an extrovert, they need a lot of affection.

5. *The best way to tell your partner about something you* don't *like is to tell them about something you* do *like.* For example: "I really like it when you…try out new recipes on me or tell me you're going to the store."

6. *When your partner lets you know he or she has been hurt or offended by you, think about your goal and choose your response.* Will you be defensive? Resentful? Humble? Sorrowful? If your goal is to be close again, the choice is clear.

7. *Be your partner's companion.* When you're married, you don't want to feel alone. Be there for your spouse. Your presence, patience, and prayers will help him or her feel loved.

8. *If you love someone you will be loyal to them no matter what the cost.* You'll always believe in them, always expect the best of them, and always stand your ground in defending them (see 1 Corinthians 13:7).

9. *Complaining about your partner won't improve your marriage.* Instead, tell your spouse what you like about your marriage and make positive suggestions.

10. *Don't suffocate your partner with possessiveness.* Remember that God is the one who owns us; He has merely entrusted your partner to your care.

Have You Ever Been Mad?

God said to Jonah, "Do you have a right to be angry about the vine?"
"I do," he said. "I am angry enough to die."
But the LORD said, "You have been concerned about this vine,
though you did not tend it or make it grow."
JONAH 4:9,10

To the following questions you'll answer yes. Everyone would.

- Have you ever been mad?
- Have you ever been mad at your parents?
- Have you ever been mad at your spouse?

But what about this one?

- Have you ever been mad at God?

Jonah was mad at God about the vine and Nineveh. (Why not stop and read this short Old Testament book?) But what about you? If you have, what were you mad about?

Have you ever thought about why we get mad at anyone? Usually it's because we're frustrated. There's some need or expectation we have that's not being met like we believe it should. "That person is not doing what I want or giving me what I want. That person is keeping me from getting my way."

Some people have been mad at God because their prayers for perfect spouses weren't answered; they tithed but still didn't get raises or lost their jobs; or God didn't come through when they needed Him the most. Remember this:

- Being mad at God reflects what we believe about who God really is.
- Being mad at God is a window into our theology.
- Being mad at God could mean we've created a concept of God from our own minds rather than from Scripture.
- Being mad at God is a lesson in futility. He doesn't deserve our anger but our love. How can we be mad at someone who's done so much for us when we didn't deserve it?

Let God deal with the source of your anger. When you tell Him about your feelings, He'll gently lead you in a new direction. Praise Him for that.

The Truth

*Be completely humble and gentle; be patient,
bearing with one another in love.*
EPHESIANS 4:2

Be honest. Do you hold some stereotypes about the opposite sex? Many people reveal their biases through off-hand comments or jokes. But even if a person is "joking," it could impact a relationship. Give careful attention to these words:

> We are often like the boy, Eustace Clarence Scrubb, in "The Chronicles of Narnia." Eustace was an annoying self-centered prig if there ever was one. And, as the story goes, he went off by himself in Narnia and was lured into a dragon's den. In this den were mountains of gold and jewels; Eustace's heart coveted the treasure. He soon fell asleep. When he awoke sometime later, he was quite thirsty. He went to a nearby pool and was surprised to see a dragon in the water. He tried to figure out how a dragon could be looking at him. To his shock and horror he realized he was looking at himself. He had become a dragon! Aslan the Lion (the Christ figure in the Chronicles) comes to the bedragoned Eustace and delivers him by extending his claws and swiping them into Eustace's dragon flesh. Tearing off huge chunks at a time, Aslan uncovers the now meek and completely humbled Eustace.
>
> The story is rich in allegory. We, like Eustace, have become hard and scaly and fire-breathing. We do not trust each other. We have embraced myths about each other.
>
> If you are a man, it takes great courage to ask God how many of your attitudes about women find their source in culture, tradition and pride. If you are a woman, you need courage to ask how many of your attitudes about men find their source in wounding. Cancer does not disappear because we choose to call it another name. Both men and women need to look at the issue of honor from God's perspective.
>
> The Scripture is clear. God's intent is for men and women to share as joint heirs, expressing together His grace and gifts to a wounded world.[1]

What is your attitude toward the opposite sex? This is something you could talk about together.

Praying for
Your Spouse

Pray continually.
1 Thessalonians 5:17

Recently I found a fascinating resource that personalizes passages of Scripture into prayer for a husband and wife. It's called *Praying God's Will for My Marriage* by Lee Roberts. Roberts takes passages of Scripture and rewords them. By reading these aloud for a while, we can learn to do this for ourselves. Here is a sampling:

> I pray that my spouse and I will be swift to hear, slow to speak, slow to wrath; for the wrath of man does not produce the righteousness of God (James 1:19-20).

> I pray that my spouse and I will always love the Lord our God with all our heart, with all our soul, with all our mind, and with all our strength and that we love our neighbor as ourselves (Mark 12:30-31).

> I pray that when my spouse and I face an obstacle we always remember that God has said, "Not by might nor by power, but by my Spirit" (Zechariah 4:6).

> I pray that if my spouse and I lack wisdom, we ask it of You, God, who gives to all liberally and without reproach and that it will be given to us (James 1:5).

> I pray that my spouse and I will bless You, the Lord, at all times; and that Your praise will continually be in our mouths (Psalm 34:1).

> I pray to You, God, that my spouse and I will present our bodies a living sacrifice, holy and acceptable to God, which is our reasonable service. I pray also that we will not be conformed to this world, but transformed by the renewing of our minds, that we may prove what is that good and acceptable will of God (Romans 12:1-2).[2]

What passages would you like to pray as a couple? Can you imagine the effect on your relationship when you bathe yourselves with God's Word as a prayer? Try this as a one-month experiment, then note the difference.

A Relationship
Bank Account

Be like-minded, live in peace.
2 CORINTHIANS 13:11 NASB

One of the metaphors used to describe a couple's interaction is that of a bank account. There are variations of this, but one is called a Relational Bank Account. As is true of any bank account, the balance in the Relational Bank is in flux because of deposits and withdrawals. Relationship deposits vary in size, just like our monetary deposits. They could be a kind word or action or a very large gift of love. Withdrawals also vary. A minor disagreement could be a small withdrawal, but a major offense could drain the account. Verbal zingers are definitely withdrawals, and so are defensive actions and attitudes.

When you begin thinking of your relationship in this way, you can be more aware of deposits and attempted deposits as well as what constitutes a withdrawal. Naturally, the larger the balance, the healthier the relationship. And just like a monetary account, it's best to have sufficient reserves in your Relational Bank Account. Unfortunately, many couples live with their balances at a debit level.

There are two types of currencies in relational accounts—his and hers. Each may have a different valuation and could fluctuate from day to day. One major difference in this type of bank account is that the "teller" or receiving person sets the values of a deposit or withdrawal.

If there is a large balance in the account, a few small withdrawals don't impact the account that much. But if the balance is relatively small or hovers around zero, a small withdrawal is definitely felt. The ideal is to keep the deposits high and the withdrawals low. Each partner needs to be enlightened by the other as to what he or she perceives as a deposit or a withdrawal.

What's the status of your bank account? Is there a surplus or are you running in the red? What is a deposit for you and your partner? What is a withdrawal for you and your partner? It may help to discuss this concept together for clarification.[3]

How Much?

*I have learned to be content whatever the circumstances.
I know what it is to be in need, and I know what it is
to have plenty. I have learned the secret of being content
in any and every situation, whether well fed or hungry.*
PHILIPPIANS 4:11,12

How much do you give to your church? It's a meddling question, but an important one. But perhaps that's not the important question at all. The most significant question is, How do you give? Is it out of obligation or a sense of joy? Paul tells us that "cheerful givers are the ones God prizes" (2 Corinthians 9:7 TLB). Have you ever discussed how and why you give as a couple? Have you discussed not only how much you give, but how you feel about giving? When it comes to giving, here are some suggestions that may impact your marriage.

Take a look at the way you give now. Is your giving from the heart or from a sense of obligation? Have you considered that giving is an activity that could draw you closer to one another as well as to God?

Have you explored other Christian ministries to give to, or do you just give to your church? There are many unique ministries that can use not only money but, your personal involvement as well. One of the joys for many couples is to find a Christian project near where they live and give a few hours a month in serving. This often leads to taking a weekend or a week to some area to minister in some form of mission work. And when this is done together, you'll find yourself praying together for this venture and having a greater desire to give to this ministry.

Some people say they really don't have that much to give, and that could be true. But are there ways you could cut back or simplify your lifestyle so you could live on less and give more?

Your Spouse,
Your Ally

A new command I give you: Love one another. As I have loved you, so
you must love one another. By this all men will know that
you are my disciples, if you love one another.
JOHN 13:34,35

It's easy to become distracted and concentrate our efforts in the wrong directions. If you remember your history, you'll recall studying the War of 1812. It was significant in the history of our country. Major General Andrew Jackson, the seventh president of our country, was serving in the Tennessee militia. During the war, the morale of his troops was terrible. They argued, bickered, and fought among themselves. One day all of these problems intensified and General Jackson called the troops together, looked at them, and said one simple sentence, "Gentlemen! Remember, the enemy is over *there!*"

This problem hasn't gone away. We see it today even in the church. There's arguing, bickering, and infighting all too often. As Christians we're called to pull for one another, to support one another, believe in one another, care for one another, pray for one another, love one another.

There's another place where people sometimes become misdirected and bicker, attack, and argue. It's called marriage. A spouse is not the enemy. Couples are not to see one another as adversaries, but as allies. In marriage we are to pull for, support, believe in, care for, pray for, and love one another.

During the days of the early church, an emperor sent out a man named Aristides to check on a group of people called Christians. He saw them in action and came back with a mixed report. But one statement he made has lasted throughout the centuries: "Behold! How they love one another."

As others look at you as a married couple, hopefully this is what they say about you.[4]

You Can
Make It Work

I can do everything through him who gives me strength.
PHILIPPIANS 4:13

Recall that eventful day when you married. Think for a minute and remember the scene of where you were. The time of day, the weather, what you ate (and how much) at the reception. Remember? What do you recall about the wedding vows? If you're like many couples you remember two words. You know what they are—three letters for two simple words that made a lifelong commitment—I do. The "I do" was made in response to promises for your marriage. Some couples follow their "I do's," but others don't.

Marriage can be tough at times. We enter it with high hopes and expectations, but when some of the expectations fail to materialize, discouragement sets in. This begins to sap the energy we need to continue working on our marriages. It's as though we left the lights on in our cars and the batteries were slowly draining until it wouldn't turn over.

At times you may think, "I don't have the energy or the strength for all this effort." You know what? You don't. That's a fact. We can't do it in our own strength. But we can do it with the strength of Jesus Christ. He gives us staying power. It could be that marriage is where we need God's power and presence more than in any other relationship!

Everyone knows marriage can be tough. That's why when God helps you create a dynamic, loving marriage, it can be such a testimony to His grace. You might know couples at work or at church who are struggling. Why not show them how it's done and point them to your power source?[5]

What Do I Do?

Moses answered the people, "Do not be afraid. Stand firm
and you will see the deliverance the LORD will bring you today.
The Egyptians you see today you will never see again.
The LORD will fight for you; you need only to be still."
EXODUS 14:13,14

We have many phrases we use to describe a predicament. Perhaps you say you're "in a jam" or "in a pickle." Or you could say you're "between a rock and a hard place." Can you imagine someone from a different country hearing these phrases and wondering, "What did he say?" Or worse yet they might hear us say we're "up a tree" or "I really painted myself in a corner with that one."

Predicaments. We've all been in one before. It's a situation that is difficult, embarrassing, and at times comical. Sometimes when we're in a predicament we don't always know what to do. It's like taking a wrong turn onto a dead-end street. There's nowhere to go. It's hard to turn around so we come to a full stop. It can happen in our work, our devotional lives, and even our marriages. And when there's no way out, we begin to panic. Look at the Scripture for today. In fact, go back and read chapter 14 of Exodus. Now here are several million people in a predicament. They were trapped by the Egyptians. Their only recourse was the Red Sea. They panicked. But look at the verse for today again. Chuck Swindoll describes the difference between our response to panic and God's:

> You know the human response to panic? First, we are afraid. Second, we run. Third, we fight. Fourth, we tell everybody.
>
> God's counsel is just the opposite. Don't be afraid. Stand still. Watch Him work. Keep quiet. It's then that He does it. He takes over! He handles it exactly opposite the way we'd do it. The Lord just taps His foot, waiting for us to wait.[6]

Wait. Just wait and watch God work in those tough times.

Running

Then Jesus declared, "I am the bread of life.
He who comes to me will never go hungry,
and he who believes in me will never be thirsty."
JOHN 6:35

We're a nation of runners. Look at the pathways and parks early in the morning or in the evening. People are running at all speeds. Marathons can draw 25,000 people! We run toward things or we run away from them. We can run toward God or run away from Him. Running takes energy no matter which direction we run.

Do you remember the story of Elijah? He ran away from God. Oh, he was used by God in a great way, but like all of us he had his ups and downs physically, emotionally, and spiritually. (Incidentally, where are you right now for each of these? Are you up or down? What about your spouse?) Elijah went through an exhausting experience as He saw God bring the fire and rains (see 1 Kings 19). He was very tired. That's when we're all vulnerable. Elijah was. He received a death threat, and he panicked. He forgot the tremendous display of the power of God he'd just seen. He was afraid—big time. He got up and ran for his life (1 Kings 19:3). That's not an unusual response when we're alone and threatened. We run. That's why it's best for married couples to face situations together. Each partner gives the other strength. Well, Elijah thought he could get away. But his running only made the situation worse. It made him even more exhausted. He wasn't running in the strength of the Lord, nor was he running to the Lord.

What is it that you try to do in your own strength? Do you ever feel that as a couple you run around so much you exhaust yourselves? We can be depleted physically, emotionally, and spiritually—and the last one is the worst. When that happens, run. Not away, not in circles, but to the source of your strength. Let God feed you. Then you can really run.[7]

Don't Be Afraid

But Jesus immediately said to them:
"Take courage! It is I. Don't be afraid."
MATTHEW 14:27

W e're a lot like the disciples, aren't we? We spend time with Jesus, experience His strength, and then how quickly we forget. Remember Matthew 14, when Jesus healed the sick and fed the multitudes? Afterward He went away to pray, so the disciples took off in a boat. In the evening a storm arose. In the midst of the thrashing waves and intense wind, Jesus walked toward His friends on the water. They saw Him and thought He was a ghost. Jesus responded immediately, "It is I. Don't be afraid." Then good old impulsive Peter got out of the boat, started toward Jesus, realized what he was doing and panicked. Listen to this analysis of what happened:

1. *Uncertain circumstances*—Almost every time I deal with fear, I face uncertain circumstances—just like the disciples did. My situation seems unfamiliar. My boat is rocking. My favorite Captain does not seem to be on board. My future is unknown.

2. *Wrong conclusions*—In the middle of my panic, I often look at the obvious instead of the supernatural. Instead of seeing Jesus supernaturally at work in the middle of my storm, I see all kinds of ghosts represented by my personal fears. Sometimes I voice my fears loudly as the disciples did. Other times I feel angry and powerless. "Where is Jesus when I need Him most?"

3. *Impulsive conduct*—Peter's "jump out of the boat" behavior reminds me of myself. Sometimes I cry, "Lord, if You are *really* here, in the middle of my panic and my frightening situation, prove Yourself supernaturally."

4. *Desperate call*—When I, like Peter, step out in trust, I sometimes take my eyes off [God] and focus on my terrorizing circumstances.

5. *Immediate calm—without delay*—He reaches out to me and says, "You of little faith...why did you doubt?" And in the security of His compassionate eye contact and warm, affirming grip, my heart begins the measured, careful journey toward accepting His perfect love.[8]

Spiritual Eating Disorders

Man shall not live by bread alone,
but by every word that proceeds from the mouth of God.
MATTHEW 4:4 NKJV

There is a whole range of eating disorders today: overeating, eating the wrong food, undereating, anorexia, bulimia, and so on. They all have their own sets of problems. But some eating disorders are manifested in a different way—spiritually!

Anorexia is body emaciation because of an aversion to food and eating. Bulimia is a binge-and-purge disorder. Steve Farrar describes these disorders in the spiritual realm.

> Spiritual anorexia is an aversion to feeding from the Word of God. It is impossible for anyone to stand and fight in spiritual warfare if they are spiritually malnourished. This is why the enemy will do whatever is necessary to keep us from reading and meditating on the Scriptures. Jesus put it this way: "Man shall not live by bread alone, but by every word that proceeds from the mouth of God."
>
> If you're not consistently taking in the Scriptures, then you'll be weak, sickly and easily overcome by temptation. You may believe in the Bible and even revere it, but if you're not feeding from the Bible, you're easy prey for the enemy.
>
> As dangerous as spiritual anorexia is, there is another disorder that is even more dangerous. Bulimia is an eating disorder that is commonly known as the binge-and-purge syndrome.
>
> Spiritual bulimia is knowing the Word of God without *doing* it....Spiritual bulimia is characteristic of those who binge on truth: it can be through books, tapes, good Bible teaching, listening to a favorite communicator on the radio. That's why the spiritual bulimic appears to be so righteous. There's just one problem. The bulimic knows the truth, but he doesn't apply it.[9]

When we're undernourished physically, the answer is to eat and digest food. When we're undernourished spiritually, the answer is to eat, digest, and put into action more of the Word. Are you balanced in your spiritual eating?

Enjoy Your
Love Life

*Drink water from your own cistern, running water from your own
well. Should your springs overflow in the streets, your streams of
water in the public squares? Let them be yours alone, never to be
shared with strangers. May your fountain be blessed, and may you
rejoice in the wife of your youth. A loving doe, a graceful deer—may
her breasts satisfy you always, may you ever be captivated by her love.*
PROVERBS 5:15-19

In his book *A Celebration of Sex*, Douglas Rosenau offers the
following insight into this passage.

> We could paraphrase this for wives:
>
> > Rejoice in the husband of your youth.
> > A gentle stag, a strong deer—
> > may his hands and mouth satisfy you always,
> > may you ever be captivated by his love.
>
> The Bible often uses water as a very powerful and fitting
> metaphor for cleansing, healing, and rejuvenating. There are
> beautiful images like "streams in the desert," "water of life,"
> and "beside still waters." What a tremendous portrayal of the
> dynamic nature of lovemaking to compare it to a cistern, a
> well, a stream, and a fountain of water. It is like a cool re-
> freshing drink from your own safe supply.
>
> In one way, your sex life is a cistern in which you have
> stored many amorous memories and a sexy repertoire of
> arousing activities. You can dip into it again and again in
> your fantasy life and love-making for excitement and fun. In
> another way, making love is like a stream or spring of water.
> Sex in marriage has an ever-changing, renewing quality to it.
>
> A routine sex life is not God's design. Renew your minds
> and attitudes, and get sexy and playful. You can make love
> four times a week for the next fifty years and still never
> plumb the surprising depths of this mysterious sexual
> "stream" of becoming one flesh.

I appreciate the words *rejoice, satisfy,* and *captivated* in the
Proverbs passage. Pleasure and fun are an intended part of
making love. Our creativity, imagination, and love allow us to
remain ever enthralled sexually with the lover of our youth.
We can be ever satisfied and captivated.[10]

Celebrate—
You're Married

The LORD God said, "It is not good for the man to be alone;
I will make him a helper suitable for him."
GENESIS 2:18 NASB

If you were going to mentor a young couple or share some marital advice with them, what would you say? Perhaps it would be words such as these. (And maybe some of these thoughts will cause you to remember your first months of marriage.)

Marriage is risky business. And it's a lot more risky today than it was back then. That's why I admire your courage to commit your whole life to someone even when marriages look shaky.

Refuse to marry? That would be like standing at the Grand Canyon and keeping your eyes closed because you were afraid to look. Imagine a child who won't play in water because she might get wet. Marriage holds too much joy, too many hopes, too much happiness, too many laughs, too much life to shy away from it.

Marriage can have a dark side. There are too many broken hearts to pretend that marriage can't hurt. But those are just the stories that get our attention. We usually fail to notice the local newspaper announcements of fiftieth wedding anniversaries or the eighty-year-old neighbor who says she loves her husband more now than the day she married him.

The potential in marriage is enormous. It is like a treasure chest. Every year you open the lid more and more to discover rare jewels you wouldn't dare dream of. Pity the person who is afraid to even peek inside.

If you start to wonder what you're getting into, remember that happens to most of us. Anxiety comes with the wedding vows. That's all right.

Your love for this person will not be deterred by the marriage flutters. Every worthwhile endeavor has its bumpy roads.

Celebrate! You have made a fantastic decision. Take each day as it comes. Don't get bogged down in yesterday or try to lead ahead into tomorrow. This is the day that God has given for your life together to begin. Live it courageously.[11]

Love Is...

1 CORINTHIANS 13
Translation by J. Oswald Sanders

If I speak with the tongues of the angels above or the tongues of the seers, but am lacking in love my words are all hollow, nor will they surpass the clatter of cymbals, the clanging of brass.

If I see as a prophet and know as a sage and read the occult as an obvious page, and the might of my faith can a mountain remove, with it all I am nothing if I have not love.

If I give to the poor all the wealth I have earned and if as a martyr my body is burned and love does not move to the gift or the pain, they profit me nothing, my bounties are vain.

Love suffereth long, and is endlessly kind;
Love envieth not nor is haughty in mind;
Love never is harsh; love seeks not her own;
and a grudge and revenge to love are unknown.
Love praises no evil, is true as the day;
love heareth, believeth, and hopeth for aye.
Though knowledge may cease, and though prophecies pale,
love never, no never, no never shall fail.
Now ever abideth the faith of the free,
and high hope, and love these dominant three;
but the greatest and happiest, soaring above
all glories, all joys, and all powers is love.[12]

Laugh a Lot

A glad heart makes a cheerful countenance, but by sorrow of heart the spirit is broken....All the days of the desponding afflicted are made evil [by anxious thoughts and foreboding], but he who has a glad heart has a continual feast [regardless of circumstances].
PROVERBS 15:13,15 AMP

Laugh a little. *No, laugh a lot!* Those are words of wisdom. Laughter is one of God's gifts. Marriage is filled with incidents that lend themselves to not just a snicker, but an uncontrolled siege of laughter. What's the laughter level in your marriage? Your marriage will supply you with many opportunities to laugh. Some of the time you may wonder if you should be laughing at the incidents or you wish you hadn't. Some of the humorous incidents you can share with others, and some are "don't you *dare* share that." Can you think of some of those right now?

A sense of humor reflects a healthy atmosphere within the home. The Scripture says, "A joyful heart is good medicine, but a broken spirit dries up the bones" (Proverbs 17:22 NASB). Solomon tells us what happens when we lose our sense of humor—we'll have a broken spirit, a lack of inner healing, and dried-up bones. When we lose our ability to enjoy life, something is wrong somewhere.

Humor relaxes. It relieves tension. It brings balance into life. It gives us a respite from the heaviness of life's concerns and griefs. Those who don't laugh tend to shrivel up like dried-out prunes.

Who tells the jokes in your marriage? Have you shared with your partner the humorous incidents that happened to you as a child?

When you laugh as a couple, remember to laugh *with* one another rather than at one another. Look for the lighter side in the seriousness of life. It will make life a bit easier.

It's Wonderful...
but Scary

A gentle tongue...is a tree of life.
PROVERBS 15:4 AMP

If you were going to mentor a young couple, what would you offer? Perhaps it would be words such as these.

Getting married is wonderful and also scary. A marriage may be made in heaven, but the maintenance must be done on earth. May you always consider each other first, before others.

Don't destroy each other with words, especially in public. Words are very powerful, they can kill love faster than roses can mend it. Always work toward the best for each other. Never leave each other without a kiss or an "I love you." Three little words, but they mean so much.

Romance is a fragile flower, and it cannot long survive where it is ignored or taken for granted. Without commitment and imagination, it will slowly wither and die. But for those who are committed to keeping romance in their marriage, the best is yet to come.

Marriage is what you make it. Under God, it must be the most important relationship in all your life. If your marriage is good, you can overcome anything—financial adversity, illness, rejection, anything. If it is not good, there is not enough success in the world to fill the awful void.

Guard it against all intruders. Remember your vows. You have promised, before God and your families, to forsake all others and cleave only to each other. Never allow friends, or family, or work or anything else to come between you and your beloved.

Marriage is made of time, so schedule time together. Spend it wisely in deep sharing. Listen carefully and with understanding when he in turn shares his heart with you. Spend it wisely in fun—laugh and play together. Go places and do things together. Spend it wisely in worship—pray together. Spend it wisely in touching—hold each other—be affectionate.[13]

Tomorrow's Concerns

*Therefore do not worry about tomorrow, for tomorrow will worry
about itself. Each day has enough trouble of its own.*
MATTHEW 6:34

You've been invited to the governor's mansion for a special reception and dinner a month from now. But the shock and excitement of the invitation is soon overshadowed by a very common question: "What shall we wear?" The anticipatory delight is soon disappointed by the concern over what rags to throw on for the evening.

You've invited guests over for dinner. It's the new pastor and his wife, as well as several other church staff members. Is your concentration and energy directed toward the enjoyment and fellowship of the upcoming event? Or does a sense of panic rise as you ask, "What are we going to serve?" and "How can we get the house cleaned in time?" Is entertaining a joy or a drudgery?

Those are legitimate questions to be asked and answered. But too often we let our concerns about the future drain our joy in the present. Some people live in a constant state of imagining the future and thus fail to derive the most from the present.

If you worry about the future, who is trying to be in control? Also consider what we worry about so much of the time. Even when Matthew 6 was written, people had concerns for food and clothes. Back then, such a concern was legitimate. Many people were barely surviving. They worried out of scarcity and survival. Most of us today, however, worry out of abundance (see Matthew 6:31-34). Which one of you is most concerned about looks? Who gets uptight the most when you entertain?

Let God into your decision-making, your concerns, and your difficulties. Let Him have an opportunity to dispel your worries, fill you with peace, and give you the ability to handle what you'll face today. Let go of tomorrow. It will be here soon enough.

Sense of Security

I give them eternal life, and they shall never perish;
no one can snatch them out of my hand.
JOHN 10:28

Pets can add a lot of enjoyment to our lives—as well as some additional work. Most families end up with at least one dog or a cat. Sometimes our pets teach us valuable lessons. For instance, have you ever noticed how a mother cat carries her kittens? It's not like a kangaroo, whose baby rides in a pouch, or a monkey, who grasps it's mother with its paws and holds on for all it's worth. A baby monkey's security depends on itself. That's risky. A kitten doesn't have to hang on—the mother grasps the baby by the neck with her teeth and carries it around. The kitten's security depends on the mother.

What does your sense of security depend upon? Work, ability, money, reputation, athletic ability? Is your security based upon your partner? What about your spiritual security—your salvation? Does it depend on your ability to hang on like a baby monkey, or does it depend on who God is and what He does? What does the Scripture teach? Sometimes we let our childhood and later experiences shape what we believe biblically and theologically, rather than just trusting in what Scripture says.

Reread the Scripture for today and consider its truth. God gave you to His Son, and your security is complete in Him. Christ paid the price for your sins—in full. Nothing is owed (see Ephesians 1:7) because God is satisfied with the payment Jesus made (see Romans 3:25). Jesus is continuing His work for you by constantly praying for you (see Hebrews 7:25). How often do you think about that fact? When you accepted the Lord, at that very moment, you were sealed with the Holy Spirit—God owns you (see 2 Corinthians 1:22).

If there is a day when you feel insecure for any reason, remember that your true security in Christ is permanent.[14]

What Do You Hear?

Having eyes, do you not see? And having ears, do you not hear?
MARK 8:18 NASB

Y ou're not listening to me. Didn't you hear what I said to you? Where was your mind?" Most of us have heard those confrontational words or similar words after we married. Not too many spouses enjoy hearing them. One reason is because often they're true. We didn't really hear—or more accurately, we tuned out. We didn't listen. We use our filters to screen what we hear, and then sometimes we fall back on the old excuse, "I didn't hear you." Here's an example of selective hearing.

A Native American was in downtown New York, walking along with his friend, who lived in New York City. Suddenly he said, "I hear a cricket."

"Oh, you're crazy," his friend replied.

"No, I hear a cricket. I do! I'm sure of it."

"It's the noon hour. You know there are people bustling around, cars honking, taxis squealing, noises from the city. I'm sure you can't hear it."

"I'm sure I do." He listened attentively and then walked to the corner, across the street, and looked all around. Finally on the other corner he found a shrub in a large cement planter. He dug beneath a leaf and found a cricket.

His friend was duly astounded. But the Indian said, "No. My ears are no different than yours. It simply depends on what you are listening to. Here, let me show you."

He reached into his pocket and pulled out a handful of change—a few quarters, some dimes, nickels, and pennies. And he dropped them on the concrete.

Every head within a block turned.

"You see what I mean?" the Indian said as he began picking up his coins. "It all depends on what you are listening for."[15]

What are you listening for? Who do you have difficulty hearing? It could be the Lord with a message that will make your life better than it is now. Not hearing your partner may protect you or get you off the hook, but when you don't hear, you never know what good things you are missing.

The Tools of Battle

And take the helmet of salvation, and the sword of the Spirit.
EPHESIANS 6:17 NASB

For hundreds of years, battles were won or lost by the use of the sword. Even when guns were used, swords still had their place. And they still do today in the life of a Christian. Paul describes the armament we need in this life, and he states that the Scriptures are our sword. When he referred to a sword, he was actually referring to a short dagger which was used in hand-to-hand combat.

When married couples come into an encounter with Satan (and he loves to attack marriages), they have the Holy Spirit, who will bring to mind the right passage of Scripture—our sword—to confront the problem. For example:

> When you're exhausted and need strength: "But those who hope in the LORD will renew their strength. They will soar on wings like eagles; they will run and not grow weary, they will walk and not be faint" (Isaiah 40:31).

> When you're struggling with fear: "But now, this is what the LORD says—he who created you, O Jacob, he who formed you, O Israel: 'Fear not, for I have redeemed you; I have summoned you by name; you are mine. When you pass through the waters, I will be with you; and when you pass through the rivers, they will not sweep over you. When you walk through the fire, you will not be burned; the flames will not set you ablaze'" (Isaiah 43:1,2).

> When you feel like you're dealing with life all by yourself: "Keep your lives free from the love of money and be content with what you have, because God has said, 'Never will I leave you; never will I forsake you'" (Hebrews 13:5), or "...and teaching them to obey everything I have commanded you. And surely I am with you always, to the very end of the age" (Matthew 28:20).

> When you feel boxed in with all sorts of impossibilities: "Call to me and I will answer you and tell you great and unsearchable things you do not know" (Jeremiah 33:3).

Why not commit these verses to memory? You'll soon see the difference they make in your struggles with the problems of life.[16]

More Isn't
Always Better

You shall not covet your neighbor's house. You shall not
covet your neighbor's wife, or his manservant or maidservant,
his ox or donkey or anything that belongs to your neighbor.
EXODUS 20:17

We always want more. We think we're satisfied, then we see something we think is better, bigger, flashier, or more beautiful. Then we covet it, which means we desire it. But coveting also means lust or passionate longing.

We live in a culture that promotes dissatisfaction and coveting. The violation of this commandment to not covet leads to the violation of other commandments. The writer of Proverbs warned us about this: "All day long he craves for more, but the righteous give without sparing" (Proverbs 21:26). Jesus warned us about it: "Watch out! Be on your guard against all kinds of greed; a man's life does not consist in the abundance of his possessions" (Luke 12:15).

We live under the misbelief that more is better and things can make us happy. We find it hard to rejoice in what others have; we want it ourselves. We envy the rich who have it all. But the problem is, they don't have it all. Most are missing that special something called peace and satisfaction.

Have you ever coveted? Probably. We all have. Often it's the big three that we covet: possessions, position, and people. And desire and greed can creep into a marriage.

We can covet and we can possess, but there's a better way. Jesus said, "Seek first his kingdom and his righteousness, and all these things will be given to you as well. Therefore do not worry about tomorrow, for tomorrow will worry about itself. Each day has enough trouble of its own" (Matthew 6:33,34).

When you're content, you won't covet—and it is possible. Paul says it's true: "I am not saying this because I am in need, for I have learned to be content whatever the circumstances.... And my God will meet all your needs according to his glorious riches in Christ Jesus" (Philippians 4:11,19).

If you want to do some good coveting, you could covet the best for someone else, such as your spouse.[17]

You're Called to
Be an Encourager

Anxiety in a man's heart weighs it down,
but an encouraging word makes it glad.
PROVERBS 12:25 AMP

One of the ways we reflect love is by being encouragers. Look at what God's Word tells us to do.

In Acts 18:27, the word "encourage" means "to urge forward or persuade." In 1 Thessalonians 5:11 it means "to stimulate another person to the ordinary duties of life." Consider the words found in 1 Thessalonians 5:14: "Encourage the timid and fainthearted, help and give your support to the weak souls, [and] be very patient with everybody [always keeping your temper]" (AMP).

Scripture uses a variety of words to describe both our involvement with others as well as the actual relationships. "Urge" means "to beseech or exhort." It is intended to create an environment of urgency to listen and respond to a directive. The word translated "encourage" means "to console, comfort, and cheer up." This process includes elements of understanding, redirecting of thoughts, and a general shifting of focus from the negative to the positive. In the context of the verse, it refers to the timid ("fainthearted" in some translations) individual who is discouraged and ready to give up. It's a matter of loaning your faith and hope to the person until his or her own develops.

"Help" primarily contains the idea of "taking interest in, being devoted to, rendering assistance, or holding up spiritually and emotionally." It is not so much an active involvement as it is a passive approach. It suggests the idea of coming alongside a person and supporting him. In the context of 1 Thessalonians 5:14, it seems to refer to those who are incapable of helping themselves. How could you do this?

First Thessalonians 5:11 states, "Therefore encourage one another and build each other up, just as in fact you are doing." Hebrews 10:25 says, "Let us encourage one another." This time the word means to keep someone on his feet, who if left to himself would collapse. Your encouragement serves like the concrete pilings of a structural support.

In what way do you need to be encouraged? How does your partner need to be encouraged?

Decisions, Decisions!

*Trust in the LORD with all your heart
and lean not on your own understanding.*
PROVERBS 3:5

William Shakespeare was born in 1564. When he died in 1616, the world around him was not very different than the world he was born into. The occupational spectrum was the same, lifestyles were unchanged, disease and life expectancy were the same, family makeup was the same. And so it has been from generation to generation for century upon century. Life has been slow and static, with the best descriptive being *same*, not changing.

But at the beginning of this century, change picked up momentum. Change is like a massive tidal wave that sweeps us up and dominates us by its own independent and autonomous strength. As a direct consequence, it has given birth to an unprecedented stress epidemic that has taxed our capacity for adaptation.

So much of daily living is now involved with the making of trivial decisions based on this incredible profusion of choice. For example, Oreo cookies—now you can buy mint, double-stuff, chocolate-dipped, giant, or regular. Toothpaste is available in 250 different varieties.

Richard Swenson said, "Not only have decisions proliferated, but the context of the decisions is often more burdensome. It is one thing to decide whether to get rippled barbecue chips or unrippled sour cream and onion; it is entirely another to decide to unplug the respirator of a loved one."

The simple decisions don't cost us much, and we make them easily: "I'll have a Big Mac, fries, and a Coke." Modernity has brought us new choices that are not so easy: whether to have children and how many; whether to buy a house and how big a mortgage to assume; whether to move and how often; whether to change jobs; whether to change churches; whether both spouses should work outside the home or not; whether to put Grandpa into a nursing home.

What are the decisions you are facing as a couple? Who is the decision-maker in your marriage? What are the decisions that stress you, and which one of you has the hardest time making decisions?[18]

What Makes a
Christian Marriage?

*Then the eyes of both of them were opened,
and they realized they were naked, so they sewed fig leaves
together and made coverings for themselves.*
GENESIS 3:7

D r. David Stoop has asked one of the most important questions that married couples need to consider...and he gives an amazing answer:

> As a therapist who enjoys working with married couples, I have had many of my presuppositions challenged and destroyed by what I have experienced in my counseling office. In far too many cases, couples have referred to their marriage as Christian, but the only thing that made their marriage Christian was the type of wedding ceremony they had chosen, or the fact that they went to the same church. Most have never even thought about what it is that makes a marriage Christian.
>
> How does the reality of Christ within your personal life affect your marriage? Most people answer that question by saying, "Well, we have a Christian marriage because we're both Christians" or "We go to church together." But when they go on to describe what happens between them, there is nothing evident that makes their marriage uniquely Christian.
>
> To me, what makes a marriage Christian is that *we as a couple are seeking to restore what was lost back in Genesis.* We become whole people again through the work of Christ, and our marriage becomes fully what it was designed to be—a complete, satisfying union of two people before God. In a marriage that is growing spiritually, both partners make the choice regularly to confront not only the shame, defensiveness, and fear that any two people are going to encounter in an intimate relationship, but also brokenness in their relationship with God. We are endeavoring to restore some part of what Adam and Eve shared together with God in the very beginning.
>
> In a marriage that is Christian, we are to seek to restore that spiritual intimacy with God, together as well as individually.[19]

What do you think about this concept?

A Love That Lasts

Love never gives up.
1 CORINTHIANS 13:4 MSG

The wonder and the promise of a love that lasts were once related to me in the writings of an older man. Listen to the message he gave to all of us as he wrote:

> I couldn't even describe what I thought love was when I was first married. Forty years is a long time to be together with one person. It's almost half of a century. All I knew then was that I wanted a love that would keep us together forever. Jean really felt those love feelings a lot of people talk about. I'm not so sure I did. But I knew that I loved her. I still do. That's me all right. We learned it's all right to be different in the style of love we had and how we expressed it, as long as we were adaptable enough to learn to put it into a package that the other person liked. I didn't do that the first twenty years and that's what created what we now call our valley of "love recessions." Sometimes the wick of our candle of love got kind of low. But it never went out. We learned to work at our love and make it stronger. And it works, no matter what anyone says.
>
> Now that we're almost in our seventies we don't know how many more years we'll have to love one another. But we'll make the most of them. I'm not a poet or much of a reader, never have been, but I found a statement that puts into words some of my thoughts better than I can. Maybe this will have a message to the next generation right behind us.
>
> > It is love in old age, no longer blind, that is true love. For love's highest intensity doesn't necessarily mean its highest quality. Glamour and jealousy are gone; and the ardent caress, no longer needed, is valueless compared to the reassuring touch of a trembling hand. Passers-by commonly see little beauty in the embrace of young lovers on a park bench, but the understanding smile of an old wife to her husband is one of the loveliest things in the world.
>
> That sums it all up.[20]

Where Is He?

He is not far from each one of us.
ACTS 17:27

More and more we seem to be in a society that reminds us of an upcoming appointment. You make an appointment at the dentist's office, and they call the day before to remind you. You make an appointment at the hairdresser's, and they call the day before to remind you. You make an appointment at a counselor's office, and they call the day before to remind you.

Why? It's simple. This is also the age of "no shows" for appointments. And when that happens, there's a vacancy in someone's schedule. That means lost income.

At sports events, when stating the attendance, announcers usually talk about the number of "no shows."

Has there been a "no show" in your marriage in some way? Sometimes discouraged couples say God was a "no show" in their marriages. They wonder where He was and is! One or both are waiting for God to show up. But surprise of all surprises—God is always there in their marriages—as He is in yours.

The two of you didn't meet by chance. He knew each of you long before you were born.

God was there watching when you first met.

God knew your thoughts about each other.

He was there at your first kiss as He was when one of you popped the question.

God was in attendance at your wedding as well as there for your wedding night. He was there blessing your marriage and desiring the best for you. He is there even now, even though you can't see Him or feel Him.

You don't have to be concerned about God not "showing up." He's never absent. Could it be that you just missed Him? Or is it possible you have failed to show up in some way because of a spiritual learning disability?

Who's really missing? Hopefully, no one. Enjoy God.[21]

Are You Childlike?

*Jesus called a little child to his side and set him on his feet
in the middle of them all. "Believe me," he said,
"unless you change your whole outlook and become like little children
you will never enter the kingdom of Heaven."*
MATTHEW 18:2,3 PHILLIPS

How's your energy level, especially for your family? Low, medium, or high? Do you know who has the most energy the majority of the time? That's right—kids.

Adults who are able to perform at high levels of energy essentially follow the same thinking and behavior patterns that young children follow. Consider the following energy-gaining traits that are true of most children.

Children search out things that are fun to do. Enjoyment and fun are high values for children. When they are doing something they enjoy, they seem to have boundless energy. What enjoyable thing have you done recently as a couple?

Children are flexible. Children can jump from one activity to another, responding to what interests them the most. They're adaptable. In what ways are you flexible?

Children smile and laugh a lot. Children know the wonderful release that comes from deep, contagious laughter.

Children experience and express their emotions freely. They let them out, often without any self-consciousness.

Children are creative. When you think of every problem as an opportunity and a challenge, you become more creative.

Children keep moving. They are physically active. Sometimes it's hard to keep up with their high energy level. What type of regular exercise program are you following? (It's more fun to do this as a couple!)

Children are constantly growing mentally and physically. It's possible to learn new skills no matter what our ages. When we stop growing and learning mentally, we don't stay at the same level. We regress.

Children are willing to take risks. They have little fear about staying at something they're not really good at.

Children dream and imagine. Why stop dreaming and imagining when you're 30 or 60 or 80? The older we become, the more we can combine our dreaming with wisdom. What dream would you like to pursue?

Jesus calls us to look at life through children's eyes. They see life as simple. Their faith is also simple. Is yours?[22]

Cleaning Out
the Clutter

Ascribe to the LORD glory and strength.
PSALM 96:7

Here's an interesting thought from David Morris in his book
A Lifestyle of Worship:

> You know what it's like when you clean out the garage (or
> perhaps you haven't yet). You discover things that have been
> misplaced for years. Then again, you find things that should
> have been trashed long ago. The clutter often leaves you puz-
> zled as you think, What in the world is *that* doing here? And
> what about those "spare parts"? We can always find room for
> one more item that has virtually *no* significance! Our thought
> is, I may need that one day. That may be true, but the fact re-
> mains that most of us tend to hold on to things much too
> long—even when their usefulness has been outlived by the
> need for more space.
>
> If we're not careful, we find that storage itself becomes
> the goal. We need more space for more stuff to satisfy the
> need for more ownership and control in our lives. Even
> when we're married.
>
> Our spiritual lives can also become warehouses for use-
> less, gratifying "stuff"—attitudes, titles, past hurts, outdated
> traditions, old accomplishments, and stale testimonies that
> don't reflect a "first love" for Jesus—we think they'll be use-
> ful down the road, but all they do is clutter up the garage.
>
> Our lives then tend to become compartmentalized. We
> develop containers for everything and call it...organization.
> This belongs to my occupational life; this belongs to my so-
> cial life; this belongs to my marital life; this belongs to my
> recreational life; this belongs to my spiritual life...and the
> storage list continues.
>
> Then Jesus comes along and says, "May I look into that
> box?"

If Jesus asked you that, how would you respond?

In His question He's trying to show us that our container
system is useless to His all-seeing eye. We pretend we can
keep secrets from God, but in the depths of our hearts, we
know there's nothing hidden from Him. That's something to
think about.[23]

Hide and Seek

And they heard the sound of the LORD God walking in the garden in the cool of the day, and the man and his wife hid themselves from the presence of the LORD God among the trees of the garden.
GENESIS 3:8 NASB

Dennis Rainey has some good insights about relationships:

Remember playing "hide and seek" when you were a kid? My cousins and I usually played it just before dark.

I remember being significantly better at hiding than I was at seeking. No one could find me. But after awhile, even the sheer joy of knowing that I had outwitted my buddies was overridden by solitude. It was this loneliness that invariably would flush me out into the open.

In the same way, most of us are more adept at hiding than seeking in our relationships. The human race is well trained in hiding—we've been doing it since the beginning of time. When Adam and Eve got into trouble in the Garden of Eden, the first thing they did was to run and hide. They hid from one another—the notorious fig leaf cover-up.

From that point on, we've worn masks in our relationships, both with God and with other human beings. We hide because we are afraid to unmask ourselves and let people see us for who we really are. We feel that if others discover our faults, they'll reject us.

No human relationship endures more hiding and hurting than marriage. It is within this most intimate of human associations that two people seek to know one another and be known. It is tragic that many people marry to stop being lonely, but soon find themselves lonelier than they were as singles.

The problem is that God did not create us to hide. In the garden, He sought out Adam and Eve. And today He pursues us and challenges us to come out of our sinful, self-absorbed isolation and yield to being discovered both by Him and by our spouses.[1]

Who Were
You Made For?

For You have made him a little lower than the angels,
and You have crowned him with glory and honor.
PSALM 8:5 NKJV

Do you like garage sales? Some people love them and go every Saturday. There was a husband in Southern California whose wife was like that. It wasn't his idea of fun, but so they could spend time together he'd tag along. One day he noticed something covered up in a garage. He lifted up the tarp and discovered an old rusty motorcycle. He asked the man how much he wanted for it. When the owner replied that it wasn't for sale, the husband said, "Well, if it were, how much would you want for it?" The owner thought a while and then said, "Oh, I'd take $35." So the transaction took place, and the husband took it home. It sat in his garage for years until his wife said, "Unless you do something with it, I'll call the thrift store and they'll take it away."

Her husband went out to look at it and figure out what was needed to get it running. He wrote down the parts and called Harley-Davidson. When he gave the number there was a long silence on the other end. The parts person said he'd call back in an hour. The husband began to worry that perhaps he had a stolen bike or maybe it was used in a crime. The parts man called back and asked him to look under the seat to see if anything was written there. He did and when he reported back what he found, the Harley-Davidson man offered the man a six-figure sum for the bike. What made it so valuable? It was made for Elvis Presley. The worth wasn't in the motorcycle; it was in for whom it was made.

It's the same with you and your partner. Your value is not in yourselves, but because each of you was made for the pleasure and joy of God. Remember that when you look at each other next time.[2]

Crossfire

*I consider that our present sufferings are not worth comparing
with the glory that will be revealed in us.*
ROMANS 8:18

You hear it in the news: "The officers entered the bank and were caught in a crossfire" or "Our peacekeeping forces were caught in a crossfire." What is crossfire? In the examples cited, it's the firing of guns from two or more points so the bullet directions cross. This immobilizes the people in the line of fire, pins them down, and makes people feel out of control. You may not have experienced the crossfire of bullets, but there are other kinds.

You're happily married and everything is going along well. Suddenly the plumbing in your house breaks down. It comes to a complete stop, and the plumber can't come for three days. Then one of your kids has some alarming symptoms and the doctor wants her hospitalized (just for observation) for a night. You get a call from your spouse's parents. One of them is in intensive care at the local hospital with a heart attack and wants you to come right away. And this is three days before Thanksgiving. Pressure? Obviously. You're in a relationship crossfire. You can't be immobilized; you're needed. So what do you do?

Gary Rosberg suggests that whenever you're in crossfire, prioritize. Who needs you the most? Your spouse? Who do you need the most? Your spouse? He or she can't do what needs to be done alone. Neither can you. Sometimes in pressure situations you see your spouse as your greatest enemy. In reality, that person is your greatest asset. Everyone else is important, but you can help them the most by being a couple's team. Ask one another, "What do you need from me?" Listen to one another. Go easy on the advice and trying to fix everything all at once. You can't and won't. Talk about it. And remember, those who handle crossfire the best do so out of a marriage that is already well constructed. Don't wait for pressure before you build. It's difficult to do those two things at once.[3]

Some
Assembly Required

Unless the LORD builds the house, its builders labor in vain. Unless the LORD watches over the city, the watchmen stand guard in vain.
PSALM 127:1

Bunky Knudsen had a reputation. It wasn't the best. He was spoiled. A rich kid living in a mansion with servants and all the gadgets a person would want.

It was summer vacation for Bunky. He was between his junior and senior years in high school. He was looking forward to a summer of ease and sleeping in each morning. But early one morning he got a call from his father who happened to be the president of General Motors. His father asked him how long it would take him to get down to the G.M. plant. Bunky thought it would take him about an hour. His father said, "Well, I've got a present for you. I want to give you a brand-new Chevrolet." His son said, "I'll be there in ten minutes."

When he arrived, his dad took him past all the assembly lines to an old, dusty warehouse in the far corner of the property. He opened the door. Sure enough, there was a new Chevrolet...in several thousand pieces.

His dad knew his son was spoiled, and it was time to do something about it. Bunky found the motivation to work from seven in the morning until ten at night. In his drive to put together this new car, he was also gaining some invaluable experience: He was learning every facet of assembling cars.

His father didn't tell him "some assembly required." Those are dreaded words when we buy something from the store. Most of us would be willing to pay a bit more if it would come assembled. It's like this in some other areas as well. God gives us what we need to live Christian lives. But we have to do some assembling. We're to work out what God has already done in our lives. We'll always be doing some assembly. There's something else we'll always be assembling...our marriages. It works and goes faster when we work as a team.[4]

Damage Control

Unless the LORD builds the house, its builders labor in vain. Unless the LORD watches over the city, the watchmen stand guard in vain.
PSALM 127:1

Many organizations, police departments, and armies have plans called damage control to keep casualties or losses to a minimum. It would be helpful for married couples to have a plan for damage control as well because there are too many pressures on marriage today, and some cave in after a while.

Is there a way for couples to strengthen themselves against the onslaughts that work against lasting relationships? Yes, there is. Let's put it in the negative first: There is nothing that can cripple a marriage quicker than spiritual emptiness. You can end up drained physically, emotionally, and even intellectually. Yes, there can also be brain-drain in marriage. When this happens, little differences grow into unsolvable irritations. You start thinking the worst and wonder if you made a mistake. Is there a preventative option? Absolutely. Both a husband and wife need another person walking with them in marriage. As someone once said, "How can you have a marriage made in heaven, unless you have some help from heaven with your marriage?"

Who is building your house? If it's the Lord you're in good shape. One author put it this way:

> The ideal marriage relationship takes on the shape of an equilateral triangle. The apex is symbolized by God, with the two equal sides representing the individual marriage partners. The base of the triangle represents Jesus Christ. The analogy infers that both partners, grounded in faith in Jesus Christ, are continually moving upward toward a loving relationship with God. The perfect picture then is two individuals moving closer to one another in the marriage relationship, while also ascending upward toward God and spiritual maturity.
>
> If this is not the case in your marriage, you are probably frustrated and perplexed, fearing that this picture may never represent your home. Do not be discouraged! It is not your job to change your mate, but God's. It is your job to remain faithful in prayer for that mate. When God straightens out His vertical relationship with your mate, the horizontal relationship with you will fall beautifully into place.[5]

Reduce In-Law
and Parent Stress

And let the peace of Christ rule in your hearts.
COLOSSIANS 3:15 NASB

What happens at family get-togethers? If you plan in advance by carefully evaluating the situation, you can make these experiences better, whether they are at your place, your parents' house or your in-laws' home. Consider these questions:

- What do you want to have happen during the get-together?
- What would you like to be different this time—yourself, your response, or the other people?
- What is possible to change?
- What have been the best times? What made them that way?

Another important question that may raise mixed feelings is: Why are you getting together? What is the purpose of the event? An honest answer to these questions may relieve some pressure. I have heard responses such as:

- "I miss them and want to see them."
- "I'm going because my husband needs to be with them.
- "They're getting older."
- "Our children need to know their relatives."
- "I'm going out of obligation. The guilt I would feel if I didn't go is worse than getting together."
- "We have a wonderful time. It's a highlight of the year."
- "I'm concerned about the upset it would cause if we tried to change anything about our gatherings, even though they do need some new life. I just go along with the rest of them."

Once you have evaluated why you are getting together, identify and modify your expectations. If you are prepared not to be surprised when the grandparents get upset because your children want to play video games instead of talking with them, you will be in a better position to help them accept each other's ways.

And if your mother-in-law complains about all the work and stress over fixing Christmas dinner every year, why let yourself be surprised and upset when she does it again? If you go to the gathering giving everyone permission to be who they are and are prepared for certain events and traditions to occur as they always have, you will be less stressed.

Getting Along
with Your Relatives

Therefore encourage one another and build each other up,
just as in fact you are doing.
1 THESSALONIANS 5:11

Do you ever have problems with relatives? Whether your long-term difficulty involves a parent, sibling, grown child, young child, or spouse, perhaps a new level of expectation and a new way of thinking would help.

One of the best ways to effect a change is to specifically pray for the person you have difficulty accepting—and for yourself, too. Ask God to begin healing this person of the root causes of the problem. And ask Him to change your own capacity to accept the difficult person. Ask God to give you a heightened degree of understanding and patience and help you deal with the traits or responses in yourself that you do not like. Here's one person's story:

> The last time I saw my older sister—the family perfectionist and keeper of the faults of others—I simply told her that it was perfectly all right for her to attempt to be perfect and expect us to be that way. It was also all right for her to point out our faults, and we would accept her doing this. But I also said that I was concerned about her because if she was this way toward us, she was probably the same way toward herself. I told her I would be praying for her that the Lord would help her discover the root cause of her being so hard on herself.
>
> I concluded by saying that I was more concerned about her way of treating herself than the rest of us. She didn't say anything and I thought she was going to cry. She called yesterday and I thought I was talking to a stranger. She wasn't critical; she was actually friendly. I can't believe the change.
>
> Be hopeful—change can happen!

Physical Problems
in Marriage

Bear (endure, carry) one another's burdens.
GALATIANS 6:2 AMP

A couple married 55 years shared these insights:

I think as we look back over our marriage, one of the most fulfilling things has been the enjoyment of each other. And the fact that God led us together and the fact that even to this day we still enjoy being together.

One thing that hindered us was my wife had an auto accident five weeks after we were married. She was in a body cast for the first year of our marriage. Her spine had been crushed. We were afraid that had we been kids (we were older, I was twenty-six and she was twenty-three) we would not have stayed together because that was a difficult time. We had no money, but we had each other.

The things that I felt that he put into our marriage were his great patience and his unselfishness of putting his family first to his best ability. You always knew what he was going to be like.

His patience with me was wonderful. I was in a brace for about six years off and on, and he had great patience with me and understanding. When I would have to lie down and take it easy for awhile, he never looked at me or came through the room saying, "Are you down again?" or "Here you go again" or anything like that.

Then he had the first of a series of heart attacks before heart surgery when he was just in his early forties. I think our physical difficulties gave us both an understanding. We were both given enough physical limitations, handicaps you may say, even though we've never felt that the other one was handicapped even with his stroke.

We're so thankful his mind wasn't affected. That has been an adjustment. The retirement hasn't been an adjustment for us because he's never really retired. So this adjusting to his stroke at this time of life has been one of the hardest. But then it's just day by day. We have each other.

How will you accept losses like this in your marriage? How have you handled the ones you've already experienced?

Chosen

Praise be to the God and Father of our Lord Jesus Christ,
who has blessed us in the heavenly realms with every
spiritual blessing in Christ. For he chose us in him before
the creation of the world to be holy and blameless in his sight.
EPHESIANS 1:3,4

Reflect back to a time when you were a bit younger (perhaps a lot younger), when you were in grade school and had to play on teams. Next to being the captain of the team, what was the best thing that could happen? Wasn't it being the first one chosen? The captain locked eyes with you, pointed his finger, and said, "I choose you." At that moment in time you knew how wonderful it was to be a chosen person.

Remember your "Will you marry me?" You chose one another. It's also wonderful to be chosen by another person to be your spouse, too. Scripture gives us numerous examples of people who were chosen for specific purposes. Abraham was one of these individuals.

Abraham was born during a time when, as far as we can tell, there wasn't much interaction going on between God and mankind. But one day, out of the clear blue sky, God spoke to Abraham. You can imagine what a shock it must have been, but there was no doubt: Abraham knew it was God. The Lord said: "Leave your country, your people and your father's household and go to the land I will show you" (Genesis 12:1).

For Abraham to have God speak to him was a miracle. But there was more! God told Abraham that he was special. Abraham was a chosen one, the patriarch of blessing. And Galatians 3:7-9 affirms that we who are in Christ are children of Abraham and heirs to the promise of blessing. Remember Paul's words in today's verse! You, too, have been chosen by God. His selection of you has nothing to do with any of your characteristics or qualities. God chose to declare you holy and blameless apart from your merits and despite your shortcomings. You weren't chosen to be perfect; God simply chose you to be with Him. Why? Because He loves you. Doesn't this make you feel great?

Pray for One Another

Therefore confess your sins to each other
and pray for each other so that you may be healed.
The prayer of a righteous man is powerful and effective.
JAMES 5:16

You've probably heard the admonition to make prayer a vital part of your life together as a couple, and perhaps you want to. But if you're like many couples, you may be wondering how to do this. Perhaps your question is, "What does a couple actually do to make this a reality?" Here are several suggestions that Dave Stoop offers:

1. *Pray for each other*. You can begin by praying for each other. The Bible doesn't say directly, "Husbands and wives pray for each other." But it does say in James 5:16 that we all are to "pray for each other so that you may be healed." Pray this for your mate:

   > *And this is my prayer: that your love may abound more and more in knowledge and depth of insight, so that you may be able to discern what is best and may be pure and blameless until the day of Christ* (Philippians 1:9-10).

   Read through Paul's letters and note his prayers. They can be a very meaningful way for you to pray for each other. If you are just beginning this discipline together, it is important that you talk about what you are doing. Simply tell your spouse that you are praying for him or her and that you are using Paul's prayer as your prayer.

   The first step may not exactly make you feel like you are praying together, but it is a good place to begin if you are not yet praying together as a couple.

2. *Pray silently—together*. Take some time alone together and begin to talk about some of your concerns. As you finish the conversation, one of you may say to the other, "Let's pray about this."

   Then have a time of silent prayer together. As you pray, you may want to hold hands as a reminder that, even though you are praying silently, you are praying together.[6]

Praying Together

Therefore confess your sins to each other
and pray for each other so that you may be healed.
The prayer of a righteous man is powerful and effective.
JAMES 5:16

Yesterday we discussed the importance of praying together. Praying for each other and praying silently are good starting points. Let's continue with what Dave Stoop suggests.

3. *Finish silent prayer out loud.* The third way you can pray together is an extension of the second way we have just described. [See May 10.] It takes us a step further in becoming more open and more comfortable praying together. Instead of ending your silent prayer with a verbal "Amen," agree that after a squeeze of the hand, one of you will finish the silent prayer out loud. Just say out loud something that acknowledges feelings of thanksgiving and praise for the knowledge that God is present with you and that he hears not only your prayers but the needs of your hearts.

4. *Write out prayers, then share them.* Another way a couple can begin to pray out loud together is for each person to first write out a short, simple prayer that is meaningful to him or her. Do this part separately. Then come together and read your prayers out loud.

5. *Pray as you talk.* In this step, we back up and include God more consciously in our preliminary conversation together. As a couple, you can simply stop in the middle of conversation and suggest "let's pray a moment." At first, you can pray silently, but then, as you become more comfortable, you can simply add God to the conversation.

6. *Pray out loud together daily.* Perhaps this is the most challenging, but it's also the most rewarding.

7. *Practice "vulnerable prayer."* This one is difficult. In vulnerable prayer, we pray about ourselves, out loud, in the presence of our spouse.

Remember, praying together does more than bring two people into the presence of God, as powerful as that is! It also knits two hearts together.[7]

You Are Special

So do not worry, saying, "What shall we eat?" or "What shall we
drink?" or "What shall we wear?" For the pagans run after
all these things, and your heavenly Father knows that you
need them. But seek first his kingdom and his righteousness,
and all these things will be given to you as well. Therefore do not
worry about tomorrow, for tomorrow will worry about itself.
Each day has enough trouble of its own.
MATTHEW 6:31-34

Your presence is a present to the world.
You're unique and one of a kind.
Your life can be what you want it to be.
Take the days just one at a time.

Count your blessings, not your troubles.
You'll make it through whatever comes along.
Within you are so many answers.
Understand, have courage, be strong.

Don't put limits on yourself.
So many dreams are waiting to be realized.
Decisions are too important to leave to chance.
Reach for your peak, your goal, your prize.

Nothing wastes more energy than worrying.
The longer one carries a problem
The heavier it gets.
Don't take things too seriously.
Live a life of serenity, not a life of regrets.

Remember that a little love goes a long way.
Remember that a lot...goes forever.
Remember that friendship is a wise investment.
Life's treasures are people...together.

Realize that it's never too late.
Do ordinary things in an extraordinary way.
Have health and hope and happiness.
Take the time to wish upon a star.

And don't ever forget... for even a day...
how very special you are.

—Colin McCarty

God has declared both you and your partner very special.
And special people need to be treated in special ways.

How Much
Do You Owe?

Forgive us what we owe to you,
as we have also forgiven those who owe anything to us!
MATTHEW 6:12 PHILLIPS

Years ago there was an old song written by Merle Travis that included the words, "I owe my soul to the company store." Many couples go through life owing everyone, or so it seems. Sometimes when we accept a favor, the person will say, "You owe me." And being in debt to someone is not a comfortable feeling. We feel pressure hanging over our heads until we can repay it. What's especially sad is that today there are many couples who have experienced financial bankruptcy. But we were never called to be people in debt. "Let no debt remain outstanding, except the continuing debt to love one another" (Romans 13:8).

Of course it's difficult to purchase a house or other large items without incurring debt, but there are many other items we could choose to wait on so we won't have to owe someone.

Who do you owe? What do you owe? There are many things we owe other than money. Is there anyone to whom you owe a letter? Do you owe someone an apology? What about owing someone a visit or a call or a bit of your time? Is there anything you owe your spouse at this time? What do you owe yourself? A bit of solitude, time to sit and read, a lunch with a friend? Sometimes we're in debt to ourselves as much as to others.[8] There are more debts to be aware of as Phillip Keller points out, and these are especially applicable in marriage:

> The debt of common courtesy for each other.
>
> The debt of promises made but never fulfilled.
>
> The debt of cheerful encouragement in adversity withheld.
>
> The debt of insensitivity for those who suffer.
>
> The debt of neglect for one another in loneliness.
>
> The debt of just not caring about others.
>
> The debt of silence, when praise is needed.[9]

Wouldn't it be wonderful to begin to live debt free!

You're a Portrait

*We, who with unveiled faces all reflect the Lord's glory,
are being transformed into his likeness with ever-increasing glory,
which comes from the Lord, who is the Spirit.*
2 CORINTHIANS 3:18

You're holding that camera in front of you. You snap the shutter and then...a strange winding noise and a piece of coated paper slides out of a slot in the camera. At first it is blank. But the seconds tick by, and soon some vague shapes begin to emerge. Gradually the process continues. Thirty seconds more and the picture takes on a unique, recognizable form...it's your partner. His or her picture developed right before your eyes. Isn't the Polaroid developing process amazing? But it's nothing new. It's the same process a gifted artist uses, only it's much more rapid and mechanized.

An artist begins with a blank canvas. A brush or pallet knife is dipped into a glob of paint, lifted to the canvas, and the application begins. For a while, that's all that seems to happen...dip, lift, and apply, dip, lift, and apply. Colors are laid over colors, outlines that are at first vague become distinct. The artist glances every now and then to the model, who is motionless to make sure what is captured on the stretched cloth is an accurate representation of the person. Slowly and gradually the face begins to resemble more and more who it is supposed to reflect.

Some portraits take hours, yet others take days or even weeks. All portraits take time. They progress slowly. You and your spouse are a portrait in progress. The artist is constantly at work refashioning, remaking, and changing you. He doesn't make mistakes. He knows what needs to be added or deleted. A still-life model or a person who has commissioned an artist doesn't peek over the artist's shoulder to give advice. He trusts, sits patiently, relaxes, and allows the expert to create.

God is the artist who is shaping us. And the finished product is more than a portrait. You're being made into the image of Jesus Christ! Let your artist work on both of you. You will praise Him for the result.

Love Is...

1 Corinthians 13
Berkeley Version

I will show you a course that runs higher.

Even though I speak in human and angelic language and have no love, I am as noisy brass or a clashing cymbal. And although I have the prophetic gift and see through every secret and through all that may be known, and have sufficient faith for the removal of mountains, but I have no love, I am nothing. And though I give all my belongings to feed the hungry and surrender my body to be burned, but I have no love, I am not in the least benefited.

Love endures long and is kind; love is not jealous; love is not out for display; it is not conceited or unmannerly; it is neither self-seeking nor irritable, nor does it take account of a wrong that is suffered. It takes no pleasure in injustice, but sides happily with truth. It bears everything in silence, has unquenchable faith, hopes under all circumstances, endures without limit.

Love never fails....

When I was a child I talked like a child, I thought like a child, I reasoned like a child; but on becoming a man I was through with childish ways. For now we see indistinctly in a mirror, but then face to face. Now we know partly, but then we shall understand as completely as we are understood.

There remain then, faith, hope, love, these three; but the greatest of these is love.[10]

How's Your Body?

Therefore, I urge you, brothers, in view of God's mercy, to offer your bodies as living sacrifices, holy and pleasing to God—this is your spiritual act of worship. Do not conform any longer to the pattern of this world, but be transformed by the renewing of your mind
ROMANS 12:1,2

How's your body today? Take a look at it in the mirror. How is the body of your spouse? Do you ever talk about your bodies?

It's interesting to note and understand what the Scripture says about our bodies.

We don't own our bodies. They're not ours. They never were and never will be. Our bodies belong to God. We are to present them to God as a sacrifice. When sacrifices were presented to God in the Old Testament, the animals offered had to be the best, without blemish. But ours is a *living* sacrifice. We're a walking-around, breathing sacrifice. People should be able to look at us and say, "That's a sacrifice to God." But will they end the statement with an exclamation point or a question mark? An exclamation point says, "You're in great shape! Wow!" A question mark says, "You're a living sacrifice? You've got to be kidding!"

Which are you? How are you treating your body? What shape are you in? We live in a health-conscious age, and what we do to ourselves is rated by our partners. What we eat or don't eat, whether we exercise regularly (four times of aerobic activity a week—sorry, golf doesn't qualify), and whether we get sufficient sleep or not contribute to the shape we're in. And it does matter to God.

Our bodies are temples of the Holy Spirit (see 1 Corinthians 6:19). They belong to God. In essence, He is saying, "Treat well what I've given to you, for in doing so, you honor Me and you become a testimony to others about your relationship with Me."

Is this something you've considered in your life?

Take It with You

I pray that you may be active in sharing your faith,
so that you will have a full understanding of every good thing
we have in Christ.... I do wish, brother, that I may have some benefit
from you in the Lord; refresh my heart in Christ.
PHILEMON 6,20

People joke around when they say you can't take possessions with you into heaven, but who would want to? What would you want to take with you for the duration of eternity? Not too many of our possessions mean that much.

Perhaps the question shouldn't be *what* would we like to take, but *who* would we like to take? Who is it that you want to spend eternity with that doesn't yet know Jesus as Savior? That puts a whole new light on the subject, doesn't it? Do you have a list of the names of other people you're praying for so you can spend eternity together? That's a good place to begin. Once their names are on the list, then your prayers can begin.

God wants us to tell others about the salvation we've been given. Of course, we want our children, spouses, and other family members to know Jesus. But what about the mail carrier, grocer, physician, barber, or manicurist? Do they know you're a Christian? Do they know the way to Jesus?

You can tell other people about Christ by the life you live in front of them—the way you drive, talk about others, or respond when an overloaded shopping cart crushes your foot as someone cuts in line at the market. How do you respond to people who mess up your orders or bills or ignore you and take the next person in line? What's your response to the smelly, dirty, street person who knocks on your door looking for work or a meal?

Our words tell others what we believe. Our behavior says volumes more. Let's share who we are, what we have, and who Jesus is. We need couples today who are different. It's all right to be noticed as a couple who stands for Jesus.[11]

Are You Exhausted?

He himself is our peace, who has made the two one
and has destroyed the barrier, the dividing wall of hostility.
EPHESIANS 2:14

Fatigue—weariness—exhaustion. It happens to all of us at some time or another. All of us feel worn-out sometimes. That's normal. We're not going to feel at the end of a day like we did in the morning. All types of weariness creep into our lives—physical, emotional, mental, and even spiritual fatigue.

Some days you may want to wave a white flag of surrender and yell, "I give up. I need someone else to take over." Some days you get weary of waiting. "I am worn out calling for help; my throat is parched. My eyes fail, looking for God" (Psalm 69:3).

Some of us get weary because of criticism and persecution. "I am worn out from groaning; all night long I flood my bed with weeping and drench my couch with tears. My eyes grow weak with sorrow; they fail because of all my foes" (Psalm 6:6,7). And sometimes criticism comes from the one closest to us...or even ourselves!

Weariness is a sign that you need to rest and refresh. If you don't, you could move into the malady called burnout. Yes, there is such a thing as burnout! And you don't recover very quickly from it.

God's word can refresh you. Stop several times a day and start receiving. Take in God's Word. Dwell on it and let it refresh you. Take a moment and read Isaiah 40:29,31: "[The LORD] gives strength to the weary and increases the power of the weak....Those who hope in the LORD will renew their strength. They will soar on wings like eagles; they will run and not grow weary, they will walk and not be faint." And listen to what Jesus said, "Come to me, all you who are weary and burdened, and I will give you rest" (Matthew 11:28).

Jesus is the one to give you the rest you need. The more you try to carry everything alone, the more exhausted you'll be. The more you give to Him in prayer (and don't take back), the stronger you'll feel. Try it!

Live as a Servant

*Here is my servant whom I have chosen,
the one I love, in whom I delight.*
MATTHEW 12:18

It's doubtful that you were raised in a home with servants. Not too many of us were. But if you did, you know that those servants had one job to perform—service.

When you signed on to be a spouse, you probably didn't realize that your job description included becoming a servant. Some positions of serving are recognized and appreciated. In others you feel taken for granted. If that's the way you feel at times, remember that someone else who came to serve was unappreciated as well. One of the more than 100 names and titles of Jesus was "servant." This role was a fulfillment of the prophecy in Isaiah 42:1.

Unfortunately, we don't live in a world that values the servant role. We'd rather get than give, take than share, or grasp than release. It's all too natural to be self-centered. But all through the New Testament we see that those who had transformed lives were servants. In Romans 1:1, Paul introduced himself as a servant of Jesus Christ. In 2 Peter 1:1, Peter introduced himself as a servant of Jesus Christ. Jude, the brother of Jesus, said the same, as did John in Revelation.

Perhaps we're all afraid of what being a servant might cost us because there are risks. We can focus on the risks involved, or we can focus on service as a privilege and a learning experience.[12]

Colonel James Irwin, a former astronaut who became a lunar pedestrian, shares that while walking on the moon he realized that when he would return to earth many would consider him an international celebrity. Realizing his role as a Christian, he records:

> As I was returning to earth, I realized that I was a servant, not a celebrity. I am here as God's servant on Planet Earth to share what I have experienced that others might know the glory of God.

If Christ, Lord of the universe, became a servant for us, can we do any less for Him?[13]

How can you become more of a servant today? Take a few moments to discuss it now.

Don't Put It Off

Do not conform any longer to the pattern of this world, but be trans-
formed by the renewing of your mind. Then you will be able to test and
approve what God's will is—his good, pleasing and perfect will.
ROMANS 12:2

Put off until tomorrow..." Wait a minute—we're told not to
put things off until tomorrow! But there are exceptions, as
Lloyd Ogilvie suggests:

> When a difficult problem must be solved or a hard choice
> must be made, tell the Lord about it, praise Him for it, and
> then put off the resolution until He has full access to your
> mind and imagination. After the initial praise, thank Him
> constantly that the answer is on the way and that, in time
> and on time, you will know what He wants you to do.
>
> A woman came to see me about her "unsolvable prob-
> lems." When we got into the specific problems, she con-
> fessed that she did not know how to pray. We talked through
> the potential of praise for each of the needs. In a time of
> prayer with her, I asked for the anointing of the Holy Spirit
> on her will and imagination. She started experimenting with
> a kind of "release through rejoicing" prayer therapy. She is a
> competent executive with a large company. Her thorough-
> ness and attention to detail were utilized in keeping a log
> which has become a kind of spiritual autobiography. She
> kept track of problems surrendered with praise. The amaz-
> ing thing to her was the new freedom to imagine solutions to
> the very problems that had brought her to see me.
>
> Henry Drummond once said, "There is a will of God for
> me which is willed for no one else besides. It is a particular
> will for me, different from the will He has for anyone else—
> a private will—a will which no one else knows about."
>
> By the use of the word "private," he did not mean that the
> will of God for each of us is separatistic, freeing us from re-
> sponsibility for others. Rather, God has a personal will for
> each of us, as a part of the eternal purpose of God.[14]

How could you as a couple follow the woman's pattern?
What might this do for your marriage?

I'll Be There for You

*Because of the LORD's great love we are
not consumed, for his compassions never fail. They are
new every morning; great is your faithfulness.*
LAMENTATIONS 3:22,23

Armenia, 1988. Samuel and Danielle sent Armand off to school. Samuel said to his young son, "Have a good day, and remember I'll always be there for you."

Hours later buildings crumbled as a massive earthquake hit. Casualties were in the thousands. People were trapped in rubble. Samuel went to Armand's school and found where his classroom used to be. He began picking up rocks and pieces of wood. When he was asked what he was doing, he said he was digging for his son. Others tried to pull him away. They told him he would just make the conditions worse and the rubble would fall in even more. No one would help him; a fireman told him he was in danger because so many fires were breaking out. But he refused to quit. He picked up one rock at a time, one piece of jagged wood at a time. He worked through the night and into the next day digging. Samuel kept working. He took a beam and wedged it under a boulder. When the boulder began to move, he heard a faint cry for help. He stopped and listened. Nothing. He began to dig again. He heard a faint voice crying, "Papa."

He recognized the voice of his son, Armand, and began to dig faster and harder. Then he saw him. He said, "Armand, come out, son." But his boy said, "No, let the other children come out first. I know you'll get me." And they came out—one after another. Finally, Armand emerged, and Samuel hugged him. Armand said, "I told the others to not worry. If you were alive, you'd come and save me, and they'd be saved, too. You promised to be there for me." And he was—for Armand and 14 other children.

Are you always there for each other? How would you like your spouse to be there for you? God is. He wants us to be as well.[15]

Comfort One Another

But God, who comforts the downcast,
comforted us by the coming of Titus.
2 CORINTHIANS 7:6

Do you know how to comfort your spouse? Does your spouse know how to comfort you? Most couples think they do, but they've never really discussed it.

Comfort is something we all need. You've probably heard Joni Eareckson Tada speak, sing, or have seen her artwork. At the age of 17 she broke her neck. She has been through so much. During one of her stays in the hospital, the thought of her paralysis and being that way for the rest of her life overwhelmed her. No one seemed to notice her fear and tears of anguish. Suddenly she heard the door to her room creak open. In the darkness she could see the shape of her best friend, Jackie, crawling toward her on her hands and knees. She took down the side rail, climbed into bed with her, held Joni and began to sing to her, "Jesus, man of sorrows, what a friend..." Those words gave her the comfort and the assurance that she would survive. Jackie was able to bring back to Joni's life the assurance of God's love for her.

What are the words that your spouse wants when he or she needs comforting? You can't always give them the answer to the question "why?" because you don't always know. And you can't always fix the problem; saying "this is what you ought to do" is not usually a comfort. And excessive talking may not help either. Just be there. Put your arm around the one you love. Listen. Hum a hymn. Hold or hug. Be silent, but available. Share that you wish you could take the hurt away. Just knowing you notice and care may be the most comforting of all.[16]

Do You Have
a Shortage?

And my God will meet all your needs
according to his glorious riches in Christ Jesus.
PHILIPPIANS 4:19

In the 1970s there was an oil embargo. We had a shortage of gasoline, or so we were told. Depending on the last number on your license plate you were allowed to go to the gas station on odd or even days. During World War II there were also many shortages in this country, and everyone learned to adjust. Most younger couples today have never faced shortages like these.

Also in the 70s, people heard the ominous radio transmission: "Houston, we have a problem here." Apollo 13 Commander Jim Lovell spoke those words and let the world know that this three-man spacecraft was in dire straits. The flight engineers went to work to figure out just how serious the problem was. It came down to a critical shortage. They were short on power. In fact, they had the equivalent of what it takes to run a coffeemaker here on earth for nine hours.

There are relationship shortages as well. Have you ever considered these?

- Some relationships have a shortage of communication.
- Some relationships have a shortage of hope.
- Some relationships have a shortage of forgiveness.
- Some relationships have a shortage of togetherness.
- Some relationships have a shortage of one expression of love.

Can you think of any other possibilities? Some couples have ranked their shortage level and abundance level on a scale of 1 to 10 to get a better handle on what they have and what they need.

If there is a shortage in your marriage relationship, talk about it together, listen to one another, then ask God to help you provide what you and your partner need. He will. You can count on it.

Here Comes the Judge

Is this the way you repay the LORD, O foolish and unwise people? Is he not your Father, your Creator, who made you and formed you?
DEUTERONOMY 32:6

J ustice is served. That's a statement we believe in this country. We've got to have justice; it's a pillar of any society. It vindicates the innocent and punishes the guilty. We hope our justice system works, but often it doesn't.

We have a system of courts: municipal courts, district courts, federal courts, State Supreme courts, and the Federal Supreme Court, the highest court in our country. If we expect justice anywhere, we expect it there. But the judges are human, too. Their caseload is overwhelming. So much so that the Solicitor General of the Justice Department chooses from thousands of potential cases waiting to be heard by this court. And this court is ten times more likely to hear a case if it's filed by the Solicitor General. And there is so much paperwork in the Superior Court system that the rules for the way a document is worded, filed, or its length can keep a legitimate case from ever being heard. Perfect justice just doesn't exist in human endeavors.

The two of you probably don't have to be concerned about the Supreme Court. However, we all have a judge of our lives. He's a fair judge. He doesn't need a brief to examine a case. He doesn't do any research. He already knows everything. He knows what you are going to say before you say it (see Psalm 139:4).

There will be a final judgment day. Read Revelation 20:11-15:

> Then I saw a great white throne and him who sat on it.... And I saw the dead, great and small, standing before the throne, and books were opened. Another book was opened, which is the book of life. The dead were judged according to what they had done as recorded in the books.... Each person was judged according to what he had done. Then death and Hades were thrown into the lake of fire. The lake of fire is the second death. If anyone's name was not found written in the book of life, he was thrown into the lake of fire.

Believers won't come before the Great White Throne judgment of sinners, but we will come before Christ's judgment seat. This isn't a judgment of sin, but of how we have served Jesus. Then we receive even greater opportunities to serve Him. Think of how most people view going into a courtroom. What a difference when you know Jesus and can look forward to His judgment![17]

Perfect Love

There is no fear in love; but perfect love casts out fear.
1 John 4:18 NASB

Do you accept your spouse totally or in part? Think about this. If you accept your partner only in part, you can love only in part. And if you love in part, your marriage will never be complete.

God's Word says "perfect love casts out fear." There is a choice picture of how love casts out fear in the book *Welcome Home, Davey*. While Dave Roever was serving aboard a gunboat in Vietnam, he was holding a phosphorus grenade some six inches from his face when a sniper's bullet ignited the explosive. This is his description of the first time he saw his face after the explosion:

> While I looked in that mirror, I saw a monster, not a human being....My soul seemed to shrivel up and collapse in on itself, to be sucked into a black hole of despair. I was left with an indescribable and terrifying emptiness. I was alone in the way the souls in hell must feel alone.

Finally he came back to the States to meet with his young bride, Brenda. Just before she arrived, he watched a wife tell another burn victim that she wanted a divorce. Then Brenda walked in.

> Showing not the slightest tremor of horror or shock, she bent down and kissed me on what was left on my face. Then she looked me in my good eye, smiled and said, "Welcome home, Davey! I love you." To understand what that meant to me you have to know that's what she called me when we were most intimate; she would whisper "Davey" over and over in my ear. By using her term of endearment for me, she said, *You are my husband. You will always be my husband. You are still my man.*

That is what a marriage is all about.[18]

The Power of Words

*There is a time for everything, and a season for every activity
under heaven...a time to be silent and a time to speak.*
ECCLESIASTES 3:1,7

Words are the window into the soul. They escort my mate into my inner being, and usher me into her innermost thoughts. Words give form and expression to our deepest thoughts. They are valuable.

We use words to paint the portrait of our love for each other: "I love the way you do your hair." A few sincere words skillfully clumped together can lift the spirit of your partner high into the heavens. Words are beautiful. They also capture the raw intensity of our passion. Words can be like the pressure valve on a steam cooker that lets off steam or the arrow through the bull's-eye that heals a wounded mate. Words are powerful.

Sometimes, though, words don't come. We cannot find the words to express our deepest feelings. Language can be inadequate to get across our meaning. Sometimes the right word eludes us altogether. Other times, it teases us by buzzing around our heads, never landing long enough to be captured. And sometimes the word that comes just doesn't measure up to the beauty of the feeling. Mark Twain said, "The difference between the right word and the almost right word is the difference between lightning and the lightning bug." Words can be inadequate.

It is the duty of husbands and wives to know the times they should speak words of encouragement, comfort, challenge, and inspiration to their spouses. In marriage we each have a responsibility for each other's nurturing. It is likewise the duty of every husband and wife to know when to remain silent. There are times of silence when the highest form of love we can express may be a hand laid gently on our mate's shoulder or hand.

Never leave a thought or feeling left unsaid that may build up and encourage your mate. It is the ministry of words. Conversely, never say something better left unsaid. There is a time for everything.[19]

Let It Go

A man's wisdom gives him patience; it is to
his glory to overlook an offense.
PROVERBS 19:11

- She forgets to write down a phone message. He forgets to phone that he will be 15 minutes late for dinner.
- He doesn't put the garage door down when he leaves for work. She doesn't mark down the checks she writes in the register.
- She eats more ice cream than he would prefer. He spends more time hammering away in his workshop than she would like.
- He thinks she talks on the telephone too much. She thinks he needs to get more exercise.
- She likes to go shopping, but never calls ahead to see if the store carries the product she wants. He hates to shop so he never lends a hand getting groceries or household items.

In every marriage, each day produces many small offenses. A great secret of successful marriage is letting the little ones go. The more we must adjudicate every small infraction of our self-styled rules and regulations, the less room we will find for love and affection. We should laugh more and legislate less.

We must be patient with one another. Humans are odd creatures. It is not only our partners who are funny ducks at times. We ourselves have many foibles that can grate on the nerves of our mates. We have many weaknesses that our spouses did not see in the early days of the honeymoon. We have many quirks that can be taken as insensitivity.

"A man's wisdom gives him patience; it is to his glory to overlook an offense." To grow in our marriages we must grow in maturity and wisdom. Overlooking an offense is not the work of the spiritually immature.

A great secret to this principle is always to strive to raise the threshold of what you deem "little." In other words, constantly seek to let bigger and bigger offenses become smaller and smaller.[20]

Don't Sweat
Tomorrow

Do not worry about tomorrow, for tomorrow will worry about itself.
Each day has enough trouble of its own.
MATTHEW 6:34

Today when young men and women interview for a prospective job, one of their questions is usually, "What are the retirement benefits? What kind of pension do you have?" Sometimes a job offer is refused because of what isn't offered 40 or 50 years down the line. Many people today are concerned, and rightly so, about the future of Social Security or whether there will be any medical payments available for them when they reach retirement age. Have you ever asked?

In other areas of life, we often fall into the pattern of worrying about the future and not enjoying today. We allow what may or may not happen years from now to rob us of our joy at the present time. But 90 percent of our worries about the future never come to pass. W. Phillip Keller describes graphically what we tend to do.

> We fret and fume and fuss about the unknown future.
> We drag tomorrow's imagined difficulties into this day.
> So we desecrate each day with stress and strain.
> Our Father never intended us to live that way.
> He gives us life one day at a time.
> Yesterday is gone.
> Only today is mine to relish at a gentle pace.
> It is too precious to overload.
>> So it is to be enjoyed in serenity and strength.
>> Put first things first.
>>> The petty distractions can wait.
>>> Time erases most of them.[21]

What can you do with the gift of today? A gentle pace is not a hurried pace. Does God hurry? No, He doesn't, but we tend to. We want to get things done and move on to the next activity. But in doing so we miss the joy of doing because we're so focused on the end result. Is this what we really want?

Perhaps we can learn to move slower through life, to enjoy each moment. When we stop worrying about tomorrow, we can experience the joys of here and now.

Living the Commandments

Then God issued this edict: "I am Jehovah your God who
liberated you from your slavery in Egypt."
EXODUS 20:1,2 TLB

Kent Hughes has written an exceptional book on the Ten
Commandments titled *Disciplines of Grace*. In fact, it's the basis
for much of our study of this passage in Exodus. He gives a
provocative summary of the first four commandments. He
calls each one a Word of Grace. Let's review the first four.

What a remarkable enabling bouquet we have in the first
four words—help us live out the Shema—loving God with all
we have. Each of the words is magisterial and foundational,
and each is uniquely powerful. But like a floral bouquet, their
maximum effort comes when they are held together, for then
comes the sweet power to love God. Consider the bouquet:

The First Word of Grace—the primacy of God: "You shall
have no other gods before me." That is, "You shall have Me!
I must be in first place." If God is first, if there is nothing before Him, you will love Him more and more! Is He truly first
in your life?

The Second Word of Grace—the person of God: "You shall not
make for yourself an idol in the form of anything...." That is,
you shall not make a material image or dream up a mental
image of God according to your own design. God wants you
to see Himself in His Word and in His Son, because if you do,
you will love Him more. The clearer your vision, the greater
your love. How is your vision?

The Third Word of Grace—reverence for God: "You shall not
misuse the name of the Lord your God." That is, "You shall
reverence God's name." Reverently loving Him in your mind
and with your mouth will elevate and substantiate your love.
Honestly, do you misuse or reverence His name?

The Fourth Word of Grace—the time for God: "Remember
the Sabbath day by keeping it holy." This tells us to keep
holy the Lord's Day. Are you week by week offering it up in
love to Him?[22]

Why not consider and discuss how these commandments
fit into your marriage?

An Indication
of Love

My beloved responded and said to me, "Arise, my darling,
my beautiful one, and come along. For behold, the winter is past,
the rain is over and gone. The flowers have already appeared in the
land; the time has arrived for pruning the vines, and the voice of the
turtledove has been heard in our land. The fig tree has ripened its figs,
and the vines in blossom have given forth their fragrance. Arise,
my darling, my beautiful one, and come along!"
SONG OF SOLOMON 2:10-13

Consider these thoughts:

Have you ever wondered why spring has always been the season for lovers, the background of romantic literature in every century? It must be because the season of spring reflects the experience of the young lovers. Everything is fresh; new life flows through the world; happiness and colors triumph over winter's boring grays. Whenever any couple falls in love, it is spring for them because their lives are fresh; everything in life has a new perspective, what was black and white is now in color; what was dark is light....

New love brings new life. Spring lovers, like spring trees, though plain and barren in winter, become full and lovely in spring.

One good indication of real love is the desire to communicate, a wish to discover all about this person whom you love so much. No detail seems too trivial to be related. No mood or feeling of one is unimportant to the other. And you care about the details and the feelings because you care so much about the person.[23]

Have you discovered everything about your partner yet? Have you sat and shared one another's family picture album asking for each picture: "How old were you?" "Where were you?" "What were you doing?" If not, why not do it today? You may literally discover a different picture of your partner.

So What If You're Different!

Bearing with one another and making allowances because you love one another.
EPHESIANS 4:2 AMP

How do you feel about the fact (yes, it's a fact) that the two of you are so different? Is it a time of celebration or consternation? There is tremendous value in learning to appreciate our differences.

In 1 Corinthians 12–14, we learn that *diversity does not necessitate division.* We can learn to maximize the value of our differences. Second, it is impossible to understand and appreciate who your spouse is without understanding his or her God-given uniqueness. Consider these thoughts:

> If I do not want what you want, please try not to tell me that my want is wrong.
>
> Or if I believe other than you, at least pause before you correct my view.
>
> Or if my emotion is less than yours, or more, given the same circumstances, try not to ask me to feel more strongly or weakly.
>
> Or yet if I act, or fail to act, in the manner of your design for action, let me be.
>
> I do not, for the moment at least, ask you to understand me.
>
> That will come only when you are willing to give up changing me into a copy of you.
>
> To put up with me is the first step to understanding me. Not that you embrace my ways as right for you, but that you are no longer irritated or disappointed with me for my seeming waywardness.
>
> And in understanding me you might come to prize my differences from you, and, far from seeking to change me, preserve and even nurture those differences.[1]

While the first two steps are important, the third one is critical. Not only do we need to acknowledge our differences and be willing to value them, but we also need to have a way to understand or make sense of those differences. And when you do, what a difference it makes in your marriage. Are you there yet?

Words to Live By

Finally, brethren, whatever is true, whatever is honorable,
whatever is just, whatever is pure, whatever is lovely,
whatever is gracious, if there is any excellence,
if there is anything worthy of praise, think about these things.
PHILIPPIANS 4:8 RSV

If you want a verse to keep you on track each day, today's reading is it. Read it several times a day—better yet, memorize it! Let's consider what it means.

The word "true" means just what it says. There are many concepts, New Age teachings, and assumptions that are deceptive.

"Honorable" is a difficult word to describe or translate. It actually refers to something that has the dignity of holiness about it. The idea in this verse is that we should set our minds upon things that are more serious, dignified, and have substance. How do you think about one another during the day?

In the New Testament, the word "just" means a state of right being or right conduct. It is also used to describe people who are faithful in fulfilling their duty to God and to people.

"Pure" describes that which is morally pure, free from defilement and contamination. It's easy for our thoughts to deteriorate when we dwell on negative ideas. Our thoughts need to be clean, especially in this society. Destructiveness in marriage usually begins here.

The word "lovely" means "pleasing, agreeable, or winsome"—thoughts of kindness, love, and acceptance as opposed to vengeful or bitter ones. How you think of your partner can determine how you act toward him or her.

"Gracious" means "of good report" or "fair-speaking." It implies that the words that go through our own minds should reflect fairness.

The word "think" means "to consider or ponder or dwell on." Colossians 3:2 advises that we should set our minds and keep them set on what is above—the higher things, not on the things that are on the earth.

So there's the plan. Workable? Yes, but don't try it by yourself. Let the Holy Spirit work with you. You'll see a big difference in your thought lives. And that can make a big difference in your marriage.

Go Ahead—
It's Your Choice

Now the serpent was more crafty than any of the wild animals the
LORD God had made. He said to the woman, "Did God really say,
'You must not eat from any tree in the garden'?"
GENESIS 3:1

Doesn't it get to you when someone changes his or her mind? Especially when it's really an important decision. It happens in life. We all do it, although some do it more than others.

Is it possible to change our minds *and* reverse the consequences of a choice made at the beginning of time that has impacted the human race since then? It's possible, and it happens in lives every day.

Let's go back to the choice. A conversation took place. It occurred between Satan and Eve, and they talked, of all things, about God. They didn't debate His attributes or if He existed. The issue was about obedience. Who would Eve obey? Who would be the lord of her life? An interesting question—and one we all need to answer.

But then Eve gave Adam the fruit, and he chose to eat it. Eve didn't have to threaten him or make any deals, Adam made his choice. It wasn't for God; it was for Satan. The first couple on earth blew it. There's no getting around it. So, from the start until now the issue has been who we will serve. Will it be God or Satan?

This choice can be subtle or obvious. There was a question that Joshua put to the people of his day, "Choose for yourselves today whom you will serve" (Joshua 24:15 NASB). Who will you serve? If you say yes to Jesus and He becomes Lord and Savior of your life, the choice that Adam and Eve made in the garden is reversed! You've chosen God to be the master of your life. Let Him be the master of your marriage.[2]

Air Holes and
"The Sorry Chair"

*"In your anger do not sin": Do not let the sun
go down while you are still angry.*
EPHESIANS 4:26

In the Arctic Ocean, seals can swim under water for many minutes. However, since they do not have gills, they must come up periodically for air. Living under thick ice, they need to have air holes through the ice in several places. To keep these vital holes from freezing over, a seal visits each one frequently enough to poke its nose through the thin crust of ice that has begun to form.

Like seals, couples need to keep their lines of communication open by paying frequent attention to any icy barriers that begin to develop between them. The survival techniques used by the seals illustrate the powerful scriptural principle in today's Scripture. In other words, keep your irritations no bigger than 24-hour-size. Deal with them before they freeze so thick and hard that you can't bump your nose through them.

In the cheese country of southern Wisconsin lies a tourist attraction known as "Little Norway." It is not a town, but a farm settled by Norwegian immigrants more than 100 years ago. A tour guide once took my wife and me around the interesting buildings on this lovely spot of land.

She walked us up one flight of stairs to the master bedroom of the main log farmhouse. Near the marriage bed stood an unusual piece of furniture, which our guide referred to as "the sorry chair." It was a small, low seat of hardwood just barely big enough for two people to squeeze a portion of their posteriors onto.

Our guide explained the custom: If the husband and wife ever went to their bedroom angry at each other, they had to sit together on that uncomfortable chair until they both said, "I'm sorry." Until that healing gesture, they could not go to bed.[3]

Stand Off

*No, in all these things we are more than
conquerors through him who loved us.*
ROMANS 8:37

Have you ever been in a collision? If it's been in a car, you know the sound. There's a terrific impact and sounds of tearing metal and the crunch of glass. Then...silence. There are other collisions you've probably experienced in your marriage. It's happens easily when you're married.

During your last intense discussion (politically correct terminology for disagreement, conflict, or argument), did you happen to say to one another, "Why don't you share with me what you want or how you see things? I'll sit and listen and won't interrupt." If you did, the problem probably went away and you now encounter fewer collisions. Most couples have to learn to do this, since most individuals would rather speak first, then listen. Each partner would like the other to "see it his or her way." But if you're stuck in a deadlock, it's like two overloaded semis approaching each other on a one-lane road. Each wants to plow ahead; each is stuck. Neither will go anywhere until one backs up to a wide spot in the road. All too often both participants believe that backing up would indicate an act of weakness. So instead of moving forward and completing the journey, they engage in a power struggle and remain stuck.

The truck driver who backs up first to the wide spot makes progress possible. Then both can move ahead. He doesn't have to conquer the other truck driver, he conquers the problem.

The person who volunteers to listen first when there's a problem makes it possible for communication to take place. Standoffs paralyze; backing up is the way to move forward. We're each called to "be a ready listener" (James 1:19 AMP). Give it a try.

Distractions

There is a time for everything, and a season for
every activity under heaven.
ECCLESIASTES 3:1

I'd planned to spend quality time with my husband the other evening, but the kids distracted me."

"I was going to spend some time talking with my wife last night, but I got distracted by something in the garage."

Sound familiar? There are so many things that cry for our attention, and distractions can be enticing. Some can even be worthwhile. But consider what the dictionary says about distraction: "a mental intrusion or cause of confusion." That's not very positive. The word is used to indicate that the person strayed off course from what he or she had intended. Distraction also means something was able to pull you away from your purpose.

Sometimes we use distractions to avoid things or situations that aren't our favorite or are distressful. They could include praying together, discussing a touchy topic, how much time you spend shopping, talking on the phone, watching TV, and playing golf. Can you think of any distractions that have nudged you off course during the past six months? Take a few minutes and think back. It could be something very simple like going outside to bring in something for your spouse... but your eyes caught the TV and you just had to stop for a moment (okay, five minutes).

We're all prone to distractions, but they cost. They cripple. Every time you're tempted to distraction, ask yourself, "Do I want this mental intrusion or confusion in my life right now?" Label them. Call them what they are. Our God is a God of order. He wants order in our lives. There is a proper time to do things—distractions are not a part of His plan. You can avoid distractions because "God did not give us a spirit of timidity... [but a] calm and well-balanced mind" (2 Timothy 1:7 AMP). You can do it![4]

Guard Your Heart

Above all else, guard your heart, for it is the wellspring of life.
PROVERBS 4:23

Guard" is an interesting word. It means "exercising great care over." We guard our possessions, our lives, our children, and our spouses because we really care about them.

Solomon tells us to be alert, mindful, ready to protect and defend our hearts—to be on guard. Why? Because our hearts are the wellspring of life. It's the source of our lives. The dictionary says a wellspring is "a fountain head or the head or source of a spring or river." If it dries up, we have no water. Death Valley in California is a great example of this. At one time a stream fed a lake there. It dried up; the lake died. There's another problem that can happen to a wellspring as well. The bottlers of Perrier water found that out in 1990. The water was not only removed from distribution on this continent, they recalled 160 million bottles of the water from around the world. This cost the company approximately $30 million. Why did this happen? The source of the bestselling water in the world had been contaminated. The workers had failed to change the filters that usually took out the benzene that is naturally present in carbon dioxide. This is the gas used to make Perrier bubbly. What was contaminated was no longer drinkable.

We have an inner source or wellspring of our lives as well. There are many toxins that can seep into our hearts, which in turn can contaminate our relationships with our spouses and with God. What we watch, what we read, how we spend our time, with whom we associate—all these things can impact our hearts.

How's your heart? How's your spouse's? Is there any way that the guarding of your hearts needs to be intensified? It may be time to talk to the Lord about this—and even to one another.[5]

Are You Sick?

Those who hope in the LORD will renew their strength.
They will soar on wings like eagles; they will run and not grow weary,
they will walk and not be faint.
ISAIAH 40:31

You don't feel well so you go to the doctor, and he or she gives you a complete physical. You complain of weakness, headaches, being tired and irritable. You look okay. You're told to come back for a complete blood workup. You don't eat anything after 8 o'clock the night before, and early the next morning you go in. The attendant takes what seems an enormous amount of blood out of your arm.

Your doctor calls and says, "Well, I've found the problem. No wonder you feel the way you do. You're anemic. That's all. It's correctable. I'll give you the treatment, you follow it, and in a while you'll be back to normal." Physical anemia isn't that unusual. Sometimes we're physically anemic because we don't take proper care of our bodies.

Our marriages can also suffer forms of anemia if we don't nurture them and pay attention to the early warning signs of problems. There are two other types of anemia that can occur. We can feel tired and worn-out in our struggles and irritable with one another. There's not much strength in the relationship itself. Marital anemia is both preventable and correctable. Sometimes it means going to a marital counselor.

The second anemia is spiritual. Our relationships with the Lord seem distant. Our prayers seem to bounce off the ceiling when we do pray. We feel empty in the worship service and wonder, "Where is God?"

Who do you go to for help when this condition hits? There's only one person—God. It's not a matter of praying more, serving more, or attending more services. God has an answer; it's simply to wait on Him. Meditate on who He is; pray from your hearts for Him to speak to you.

Discuss what "waiting on the Lord" means to both of you.[6]

Feeling Inferior?

We are God's workmanship, created in Christ Jesus to do good works,
which God prepared in advance for us to do.
EPHESIANS 2:10

"Our brand is superior." "That brand is inferior to this one." "Don't buy an inferior car. This is the one for you." The ads shout to us telling us we need to have the best of everything. Sometimes we develop the attitude that in order to be satisfied everything we have must be perfect and better than everyone else's. Sometimes this even includes our partners! And if they're not perfect, well let's change them!

There is something about feeling inferior that impacts our marriages. It's when one spouse—or both—believes she or he is inferior. Some people come into marriage out of a background that would make anyone feel inferior. Many struggle with feelings of inadequacy. But remember, the feeling of inadequacy is just that—a feeling. There's a much better foundation to base your opinion on, and that's the Word of God. The Bible says we're worth a lot! Charles Stanley describes our value so well when he says:

> God bases our worth not on what we have but on who we have, Jesus Christ as our personal Savior and the Holy Spirit as our ever-present Comforter and Counselor.

> God bases our worth not on our performance or achievements but on whether we have received His free gift of grace and forgiveness in our lives.

> God bases our worth not on who we know or where we live or how we look but on whether we know, follow, and trust Jesus Christ as our Lord.

> God says we need only to receive His love and to accept what He has done for us in order for us to be fully acceptable in His eternal kingdom.

> If you ever catch a glimpse of how much God loves you, desires to be with you, and has prepared good things for you, you'll find yourself with confidence and inner assurance that can't be matched.[7]

If you and your spouse are valued that much by God, how should you treat one another?

Keep on Walking

As a prisoner for the Lord, then, I urge you to live a life
worthy of the calling you have received.
EPHESIANS 4:1

Have the two of you ever gone for a walk together? This usually begins in courtship. Couples stroll along in a leisurely fashion while they talk, look into one another's eyes, and feast on each word said, somewhat oblivious to their surroundings. There's no urgency to get somewhere. They're delighting in the process.

Let's change the scene to A.M. (after marriage). One suggests going for a walk. The other says, "Why? What's the purpose?" Eventually they go for their walk, but this time their arms aren't wrapped around one another. In fact, one is five strides ahead of the other and saying, "Walk faster" (usually it's the husband). The other one is looking around, taking in the surroundings, and saying slow down.

Walking is a way of describing the Christian life. Perhaps you've been asked the question, "How's your Christian walk?" It means, "How are you doing in your Christian life?" In the Scripture, to walk means basically to conduct your life in a certain way. Ephesians 4 and 5 talk about our walk. Ephesians 4:1,2 tells us to walk worthily. It's saying make sure the way we behave fits our calling. Ephesians 4:17,18 tells us to walk differently from nonbelievers. Other verses tell us to not be conformed to this world. The Message says it this way: "Don't become so well-adjusted to your culture that you fit into it without even thinking" (Romans 12:2). Ephesians 5:1,2 tells us to walk in a loving way with a sacrificial, other-centered love. Finally, Scripture tells us to walk in faith. To walk like this, we need God's will and direction for our lives.

How are you walking? The best place to practice your walk is in your marriage. It works. And the next time you decide to go walking together, one of you suggest, "Let's walk together like we did before we married." Who knows what might transpire?

You Can't Take It with You

The earth is the LORD'S, and everything in it, the world, and all who live in it.
PSALM 24:1

Have you heard the story of the dying man who wanted to take all of his money with him when he died? It wasn't all that much, but he was bound and determined it was going with him wherever he went. So he called his pastor, his doctor, and his attorney to come to his home where he lay dying. He gave each one of them an envelope with 10,000 dollars in it with the instruction to put the envelopes in his coffin at the funeral service.

In a few weeks, the man died. Each of the three did what they had agreed to do. Later they met for coffee to talk about the experience. The minister said, "I'm sure that Frank would have wanted to help out with the new church organ had he lived, so I took out 2,000 dollars and placed 8,000 dollars in the coffin!"

The doctor said, "Well, I know he appreciated the care I gave him, and I know he was interested in the new clinic. So I took out 5,000 and put 5,000 in the coffin."

The lawyer said, "Well, I'm two steps ahead of you. I took out what each of you put in the coffin, kept my 10,000, and put a check in the coffin for 30,000 dollars."

Everyone wanted to hang on to the cash, and a lot of couples live their lives that way, too. Accumulate, gather, retain, amass as much as possible. And it may not just be cash. Cars, clothes, furniture, jewelry, and real estate can also indicate the drive to own as much as possible. If we're not Christians, that's an understandable philosophy. But if we're Christians, we must have a different approach called stewardship. This means asking God what He wants us to accumulate.

You don't own yourself; God owns you. He owns everything. So take the stress and pressure off yourself and remember you're just managing what God has entrusted to you. He doesn't want you to try to bring it with you. He only wants you.[8]

Life Is a War

Knowing their thoughts, Jesus said, "Why do you entertain
evil thoughts in your hearts?"
MATTHEW 9:4

Listen to the words of one couple and their perspective on
life:

> My wife and I have come to see life more and more as a
> war. Ultimately, our battle is with the forces of evil, but on a
> daily level war involves a struggle with time, money, prior-
> ities, health, and unplanned crises. If we are to fight as allies,
> then we must grow in greater intimacy. To this growth we
> devote our time before dinner. This time is sacred and rarely
> crowded out by other activities. It is our "R and R" to return
> to fighting well.
>
> This has required repeated instructions to our children
> not to interrupt us. It requires us to let the phone ring, to
> let guests wait for their hosts to return, and to offend count-
> less others who see that as a selfish venture. In fact, it is a
> refueling time that allows us to engage with our world with
> a clearer loyalty to one another, a deepened passion for
> what is good, and a sense of rest that can come from no
> other place.
>
> The time is seldom less than a half-hour, and occasionally
> it may stretch for an hour. We usually begin by catching up
> on the events of the day. Soon, the events become the
> springboard for conversation about what was provoked in
> us that caused distress or delight. Often my wife will have
> read or thought about things that she recorded in her jour-
> nal, and she will read to me. Other times I will want her to
> listen to something I have written. We find it crucial to read
> out loud together. It not only crystallizes our vague strug-
> gles, but it also records our progress together through life.
>
> Our time is unstructured, but it is not uncommon for us
> to move from our events to feelings, from a struggle to joy,
> or from reading to prayer. In conclusion and consummation
> we call on God to deepen our hearts for him. We return to
> our family and world refreshed in our sense of being inti-
> mate allies.[9]

Accountability

Each of us will give an account of himself to God.
ROMANS 14:12

We're all accountable to someone. It could be our employers, our families, or even our friends. We're definitely accountable for our money through the wonderful and kind auspices of the Internal Revenue Service. And we're accountable to God, especially in the future.

But what about the kind of accountability you can choose to have in your life or not? Accountability to your spouse. Have you ever considered the fact that you are accountable to one another? Accountability includes the type of relationship in which your spouse can ask you personal questions so you stay on track. (You can ask him or her similar questions as well.)

We all need to answer to someone so we can reflect the presence of God in our lives in a genuine way. When we don't have someone to answer to, we're more likely to blow it. It's that clear and simple. We all like to be in charge of our own lives, to be our own bosses, but we are all blind and deaf to some of our greatest areas of need. Other people can challenge us, support us, confront us, encourage us. As believers we are called to be accountable in many ways.

> Brothers, if someone is caught in a sin, you who are spiritual should restore him gently. But watch yourself, or you also may be tempted. Carry each other's burdens, and in this way you will fulfill the law of Christ (Galatians 6:1,2).

> Two are better than one, because they have a good return for their work: If one falls down, his friend can help him up. But pity the man who falls and has no one to help him up! (Ecclesiastes 4:9,10).

> Wounds from a friend can be trusted, but an enemy multiplies kisses....As iron sharpens iron, so one man sharpens another (Proverbs 27:6,17).

What about it? Is accountability a part of your marriage? If not, think about it, talk about it, pray about it, and practice it.

Follow the Rules

Do not think that I have come to abolish the Law or the Prophets;
I have not come to abolish them but to fulfill them. I tell you the truth,
until heaven and earth disappear, not the smallest letter,
not the least stroke of a pen, will by any means disappear
from the Law until everything is accomplished.
MATTHEW 5:17,18

We live in a world of lawbreakers. Some believe laws were made to be broken. Some rules are fair; some rules are unfair. They restrict, they confine, they regulate, but they also provide structure and order. What about the laws God has given us? Do you see them as restrictive or beneficial? Hampering you or making your life better? Difficult to keep or easy? Few people consider God's laws today, but they will bless you if you follow them. David gave us a thorough description of the benefits of the law.

> The law of the LORD is perfect, reviving the soul. The statutes of the LORD are trustworthy, making wise the simple. The precepts of the LORD are right, giving joy to the heart. The commands of the LORD are radiant, giving light to the eyes. The fear of the LORD is pure, enduring forever. The ordinances of the LORD are sure and altogether righteous. They are more precious than gold, than much pure gold; they are sweeter than honey, than honey from the comb (Psalm 19:7-10).

What do God's laws do? *They reveal His holiness.* They invite us to be holy. Their purpose is to help us know the lawgiver better and to make our lives full. Are there laws or rules you live by in your marriage? What are they?

Love Is. . .

1 Corinthians 13
Cotton Patch Version

Though I speak with the tongues of men and of angels, but have no love, I am a hollow-sounding horn or a nerve-wracking rattle. And though I have the ability to preach and know all the secrets and all the slogans, and though I have sufficient faith to move a mountain, but have no love, I am nothing. Even though I renounce all my possessions, and give my body as a flaming sacrifice, but have no love, I accomplish exactly nothing. Love is long-suffering and kind. Love is not envious, nor does it strut and brag. It does not act up, nor try to get things for itself. It pitches no tantrums, keeps no books on insults or injuries, sees no fun in wickedness, but rejoices when truth prevails. Love is all-embracing, all-trusting, all-hoping, all-enduring. Love never quits....

For example, when I was a child, I was talking like a child, thinking like a child, acting like a child, but when I became an adult, I outgrew my childish ways. So, on the childish level [i.e., *without love*] we look at one another in a trick mirror, but on the adult level [i.e., *with love*] we see face to face; as a child [i.e., *without love*] I understand immaturely, but as an adult [i.e., *with love*] I'll understand just as I'll be understood. Now these three things endure: faith, hope and love; but the greatest of all is love. Seek diligently for love.[10]

God Gave the Law in Love

I am the LORD your God, who brought
you out of Egypt, out of the land of slavery.
EXODUS 20:2

Have you ever wondered what it would have been like to have been there when God gave the Ten Commandments to Moses?

> On the morning of the third day there was thunder and lightning, with a thick cloud over the mountain, and a very loud trumpet blast. Everyone in the camp trembled. Then Moses led the people out of the camp to meet with God, and they stood at the foot of the mountain. Mount Sinai was covered with smoke, because the LORD descended on it in fire. The smoke billowed up from it like smoke from a furnace, the whole mountain trembled violently, and the sound of the trumpet grew louder and louder (Exodus 19:16-19).

Try to picture it in your mind. See it. Hear it. Smell it. Feel it. The children of Israel did. Have you been in a thunderstorm that was so intense that the sounds rolled and roared? Have you seen the lightning flash from peak to peak and then flash with continued displays of sheet lightning? Have you felt the rumble and shake of an earthquake? Put all these together and you have the scene.

The giving of the law reveals God's gracious nature. He did not have to do what He did. He chose to. What God did is what He has always done for us in His grace. When the law was given a second time, Moses reminded the people of this:

> But it was because the LORD loved you and kept the oath he swore to your forefathers that he brought you out with a mighty hand and redeemed you from the land of slavery, from the power of Pharaoh king of Egypt (Deuteronomy 7:8).

God directs His grace to you today because He loves you. The children of Israel couldn't earn God's love, and neither can you. God paid the way for His people then; He pays it now.

Words to Live By

The tongue of the wise commends knowledge,
but the mouth of the fool gushes folly.
PROVERBS 15:2

A wife was browsing through the public library looking for interesting books. Her eye was drawn toward what looked like a mystery called *The Case of the Flapping Tongue.* The author's name was...Solomon. She opened the book and, much to her surprise, discovered that it was a selection of verses from the book of Proverbs. As she glanced through the book she was surprised to discover that the words "tongue," "mouth," "lips," and "words" were used in Proverbs almost 50 times.

The book of Proverbs is a wonderful, practical book for couples to live by—especially in what they say to one another. Our mouths can be used in healthy or unhealthy ways. Let's consider what Proverbs says about an uncontrolled tongue.

Deceitful flattery: "Food gained by fraud tastes sweet to a man, but he ends up with a mouth full of gravel" (Proverbs 20:17).

We want to stay clear of flattery because it reflects insincerity and sometimes backfires. When your partner asks you a direct question, be honest (also be kind).

Gossip and slander: "He who conceals his hatred has lying lips, and whoever spreads slander is a fool" (Proverbs 10:18).

God has some very strong words to say about gossip. It's easy for couples to fall into this pattern.

Angry, strifeful words: "An angry man stirs up dissension, and a hot-tempered one commits many sins" (Proverbs 29:22).

Anger and strife usually reflect stubbornness and rigidity. It doesn't build love in a relationship.

Boasting: "Like clouds and wind without rain is a man who boasts of gifts he does not give" (Proverbs 25:14).

Calling attention to ourselves usually pushes others away from us.

Talking too much: "When words are many, sin is not absent, but he who holds his tongue is wise" (Proverbs 10:19).

When we talk, we aren't listening. It's only when we listen that we learn.

Are any of these familiar? Do any of them appear in your marriage?

Words of Wisdom

*We all stumble in many ways. If anyone is never at fault in what he
says, he is a perfect man, able to keep his whole body in check.*
JAMES 3:2

Control. Highly desired, frequently absent, sometimes
overused. But when it comes to controlling our mouths, it's essential. A mouth out of control is like a runaway train ready to
jump the track and create havoc all around. But a mouth in
control can be a joy and encouragement. If you want some
guidance on how to respond to your spouse, look to the book
of Proverbs.

First, all of us are to give wise counsel and sound advice:
"The lips of the righteous know what is fitting, but the mouth
of the wicked only what is perverse" (Proverbs 10:32). "The
lips of the wise spread knowledge; not so the hearts of fools"
(Proverbs 15:7).

We are called upon to give reproof, a rebuke, and especially
spiritual exhortation: "He who listens to a life-giving rebuke
will be at home among the wise. He who ignores discipline de-
spises himself, but whoever heeds correction gains understanding" (Proverbs 15:31,32).

We're also asked to say the right words at the right time: "A
word fitly spoken and in due season is like apples of gold in
settings of silver" (Proverbs 25:11 AMP).

Did you know that the Word of God also asks us to have a
sense of humor? "A happy heart makes the face cheerful, but
heartache crushes the spirit.... All the days of the oppressed are
wretched, but the cheerful heart has a continual feast"
(Proverbs 15:13,15). Humor is healthy; it's a lifesaver. We need
to laugh not a little, but a lot. As one man prayed, "Lord,
loosen us up and activate our funny bones." Humor helps us
survive. And we need to make sure we laugh at ourselves as
well.

Which of these verses will you ask God to help you apply
today?

How Are You Handling Aging?

Even to your old age and gray hairs I am he,
I am he who will sustain you.
ISAIAH 46:4

You're growing older, aren't you? It's all right to admit it—even if we don't really like to acknowledge it. We live in a society that celebrates the vitality of youth. But we all hit our 30s, 40s, 50s, 60s, and beyond eventually. (If we don't hit them, it's because...well, we know the alternative.) We have a condition in this country described as "the graying of America." More and more people are in their 60s. The people in this age bracket face new stresses, problems, and challenges. You know what some of them are if you are approaching this time or if you have aged parents. Health issues, retirement, and memory loss seem foremost in our minds.

How we face and handle aging is a choice. We can take the pessimistic approach or the biblical approach. Old age can be a time of strength, as reflected in Isaiah 46:4, the theme verse of today's devotion.

E. Stanley Jones, in his book *Christian Maturity*, shares how this promise of God from Isaiah was fulfilled in his advanced years. He writes that God said to him when he passed 70: "I'm giving you the best ten years of your life—the next ten ahead." Jones adds: "Two of them have passed and they have literally been the best two years of my life. Eight to go!...Practically all my question marks have now been straightened out into dancing exclamation points."[11]

We can live in the past and dread our future or look toward the future and live with faith and hope. Have you ever considered that there just might be joy in aging? Remember the promise of God, "They will still bear fruit in old age, they will stay fresh and green" (Psalm 92:14).[12]

A Marriage
Based on One Verse

*Be kind and compassionate to one another,
forgiving each other, just as in Christ God forgave you.*
EPHESIANS 4:32

What a verse to help couples! How can we apply it in the daily living between a husband and wife? Here are some possibilities.

Cancel debts. Forgiving other people just as God in Christ has forgiven us means canceling the debts. It means resisting the impulse to bring up the past. It may mean asking our spouses to forgive us if we bring up old problems on impulse in the heat of an argument.

Be kind. Webster's dictionary defines kindness as being sympathetic, gentle, and benevolent. Forgiveness springs much easier from an attitude of kindness than from an attitude of defensiveness. When we feel threatened, we naturally get defensive. Replacing defensiveness with kindness means we become vulnerable to being taken advantage of again. That's why being kind is sometimes difficult. It takes a strong person to be gentle, and sometimes we don't feel all that strong. But we are called by Scripture to be kind, so we are promised strength as well. Psalm 28:7 says, "The LORD is my strength and my shield; my heart trusts in Him, and I am helped; therefore my heart exults, and with my song I shall thank Him" (NASB).

Be tenderhearted. Being kind implies some vulnerability, but being tenderhearted implies even more vulnerability. It means absorbing some hurts so our spouses can grow. It means letting our walls down and inviting our partners to feel our emotions with us. It also means feeling their emotions with them. When we are tenderhearted, it becomes much easier to forgive.

The opposite of tenderheartedness is hardness of heart. In Mark 10:4,5, Jesus says hardness of heart was the reason Moses wrote the law on divorce. In other words, tenderhearted couples don't need divorce. Tenderhearted people can forgive. No one has found a better way to live yet.

Sensitive to
the Extreme

A quick-tempered man does foolish things, and a crafty man is hated.
PROVERBS 14:17

You've met quick-tempered and crafty people before. Who are they? Those people who have the highly refined, super-sensitive antenna sticking out, who interpret whatever you say, whatever you do, however you look as a personal vendetta against them. These individuals have a highly refined capability of finding slights, insults, put-downs, and degrading comments where none were ever intended or they just don't exist! Then they misinterpret and react defensively, aggressively, or both.

A critical person demands an apology, yet counterattacks. And if the response isn't to his or her satisfaction, watch out. The arsenal of weapons is unleashed. The silent treatment is one of their choices. So is slamming the door, questioning your parents' abilities as parents, and cutting off marital privileges.

Hopefully you're not an overly sensitive person. Hopefully your spouse isn't an overly sensitive person. It's hard enough contending with a sibling or parent who's this way, let alone having this happen within marriage. If some people are overly sensitive, what can they do? Reflect on these questions:

1. Is there a tendency to imagine the worst or to interpret something as an insult?

2. Is the Holy Spirit called on to bring a balance into the perceptions?

3. Has prayer occurred for a proper response if there has been an offense?

4. Has the offending person been asked, "Could you please clarify that?" or "Could you say that in a different way, please?"

5. Has the following passage been put into practice? "A man's wisdom gives him patience; it is to his glory to overlook an offense" (Proverbs 19:11).

Instead of assuming the worst, assume the best. It's a totally different outcome![13]

Ownership

Has not [the LORD] made them one? In flesh and spirit they are his.
MALACHI 2:15

This is my wife." "This is my husband." How often we use these phrases. They imply ownership. We also talk about "my" marriage relationship or "my" marital rights. Ownership is a big issue, and it can create big disputes.

There was a massive lawsuit years ago between the states of New Jersey and New York. It was over who owned most of Ellis Island in New York Harbor, the place where millions of immigrants entered our country. When this island was first developed it was quite small, just over four acres, and New York state had the deed, but the surrounding bay was given to New Jersey. However, over the years, as soil was carried out by barges and dumped, the island grew to 24 acres. Then the problems began—both states claimed the property belonged to them. Property rights were the issue, and the lawsuits cost millions.

Property rights conflicts can also occur in marriages. People tend to be territorial. Certain rooms or areas become "claimed." That's okay. Every couple has to work through that issue. But what you don't—and can't—own is the marriage relationship. That belongs to God. Look at today's Scripture. This means a married couple does *not* have the right to do with their marriage what they want. God doesn't grant an ownership of a marriage to the couple. God created the marriage; it's His. He brought you together, witnessed your vows, and blessed you. Perhaps our marriage certificates should have a phrase added—"Property of God."[14]

How do you feel about this? Are "rights" an issue in your marriage?

Humility
Does Wonders

When pride comes, then comes disgrace,
but with humility comes wisdom.
PROVERBS 11:2

Are you a basketball fan? Even if you're not, you've probably heard of Michael Jordan. He was listed as the world's greatest athlete in the 80s and 90s. His sport was basketball, and he was amazing. But then he retired and decided to try his hand at baseball. The result was probably not what he expected.

His performance was an about-face from the basketball court. He struck out again and again, dropped easy fly balls, and even referred to the umpire as the referee. Realizing he wasn't ready for the major leagues, he was sent to the minors but only batted .200 for the entire season. That just didn't make it. Why did he try baseball? Perhaps he wanted to fulfill a dream his father had for him. Perhaps he felt it would be easy to transfer to this sport because of his outstanding capabilities. But it was a disaster. Eventually he quit and returned to basketball. Michael learned there are limits we all have to face in life even with the best of abilities. It was a painful experience no doubt, but it gave him the wisdom and humility to stick with what he could do best. Was it a failure? Perhaps. Whether it's called a failure or a learning experience, it can have the same result.

You'll also experience some setbacks and embarrassing times in your marriage. In fact, you probably already have! What have you learned through them? Some have learned modesty. We can't do it all; there are limitations. You may have learned to be more cautious or to take a much longer time for preparation. You can't do it all. When your spouse has more capability than you, don't compete. Instead, be thankful, admit it, and relax. And when you fail, rather than reliving the experience, learn from it.[15]

Become a Child

Truly I say to you, unless you are converted and become like children, you will not enter the kingdom of heaven. Whoever then humbles himself as this child, he is the greatest in the kingdom of heaven.
MATTHEW 18:3,4 NASB

We think children learn from adults, but it's also true we can learn much from children about love and life. Consider these words and how they can apply to your marriage.

A child has not made up his mind yet about what is and what is not possible. He has no fixed preconceptions about what reality is; and if someone tells him that the mossy place under the lilac bush is a magic place, he may wait until he thinks that no one is watching him, but then he will very probably crawl in under the lilac bush to see for himself. A child also knows how to accept a gift. He does not worry about losing his dignity or becoming indebted if he accepts it. His conscience does not bother him because the gift is free and he has not earned it and therefore really has no right to it. He just takes it, with joy. In fact, if it is something that he wants very much he may even ask for it. And lastly, a child knows how to trust. It is late at night and very dark and there is the sound of sirens as his father wakes him. He does not explain anything but just takes him by the hand and gets him up, and the child is scared out of his wits and has no idea what is going on, but he takes his father's hand anyway and lets his father lead him wherever he chooses into the darkness.[16]

A prayer for today:

Lord, make me childlike. Deliver me from the urge to compete with another for place or prestige or position. I would be simple and artless as a little child. Deliver me from pose and pretense. Forgive me for thinking of myself. Amen.[17]

Choosing Hope
Over Futility

*If there is anything worthy of praise, think on and weigh
and take account on these things [fix your minds on them].*
PHILIPPIANS 4:8 AMP

As Christians, we are called to be people of hope rather than
despair. We are called to be people who confront obstacles and
find ways to overcome them rather than to resign ourselves to
a sense of futility.

It's strange, but I've found some people who don't really
want to discover the exceptions to problems. Perhaps they
don't want to hope for fear they'll be disappointed. Some
see the exceptions as just that—rare exceptions that just happened. But we also struggle with selective remembering,
and what's painful tends to lock in and persist in our minds
and hearts. We emphasize failures instead of successes. But
it doesn't have to be this way! We can choose another direction. Let's consider some advice many marriage counselors
offer to assist couples in having fulfilling relationships.

> I've never worked with any couple that doesn't get along
> some of the time. We all get along well part of the time, and
> I realize for some it might be just 20 percent of the time.
> That's all right. It's enough. In order to have a lasting mar-
> riage, *the first step to take is to discover what each of you are do-
> ing during the times you do get along.* You can do this by
> yourself or with your partner. Brainstorm and figure out
> what each of you was doing before and during that time. Be
> sure to concentrate more on what *you* were doing than on
> what your partner was doing. This is the beginning point
> for any change. What were you thinking and feeling when
> you were getting along? Plan to do more of it...regardless of
> what your partner does. Focus on the good times you share
> together.
>
> In turn, this will strengthen your relationship. It's a step
> of encouragement because it lets you know you've been do-
> ing something right after all.

Perhaps this is an example of what Paul was talking about
in the verse for today. Why not read it again?

Love's Beginnings

How fair you are, my love, [he said], how very fair!
SONG OF SOLOMON 4:1 AMP

Harold Myra was the publisher of *Christianity Today* and middle-aged when he wrote "An Ode to Marriage." This poem illustrates the problems and potentials of midlife marriage.

Remember how our love began?
Years ago, I offered you my arm
that September night we first
    went out.

You reached for it
as we leaped a puddle together.

Then you walked just close enough
to show you liked it.

I glimpsed your face under
    the streetlight,
excitement splashing gently on it

No commitment—just beginnings.

My arm pulled you that
    January eve
tight beside me in that car.

Midnight. Time to leave.
"Good night" wasn't quite
    enough,
and our lips touched gently
in a kiss as light as angel cake.

"I like you," it said.
but nothing more.

November air had rough-scrubbed
    our faces.
As we wrestle playfully
in your parent's farmhouse.

That moment I knew
and breathed into your hair,
"I LOVE YOU."

The words exploded around us.
They meant far more than
    "you're nice."
They meant commitment.
Your words came back to me
in firm, sure sounds:
"I love you, too."

And our kiss of celebration
was the beginning of a new
    creation.

Yes, I chose you.
Out of all the lovely girls I knew.
I chose you.

How marvelous are the women
    of planet Earth,
hair flaring in the wind
rich browns and golds
a thousand delicious shapes
girls who laugh saucily
girls who read Browning
girls who play sitars
girls who fix carburetors.

Of all those fascinating
    possibilities,
I chose you....[18]

Love Lives

How fair you are, my love, [he said], how very fair!
SONG OF SOLOMON 4:1 AMP

Here's more of Myra's poem we looked at yesterday.

Then the wedding
flying rice and honeymoon
days and nights together.

Two persons
as unalike as birch and cypress
had chosen each other.

The heavens laughed
and the sands of earth
lay ready for the tender feet
of our newborn self.

Does time change all that?

Were we naive? Now, after we
    have loved, argued, laughed,
    given birth,
what does it mean
when I hold you and say,
"I love you"?

Without the young-love ecstasy,
    is it required rote
or reaffirmation of our new
    creation?

"I love you."

My temples don't pulse as I say it.

My body does not ache for cou-
    pling,
not as it did.

Yet the words carry more
fact than ever they did in
    courtship.

They embrace a million moments
    shared....

"I love you."

It sounds trite—
but not if it's remembering
the thousands of strands
of loving each other when we
    don't feel lovely,
of holding each other,
of winking across a room,
of eating peanut butter sandwiches
    beside the surf,
and of getting up in the morning
    thousands of times, together,
and remembering what we created
the day we first said "I love you,"

Something permanent
and growing
and alive.[19]

Dealing
with Transitions

Be still and rest in the LORD.
PSALM 37:7 AMP

Some people wish life were like a DVD player. Then, whenever they find a particular stage especially satisfying, they could just hit the pause button and remain there awhile. But life is not a series of fixed points. Stable periods in life are actually the exceptions; transitions are the norm. Dr. Charles Sell uses an apt analogy to describe these normal transitions in life:

> Transitions are mysterious, like an underground passageway I once saw in a tour through a castle. The castle's rooms were gigantic, the woodwork extravagant, and the huge beams in the inner part of the towers projected massive strength. But what captivated me the most was that underground tunnel. A half-mile long, the escape route led from the castle to the stables. It was strikingly different from the rest of the castle.
>
> The vast ballroom offered its visitors the feeling of dignity. A sense of comfort overtook us in the luxurious bedroom suites. Serenity filled the garden room. But the secret tunnel was mysterious and unnerving. It held no comfortable chairs because it was not a place to rest. No artwork adorned its moist, dark stone walls. It was not a place to browse. The tunnel was not made for stopping. It was for those en route with a sense of urgency. It turned your mind to either the past or the future: either you would concentrate on the extravagant castle you were leaving behind or on the stables ahead.
>
> Life's transitions are like that, going *from* somewhere *to* somewhere. The present circumstances may seem like a void. It would be pleasant to turn around and go back to the security left behind. But because that is impossible, it is necessary to keep groping for what is ahead; then there will surely be a resting place.[20]

What are the transitions you've experienced in your marriage? How have you handled them?

Avoid the "Takens"

And become useful and helpful and kind to one another.
EPHESIANS 4:32 AMP

A friend of mine described "takens" in this way:

People in long-term marriages tend to take each other for granted. The most common of the "takens" include:

You will always be here for me.
You will always love me.
You will always be able to provide for me.
You will always be the same.
We will always be together.

Making these assumptions in a marriage is living more in fantasyland than on reality ridge. People who take things for granted are seldom appreciative of the everyday blessings in their lives. After a time, they come to believe life owes them these little gifts. They seldom say thank you for anything.

When you take someone for granted, you demean him or her. You send the unspoken message, *You are not worth much to me.* You also deny this person of the gift of human appreciation. And to be loved and appreciated gives all of us a reason to live each day. When that gift is withdrawn or denied over the years, our spirits wither and die. People may endure this hardship and stay married forever, but they are only serving a sentence. In long-term marriages where one or both spouses are continually taken for granted, a wall of indifference arises between husband and wife. The longer the marriage, the higher the wall and the greater the human isolation. The way out of this woodpile is simple but crucial:

Start saying thank you and showing appreciation for anything and everything.

Be more consciously tuned-in to what is going on....

Become more giving and affirming.[21]

Keep in mind that in a healthy marriage...

- You look out for "number 2" rather than "number 1."

- You energize your spouse.

- You eliminate blaming and shaming.

- You are willing to learn from your partner.

- You end your disagreements with a feeling of resolve.

- You feel better after a disagreement.[22]

Your Life Story

Teach me your way, O LORD; lead me in a straight path.
PSALM 27:11

Many of King David's prayers were turned into psalms. One day he prayed, "Show me, O LORD, my life's end and the number of my days; let me know how fleeting is my life" (Psalm 39:4). Wow! Would you like to know exactly how many days you have left? And what about how you will leave this world? Perhaps this is an uncertainty most of us can live with!

Dr. Gary Chapman suggested an interesting exercise: Take a paper and draw a line just like this one:

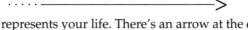

This line represents your life. There's an arrow at the end of it. Do you know why? Your life doesn't end; it continues on for eternity. Notice the dots at the left of the line. The first dot is there to represent the day you were born. The second is the day you met your spouse. The third is when you married. The fourth is when you had children. The last dot represents something that hasn't happened yet—the day you die.

See how close the dots are at the beginning of the line? There's not much space. Actually the dots are amplified and the line is condensed because we can't really comprehend the entire line.

This is how God sees our lives. He's the one who gives us the line. It's a line to live for eternity. We make the dots the focus of our lives; we live for them. Do you ever wonder what God wants us to live for? Could it be He wants us to live for the line rather than the dots?

Look at this line:

Your spouse ..... ————————————————>

There's only a short amount of time on earth to enjoy and edify your spouse, isn't there? Perhaps the message is you're living for eternity. And while you're here make the best use of your time.[1]

Fog Banks

For you were once darkness, but now you are light in the Lord.
Live as children of light.
EPHESIANS 5:8

Fog is interesting. It's made up of misty moisture that puts a chill in the air and sometimes makes you shiver. It can take the curl out of your hair and block your vision when you're driving to the extent that you have to come to a stop. The sun can be shining brightly, but you'd never know it. All you see is, well, not much. Even sound is distorted. It seems as though there's a heaviness in the air. It doesn't take much moisture for the fog to bring everything to a halt. Were you aware that a dense fog covering seven city blocks to a depth of 100 feet contains less moisture than a glass of water?

Ships have crashed on rocks or run into reefs because of fog. Planes have crashed into mountains.

In central California there is a type of fog called the *Tule Fog*. It seems to rise off the ground and completely blacks out both Highways 5 and 99. When it hits, some of the worst multicar accidents in California can happen.

Sometimes husbands and wives can feel as if they're floating around in a fog bank, not knowing which way to turn. Sometimes a gray gloom drifts into marriage relationships. It may chill the love and closeness of the relationships. Or it could be there's a fog hiding the truth of who God is and what He wants for us. It happens.

Do you know what to do with fog? You can wait until it lifts, but that puts you at its mercy. Or you can drive out of it or climb above it. When you do that you have a sense of direction, light to show you the way, and warmth. We can't do much about the weather and that kind of fog. We can do a lot about the types of fog in marriage—don't let it settle in.[2]

The Gift of Passion

God created man in his own image.
GENESIS 1:27

Here's the question of the day: Are you a passionate person? Yes or no? Would your spouse say you're passionate? Ask one another. Now define what you mean by passionate. The dictionary says it's having or showing strong feelings or resulting from, expressing, or tending to arouse strong feeling; ardent; intense; impassioned. It also means readily aroused to sexual activity: sensual.

Now some of you may be thinking, "Yes! That last part is me. I can identify with that!" But what about the other definitions? Don't those apply as well?

Some people say "Hey, I'm just not wired for all that emotion stuff. That's not me." Well, here's another question: Were you created in the image or likeness of God? The answer is yes, because we all were. Where do we get our capability to experience emotions? Where do we get the capacity to love, hate, grieve, and weep? We received this from God. Our God is a God of passions.

Perhaps you never thought of God as passionate. We know He loves. We see this in John 3:16, "For God so loved the world..." We know He hates because Proverbs 6:16 talks about seven things God finds detestable: "haughty eyes, a lying tongue..." We know He laughs: "He who sits in the heavens laughs" (Psalm 2:4 NASB). We know He cries: "Jesus wept" (John 11:35). The Scripture tells us God embraces, kisses, shouts, whispers, sings, and grieves (see Luke 15:20; Jeremiah 25:30; 1 Kings 19:12; Zephaniah 3:17; 1 Chronicles 21:15).

Our emotions are good even though we may not understand them. If you're more reserved and your spouse is expressive, you may have conflicts over this. Even though women are wired to experience emotions and encouraged to do so more than men, both sexes were created to be people of passion. If one of you hasn't yet developed your understanding and expression of your emotions, let it occur. It may be uncomfortable, but it will enrich your life—and your marriage.

A Prayer
of Responsibility

So I say, live by the Spirit, and you will not gratify the desires of the sinful nature. For the sinful nature desires what is contrary to the Spirit, and the Spirit what is contrary to the sinful nature....But if you are led by the Spirit, you are not under law.
GALATIANS 5:16-18

This is a prayer for you to read aloud today or even each day for a week. You'll see the results.

Lord,

You have given me everything good in my life, especially my spouse. Remind me that I haven't done it and that I'm not You. I pray now for a greater sense of responsibility.

Help me to remember my sense of responsibility to myself.

Help me to never do anything so I lose my self-respect or bring shame on my marriage.

Help me to never let myself down by doing anything which attacks my spouse.

Help me never to do anything that I would spend the rest of my life regretting.

Lord, I want to always remember my responsibility to those I love and those that love me and those that don't.

I want to be faithful so I don't disappoint those that love me.

Help me not to fail my partner who depends on me.

Keep me from being a source of grief to my partner.

Lord, sometimes it's difficult to be faithful, but I know that You can keep me faithful. Thank You that it's not just up to me!

Help me not to be a person who remembers my rights and forgets my responsibilities.

Help me not to be a person who wants to get everything out of life without putting anything into it.

Help me not to be someone who doesn't care what happens to others.

Remind me that I am responsible to You and will answer to You for the way I use what You have given to me. May I always honor and respect my partner.

And help me each minute of the day to remember how much You love us and how Jesus died for me. I praise You.

Amen.[3]

Candor

Wounds from a friend are better than kisses from an enemy!
PROVERBS 27:6 TLB

"Give it to me straight, I can take it." Is there anyone in your life who will tell it to you like it is? Have you got someone who will level with you and with whom you can level? Is the relationship stronger because of the honesty? Hopefully you do—and it's your spouse. That's what Proverbs 27:6 is talking about. We may not want to hear the truth, but we're better off because of what was said. Proverbs states: "A rebuke to a man of common sense is more effective than a hundred lashes on the back of a rebel" (17:10 TLB). It feels good to have someone flatter you, but it can cause problems: "Flattery is a trap" (Proverbs 29:5 TLB). So let's apply this to marriage.

Candor is being open and truthful so that when the truth is expressed, it builds the marital relationship. You see, candor comes because of our care and love for our partners. We want the best for them. We have their well-being in mind. Ephesians 4:15 describes how we can share with another: "But speaking the truth in love..." (NASB). This wording means that when you've spoken the truth, your relationship is cemented together better than before. That's a healthy relationship. Candor, mutual candor, is a sign of a close friendship. It's necessary in marriage. You'll be a different person and so will the other when candor is present. You'll change. You'll grow. Again Proverbs states the result: "A friendly discussion is as stimulating as the sparks that fly when iron strikes iron" (27:17 TLB).

Keep in mind that your response to the candor of your spouse will make a difference. Defensiveness kills candor. Responses such as "Let me think about that" or "That's something to consider" keep a marriage going.

Can you take the truth? Should you take it straight? Why or why not? Will you build a better marriage with candor? Definitely. One last thought: If you really want to have someone give it to you straight, take a look at God's Word.[4]

She's a Good Find

He who finds a wife finds what is good
and receives favor from the LORD.
PROVERBS 18:22

Years ago certain male phrases were common. "I need to find me a wife." And when that happened you might hear, "I done found me a wife." How does a man "find" a wife? It's an interesting concept. Finding or acquiring anything is just the first step.

There are many items that you acquire in life that come with an owner's manual. If you buy a new car, refrigerator, outboard motor, sewing machine, or computer, you can count on also receiving a manual that gives you the operating instructions. And you need these in order to have your new purchase operate properly. The problem is that some people never get around to reading the owner's instructional manual so the item either doesn't work properly or soon breaks down.

A man who "finds" or acquires a wife is in the same situation—with one major exception. *He doesn't own her!* Marriage is a partnership of equal subordination. But husbands do need something to help them understand their wives. Most men struggle with this. They say, "I just don't understand women. They're really different. God sure created them weird!" Women aren't weird; they're just unique.

Every husband is commanded by Scripture to learn to understand his wife. First Peter 3:7 says, "By the same token you husbands need to live understandingly with your wives" (BERKELEY). Phillips' version says, "Try to understand the wives you live with." How can a husband do this? There are three things to do:

- Study the Word of God—it tells you how to respond.
- Study books that tell you about women.
- Study your wife—she's unique. Let her help you.

Do You Want to Know the Future?

Pharaoh said to Joseph, "I had a dream, and no one can interpret it.
But I have heard it said of you that when you hear a dream
you can interpret it." "I cannot do it," Joseph replied to Pharaoh,
"but God will give Pharaoh the answer he desires."
GENESIS 41:15,16

The future is intriguing. Some people are more enthralled with what might happen in the future than what they're experiencing today. The anticipation, the expectations, the mysteries of the unknown are more exciting than the reality of the now. That's why fortunetellers have always existed. Some people are willing to pay good money for a mysterious person to gaze into a crystal ball or look at some cards or go into a trance in the hope of discovering a hint of what might happen.

Haven't we all wanted a glimpse of the future at some point? Especially if it was going to be good. Have you ever said, "I just wish for a moment that I could see..."? Have you ever wondered what your spouse would look like 10 or 20 years from now? Or have you ever wondered what you will look like 10 or 20 years from now?

Focusing on the dreams of the future takes us out of the mundane of the present, but it also robs us of energy that could be used to solve the problems of the present.

We're not supposed to be living stuck in the past or too busy fantasizing about the future to experience the present. What occurs in the present will help shape our future. Dreaming about a live, vibrant marriage in the future is an acceptable goal if we're working to create that right now.

There is one who knows the future: God. And there is something that we can and do know about the future: If we know Jesus, we'll be with Him forever. That's all the knowledge we need.

"Affluenza"

Don't weary yourself trying to get rich.
Why waste your time?
PROVERBS 23:4 TLB

In the 1918–1919 influenza epidemic, millions of people died. While couples are still affected by influenza epidemics today, they are at a higher risk of another epidemic...*affluenza.* That's right, affluenza, not influenza—and it's contagious! Here are the symptoms:

- Desiring to have more, regardless of what we have
- Striving to be successful without being contented
- Placing career over family
- Refusing to be satisfied with less than the best
- Refusing to follow the biblical guidelines to live our lives to God's glory[5]

Most people today value what they don't have more than what they do have. They look at what their friends have and say, "We need that." Some people "need" to buy lots of clothes. Others "need" the latest model car. Still others "must have" the computer with the latest chips and software. But the truth is that they don't need it—they *want* it. God's Word has something to say about our need to accumulate things:

Those who love money will never have enough. How absurd to think that wealth brings true happiness! (Ecclesiastes 5:10 NLT).

People who long to be rich fall into temptation and are trapped by many foolish and harmful desires that plunge them into ruin and destruction (1 Timothy 6:9 NLT).

No one can serve two masters. For you will hate one and love the other, or be devoted to one and despise the other. You cannot serve both God and money (Luke 16:13 NLT).

Our contact with cultural values alone puts us in danger of catching affluenza. We need to be on guard, to inoculate ourselves against the illness. Part of the inoculation comes from taking an honest look at where we are and understanding that accumulating things doesn't truly satisfy our desires.

Are You in Shape?

Endure hardship with us like a good soldier of Christ Jesus.
2 TIMOTHY 2:3

Today's session is more personal than usual: meddling. Are you in shape? Is your spouse in shape? (Remember, speak the truth in love. Today's devotion is not meant to create dissension!)

There are times when some of us look into the mirror, and we think—or hope—we're in a house of mirrors at a carnival. You know—the mirrors that stretch, distort, expand, and elongate our shapes. If perchance you might just be carrying around a few extra ounces (or pounds!), it may have an impact on your life. Extra weight can hinder our reflexes, dull our responses, slow us down.

We are a shape- and weight-conscious society. It seems as though the majority of our population gets on the scales (part of the country tilts at that time) and vows to lose weight. There are many ways to do this. Step right up and select your menu (wrong choice of word—sorry).

Diet—You can starve it off.

Exercise—You can sweat it off.

Pills—You can medicate it off.

Liposuction—You can suck it off.

Stomach surgery—You can block it out.

They are all extreme in one way or another.

Let's ask the question again with a variation. Are you in shape spiritually? It's even more important to be in shape this way. The apostle Paul warned us: "Be self-controlled and alert. Your enemy the devil prowls around like a roaring lion looking for someone to devour. Resist him, standing firm in the faith" (1 Peter 5:8,9). If this is what you're facing, get in shape and stay in shape. Read the Word together. Pray together. Fellowship together. It works.[6]

An Arranged Marriage

And show her honor as a fellow heir of the grace of life.
1 PETER 3:7 NASB

A wedding is one thing; a marriage is another. What a difference between the way things start in a home...and the way they continue. In his book *Secrets to Inner Beauty*, Joe Aldrich describes the realities of married life.

> It doesn't take long for the newlyweds to discover that "everything in one person nobody's got." They soon learn that a marriage license is just a learner's permit, and ask with agony, "Is there life after marriage?"[7]

Marriage begins like a romantic, moonlight sleigh ride smoothly gliding over the glistening snow. It's living together after the honeymoon that turns out to be rough backpacking across rocks and hot sand. Philip Yancey offers these insights:

> In the U.S. and other Western-style cultures, people tend to marry because they are attracted to another's appealing qualities: a fresh smile, wittiness, a pleasing figure, athletic ability, a cheerful disposition, charm. Over time, these qualities can change; the physical attributes, especially, will deteriorate with age. Meanwhile, surprises may surface: slatternly housekeeping, a tendency toward depression, disagreements over sex. In contrast, the partners in an arranged marriage [over half of all marriages in our international global village fit this description] do not center their relationship on mutual attractions. Having heard your parents' decision, you accept that you will live for many years with someone you now barely know. Thus the overriding question changes from "Whom should I marry?" to "Given this partner, what kind of marriage can we construct together?"[8]

What would it have been like if your marriage had been arranged? Whether it was arranged or made by choice, every marriage needs to be constructed. What kind would you like to construct? Talk it over.[9]

Nothing Hidden

Love never fails. But where there are prophecies, they will cease;
where there are tongues, they will be stilled;
where there is knowledge, it will pass away.
1 CORINTHIANS 13:8

Eric Liddell, a missionary whose life was chronicled in *Chariots of Fire*, raises an important issue:

> Nothing breaks up the joyous nature of a home so much as having to hide things from one another. Husband and wife should be able to face *everything* together, keeping nothing back. It is a sad day when this crystal-clear relationship is broken. It is a sad day when the child has to hide anything from the parents. It is a sad day when the parents have to deceive their children or frighten them in order to gain their obedience.
>
> There must be loyalty. Loyalty often demands courage. Stand by one another in difficulty, hardship, and loss. Stand by one another when the world cheers, ridicules, or neglects. Trust grows out of honesty and loyalty. A trusting and confidential environment makes for happiness. Children, honor your parents with obedience. Parents, by transparent honesty, inspire your children to trust.
>
> Love is the essential element in the Christian home. Efficiency, cleanliness, luxury cannot make up for the lack of love....Love is interest in what the other members of the families do—joys and sorrows, struggles and achievements are shared by all. Love anticipates. It sees beforehand how it can help to lighten another's load; it is always willing to go out of its way or to make time to help. Love never harbors resentment, is not easily hurt, is always ready to forgive. Where love is, God is.
>
> *Remember the marriage vow—the twofold, lifelong promise given.* "Wilt thou love, comfort, honor her [him], and keep her [him], in sickness and in health; and forsaking all others keep thee only unto her [him] so long as ye both shall live?" "I will."
>
> Ask yourself, "Am I keeping this promise in the letter and in the spirit?" When love is dethroned and the relationship is wrong at the center, how can the home be happy? Love is the secret of a happy home.[10]

Power Source

We preach Christ crucified, to the Jews a stumbling block and to the Greeks foolishness, but to those who are called, both Jews and Greeks, Christ the power of God and the wisdom of God.

1 CORINTHIANS 1:23,24 NKJV

Power failure. The lights dim and then go out. The sounds of machinery—the refrigerator or air conditioner—come to a halt. An eerie silence hangs in the air. Usually it happens when the people tapping into the power source overload it. Or it could be that there's a short in the system or a transformer that wore out. Sometimes it's just a simple thing such as a person tripping over a cord and unplugging it from the wall socket. But no matter what the cause, a power outage is no fun. Your life is totally thrown off course.

In relation to our personal lives, there are two important questions to consider. First, who's your power source? Is it you? Your spouse? The Lord? Some of us go through life connected to a real power source, and others run their lives on a portable battery pack powered by their own energy. And naturally the latter run out of juice after a while. But when your source is the Lord, there's never any lack of potential power. He gives us the gift of power—the Holy Spirit.

The second question is this: Are you plugged in? Would your spouse agree? An electric saw won't work by running the blade back and forth by hand. It's got to be connected. We're connected when we pray, listen, and read the Word. Busy? Yes, we all are. We can pray lying down, sitting, standing, walking, or driving. We can read at any time just for a minute at a time. Those who begin their day with Jesus realize they are connected to a power source that won't overload or run out. That's a pretty good source.[11] And it does wonders for your marriage.

Criticism or
Encouragement?

Therefore encourage one another and build each other up,
just as in fact you are doing.
1 THESSALONIANS 5:11

Read these thoughts out loud to each other meditatively. One of you read a point and the other make a comment. On the next idea switch roles, and so on, until you have read and commented on each idea. Conclude in prayer.

An almost mystical intimacy develops on the back of shared sorrows.

The deepest expression of our love comes through our willingness to share in the tedium of each other's daily routines and frustrations.

At the end of life what counts is not the accomplishments and accolades attained, but the people we have touched and the relationships we have developed.

It is better for a man to make a small income with dignity than to bluff about his position or resources and lose the respect of his wife. It is good for a wife to bear patiently while her husband struggles through the dark hour of unemployment.

Bitterness strangles the lifeblood out of a marriage—literally dries up our bones—and makes the words of our mate like fingernails on a chalkboard. Bitterness and intimacy cannot grow in the same heart....

When husband and wife are more focused on pleasing each other than getting their own way, God will free them up to mutually love and respect each other.

Simply put, if a couple continually quarrels and fights, one or both have not yielded themselves to the Holy Spirit. The secret to a peaceable marriage is to deny ourselves, take up our cross, and follow Jesus. We must walk rightly with the Spirit before we can walk rightly with our mate.

When our mate has strengths we should affirm him or her, but never pressure him or her to perform. To criticize our mates at the point of their strength is to kill their courage.[12]

Irritations

I know what it is to be in need, and I know what it is to have plenty.
I have learned the secret of being content in any and every situation,
whether well fed or hungry, whether living in plenty or in want.
PHILIPPIANS 4:12

A speck of dust gets in your eye and what does it feel like? Irritated. That's what it should feel like so you become aware of the problem. But not all irritation has that positive element. Sometimes you or your spouse may feel irritated over the little things of life or circumstances that just can't be changed.

Irritation comes when something just isn't quite right. The garage door won't work right, the day you wanted to play golf was rainy, you broke a nail before the party, your spouse was supposed to fill the car with gas and now you have to stop and do it, you phone a company because of a mistake it made on your bill and after pressing 1 and the pound key eight times to get a real live, breathing person you are disconnected.

Welcome to Daily Life 101. It's easy to gripe and complain about this stuff. When you and your spouse talk over a meal or while doing some task, is grumbling and irritation expressed? If, by some remote chance, they are, how does it help your marriage relationship? If, on the other hand, you've learned as many couples have how to apply Philippians 4:12 to your marriage, you're in good shape.

Every person and every couple has a choice. Change what can be changed, and if it can't be changed, accept it, learn from it, and look for God's blessings in the rest of your life. Praise God, not just when things go well, but all the time!

Love Is...

1 CORINTHIANS 13
Twentieth Century New Testament

If I speak in the "tongues" of men—aye, and of angels, too—but am without Love, I have become mere echoing brass, or a clanging cymbal! Even if I have the "prophetic" gift and know all secret truths and possess all knowledge, or even if I have such perfect faith as to be able to move mountains, but am without Love, I am nothing! If I give all that I possess to feed the hungry, and even if (to say what is boastful) I sacrifice my body, but am without Love, I am none the better!

Love is long-suffering and kind. Love is never envious, never boastful, never conceited, never behaves unbecomingly. She is not self-seeking, not easily provoked, nor does she reckon up her wrongs. She has no sympathy with deceit, but has full sympathy with truth. She is proof against all things, always hopeful, always patient.

Love never dies....

When I was a child, I talked like a child, thought like a child, reasoned like a child; now that I am a man, I have cast childish ways aside. As yet we see things dimly, reflected in a mirror, but then—face to face! As yet my knowledge is incomplete, but then it will be as full as God's knowledge of me is now. So then Faith, Hope, and Love last on—only these three—and of them the greatest is Love.[13]

The First Commandment

You shall have no other gods before me.
EXODUS 20:3

Nothing, absolutely nothing is to come before God. The first commandment is plain and simple...and easy to break. Today, gods have multiplied. Some people worship the earth; many worship Elvis Presley. Everyone today has a god, whether they call it god or not. I've seen married couples who put their spouses before God. A famous preacher from years ago, G. Campbell Morgan, said:

> It is as impossible for a man to live without having an object of worship as it is for a bird to fly if it is taken out of the air. The very composition of human life, the mystery of man's being, demands a center of worship as a necessity of existence. All life is worship....The question is whether the life and powers of man are devoted to the worship of the true God or to that of a false one.[14]

What you place first in your life may be your god. It could be your job, wife, husband, golf, an accumulation of the things that make up the "good" life, or sex. Anything that takes priority over God has removed Him from the throne. When God said you shall have no other gods before me, he was saying you shall have *Him!*

Do you understand what it means to have God—to love Him? Everything we do is to be done to honor and glorify Him. It's our life calling, and this is expressed best by David:

> O God, my God! How I search for you! How I thirst for you in this parched and weary land where there is no water. How I long to find you! How I wish I could go into your sanctuary to see your strength and glory, for your love and kindness are better to me than life itself. How I praise you! (Psalm 63:1-3 TLB).

How can you make sure God is your only god today?[15] In what way does God have first place in your life?

The Second Commandment

You shall not make for yourself an idol in the form of anything in heaven above or on the earth beneath or in the waters below.
EXODUS 20:4

Do the Ten Commandments have a place in your marriage? Let's consider the second one. This commandment is not the same as the first one. The first one forbids the *existence* of other gods. But this commandment forbids the *making* of other gods. In other words, we are not to purposely create other gods. Verse 5 takes this commandment even further.

> You shall not bow down to them or worship them; for I, the LORD your God, am a jealous God, punishing the children for the sin of the fathers to the third and fourth generation of those who hate me (Exodus 20:5).

This commandment may bother you because we have pictures and objects in our churches and our homes. It's all right to use them as *visual reminders* created by human perception. But the commandment does forbid the use of objects such as pictures and statues of Jesus and of God in private and public worship.

Images limit God, yet He is limitless. Images obscure God's glory. They are made to reveal God but they actually do the opposite—they hide the real God. Did you know that it's possible to buy a machine-washable Jesus doll? There are also plans to bring out a God doll that is a white-haired, white-bearded, white man in a rainbow colored robe with all the animals of creation flowing from Him. When an idol is created, it is usually supposed to offer something. Not only do these dolls not do that, they actually take away from what we have.

The God who created the universe, the God who created us, cannot be confined to a man-made image. When we try to create something to represent God, we detract from the worship of who He really is. We cannot see Him. He is above being seen. That adds to His holiness and majesty.

Sometimes married couples create other idols that detract from worshiping God. What do you think they are? Are there any improper images in your lives?

Misusing
God's Name

*You shall not misuse the name of the LORD your God, for the LORD
will not hold anyone guiltless who misuses his name.*
EXODUS 20:7

The children of Israel had such respect and reverence for
some of the names of God that they wouldn't even use them.
The name of Jehovah was so sacred that in the Israelite culture
it was said only once a year by the priest when he gave the
blessing on the Day of Atonement. But today this commandment is viewed by many as a joke, judging by the way it is ignored, mistreated, and violated. You can hardly find a movie
or TV show that doesn't ignore this commandment. In some
films it's violated several hundred times! Who even bothers to
think about it anymore? Times have really changed.

There are many ways we personally violate this commandment. We may use God's name in an insincere or empty way.
We may take an oath in God's name and break it. When we do
these things a violation of this commandment has occurred.
Leviticus 19:12 says: "Do not swear falsely by my name and so
profane the name of your God. I am the LORD." Scripture is
very clear that when we use God's name irreverently, we violate the commandment. What do you say when you hit your
thumb with a hammer? "Ouch!" or something else? Some
people have a highly developed skill of swearing using God's
name. Lord Byron said, "He knew not what to say, so he
swore." Someone has said that "swearing is a substitute for the
inarticulate." Have you listened to yourself lately? Another violation is using God's name to curse others. When you damn
someone using God's name, this commandment is violated.
Sometimes a person can become so incensed that he or she
does this by habit—either thinking it or saying it. There are
consequences for this. Read Exodus 20:7 again, and then look
at this verse: "But I tell you that men will have to give account
on the day of judgment for every careless word they have spoken. For by your words you will be acquitted, and by your
words you will be condemned" (Matthew 12:36,37).

Sobering, isn't it?

The Sabbath
and Rest

Remember the Sabbath day by keeping it holy. Six days you shall labor and do all your work, but the seventh day is a Sabbath to the LORD your God. On it you shall not do any work, neither you, nor your son or daughter, nor your manservant or maidservant, nor your animals, nor the alien within your gates.

EXODUS 20:8-10

Rest. God is saying that once a week we need to take a break. He is saying there is more to life than work. He is also urging us to follow His pattern: "For in six days the LORD made the heavens and the earth, the sea, and all that is in them, but he rested on the seventh day. Therefore the LORD blessed the Sabbath day and made it holy" (Exodus 20:11). Since God is God, He didn't need to rest as we know it. He certainly wasn't worn-out. He just decided to take a break. And He wants us to, also.

We need rest physically. There is a rhythm to the seventh day of rest that is the best balance of work and rest, even though people have tried other plans and failed.

Spiritually we also need this time to refocus our lives. For the children of Israel this was a day to celebrate their redemption and liberation. God wanted the people to spend the day looking to Him and thanking Him for being liberated. Listen to what the LORD said to Isaiah: "If you keep your feet from breaking the Sabbath and from doing as you please on my holy day, if you call the Sabbath a delight and the LORD's holy day honorable, and if you honor it by not doing your own way and not doing as you please or speaking idle words, then you will find your joy in the LORD...."

What do you do as a couple on this day? Is it "catch-up time" or a frenzied shopping spree? Do you spend more hours together as a couple? The Sabbath is a day that belongs to God. Who comes first on that day, in your marriage? It's a day to serve, worship, rejoice, and rest. Talk about this together and evaluate your approach to this special day. Do you need to make any changes?

The Fifth Commandment

Honor your father and your mother, so that you may live long in the land the LORD your God is giving you.
EXODUS 20:12

The emphasis of the fifth commandment is on loving others. The first four are on loving God, which makes it possible to fulfill the next six. If you have a right relationship with God you can have right relationships with others—and it begins with your parents.

Honor. We don't use this word much today, nor do we practice it. The Hebrew word comes from a verb that means "to be heavy." In a sense, you give weight to people you honor or hold in high esteem. You elevate them. You see them as important.

When children honor their parents, they're to obey them. Ephesians 6:1 says, "Children, obey your parents in the Lord, for this is right." But now you're an adult, not a child. How can you honor your parents today? When you're an adult you reverence your parents. There are four ways to do this.

Respect them. "Each of you must respect his mother and father, and you must observe my Sabbaths. I am the LORD your God" (Leviticus 19:3). How? Speak kindly to your folks and about them.

Provide for them. Don't neglect your parents when they are older. Give them time, attention, love, your listening ear, as well as help for their physical needs.

Treat them with consideration. Make their remaining years easier. Encourage them to spend your inheritance on themselves!

Make them proud. Give them something to be proud of. "The father of a righteous man has great joy, he who has a wise son delights in him. May your father and mother be glad; may she who gave you birth rejoice!" (Proverbs 23:24,25).[16]

How is your relationship with your parents now? How is your relationship with your in-laws? In what ways are you honoring them?

Life Is Precious

You shall not murder.
EXODUS 20:13

If you live in America, you live in a country where the future is excellent—for murder. The American culture kills. Look at the statistics. Violence of all types, including terrorist attacks, are on the rise. The atrocity and mayhem of the Oklahoma City bombing, the terrorist attack on September 11, 2001, and the highly publicized killings of family members and students stare us in the face.

Life is precious. Mankind was made in the image of God. "So God made man like his Maker. Like God did God make man; man and maid did he make them" (Genesis 1:27 TLB). Life is sacred. We have been called to cherish, honor, and protect our own lives and the lives of others.

The Scripture says no to *homicide.*

The Scripture says no to *suicide*, which is not only violence toward oneself, but against any remaining family members and friends. Even medically assisted suicides for the ill and elderly are wrong, regardless of what currently prevails in our society.

The Scripture says no to *feticide*—abortion. It's a direct sin against God. Sometime and somewhere we will all have to take a stand on this issue. God's Word comes first.

You may be thinking, "This is a great commandment, but for someone else. I'm no murderer." True. But consider these words from Jesus that apply to all of us:

> You have heard that it was said to the people long ago, "Do not murder, and anyone who murders will be subject to judgment." But I tell you that anyone who is angry with his brother will be subject to judgment. Again, anyone who says to his brother, "Raca," is answerable to the Sanhedrin. But anyone who says, "You fool!" will be in danger of the fire of hell (Matthew 5:21,22).

Haven't we all had anger and contempt in our hearts against others? It can happen in marriage as well. Haven't we all had thoughts of violence in our hearts for others? That's where it all begins—and thoughts do lead to actions.[17]

How do you think about one another?

The Seventh Commandment

You shall not commit adultery.
EXODUS 20:14

One of the best books written for couples on the sexual relationship is Doug Rosenau's *A Celebration of Sex*. Read what he has to say about the seventh commandment.

> A great marital partnership has room for only two people in it. Commitment is vital to intimate companionship, and the creation of good boundaries is irreplaceable for a fantastic marriage and sex life.
>
> *Adulterate* means "to contaminate by adding a foreign substance or watering down of the product." You can adulterate your marital companionship in many ways other than having a sexual affair. You can adulterate your marriage by overcommitting to work, children, or church.
>
> God's injunction of "thou shalt not commit adultery" is often portrayed in terms of a protective fence that guards the beautiful marital and sexual garden. So often we look at fences as something to jump so we can get to greener grass. Actually, the no-adultery fence is there so you can have the intimacy to create an unbelievable relationship within that enclosure—a deeper level of emotional and sexual connecting that can occur and flourish only in an intimate marriage. It protects you from contaminating elements that can threaten the quality of your companionship.
>
> The more important commitments to your mate come in a series of daily choices. Every day when you say, "I have my mate," and refuse to entertain thoughts about someone else, you are reaffirming your commitment. You are allowing sex to be relational and setting good boundaries as you choose to control your sexual impulses and preserve sexual integrity.
>
> These choices are not always huge and obvious, but they create the glue that keeps a marriage and sexual relationship together. Daily you have to choose not to adulterate and water down your companionship.[18]

Don't Steal

You shall not steal.
EXODUS 20:15

What would happen if a group of people were walking along and someone came up behind them and yelled, "Stop! Thief!" Most would probably stop, and rightly so. Haven't all of us stolen something at one time or another?

If the IRS had all the money people owed and every company had all the money stolen by employees, we'd be in great shape financially. "Don't steal" covers many kinds of thefts.

If you stole anything in Old Testament times, you were in for a rough time. If you took and disposed of a sheep or ox, you were required to give back four sheep or five oxen. And if the original animal was found, the restitution was double (see Exodus 22:1-4).

Today theft is common...and subtle. In the book *The Day America Told the Truth*, the authors conclude this about workers in our country:

- The so-called Protestant ethic is long gone from today's American workplace.

- Workers around America frankly admit that they spend more than 20 percent of their time at work totally goofing off. That amounts to a four-day work week across the nation.

- Almost half of us admit to chronic malingering, calling in sick when we are not sick, and doing it regularly.[19]

Stealing is not limited to shoplifting or taking all the cash out of a cash register. It's much easier to steal time—long breaks and lunch hours, coming in late to work, and leaving early. Not working up to our full capacity is theft. What about the personal use of the fax machine, photocopier, phone, or supplies? It happens all the time.[20]

Theft can happen in marriage, too. It may occur and we're not even aware of its occurrence. We can steal time that our marriages and spouses need. We can steal energy that could be devoted to our relationships but is diverted to other activities. We can steal kindness and love that should go to our spouses, but others receive the benefits. And we can steal thoughts that should be directed toward our mates. The commandments do apply to our marriages.

Husbands
Need Encouragement

Therefore encourage one another and build each other up,
just as in fact you are doing.
1 THESSALONIANS 5:11

Several husbands shared how their wives were encouragements to them. Here are their words:

> "She calls me several times a week at work to see how I am doing and to tell me that she has faith in me. That is very encouraging, especially if I am struggling that day. She also calls to share her trials to give me a chance to encourage her. This in turn encourages me because it makes me feel like she really cares about what I have to say."

> "She understands my physical pain, supports me with her energy, and does what she can to take over some of the things I do to make life easier for me. She supports decisions I've made and helps in implementing and carrying out the course of action we've chosen. She's there to talk to and voice her opinion."

> "My wife has been doing several things that I can think of to encourage me. Every time I do something that according to her was done very well, she makes positive remarks regarding these things. To help celebrate my successes, she initiates a great night of lovemaking. That's a wonderful encouragement."

> "My wife encourages me by wanting to spend time with me going places I like to go (i.e. art shows, ball games, movies, etc.). She stays busy on her own doing something almost all the time (chores, time with kids, etc.). She meets all my desires and needs in intimate ways. It's satisfying and something I look forward to."

> "We talk every evening fifteen minutes to an hour, and she has both a listening ear and affirming responses, as well as an open and honest way about her. She is complimentary, faithful, loyal, dependable, and committed to making the marriage and family work. And our relationship is not a competition."

To the husband: How would you like your wife to encourage you?[21]

Speak the Truth

Therefore, rejecting all falsity and being done now with it,
let everyone express the truth with his neighbor, for we are
all parts of one body and members one of another.
EPHESIANS 4:25 AMP

Did you hear about the speaker who was introduced as a very sharp businessman? The one introducing him said that his business was growing and selling potatoes in Maine. The previous year gave him a profit of $25,000. After a long, elaborate introduction the speaker got up and said, "Before I get started let me make a few changes to the introduction. First of all the business wasn't in Maine, it was in Texas. It wasn't potatoes, it was oil. It wasn't $25,000. It was $250,000. It wasn't profit, it was a loss. And one final thing—it wasn't even me, it was my brother."

How far off can someone be? This was humorous, but some mistakes aren't. We need people who are absolutely truthful—people who don't speak with forked tongues. The problem is our society doesn't really believe in absolute truth. Surveys taken even among Christians show that many people do not see any problem in shading the truth a bit. But in marriage we've got to be 100-percent truthful, even if it hurts or we're concerned about the consequences. Consider these two situations:

1. When you ask a question, are you really asking for a truthful answer? Are the questions, "How do you like my new outfit?" and "Do I look fat?" really honest queries or just hints for compliments or affirmations?

2. When you forget to pick up something or fix an item, do you come right out and say, "Oops, I'm sorry. I forgot"? Or do you give excuses or project blame back to the questioner?

Sharing a portion of the truth can lead a spouse to believe something other than the truth. We need to be so careful in our communications. Truth is the foundation for trust.[22]

Temptation in
Your Marriage

*No temptation has seized you except what is common to man.
And God is faithful; he will not let you be tempted beyond
what you can bear. But when you are tempted, he will also
provide a way out so that you can stand up under it.*
1 CORINTHIANS 10:13

One thing is as certain as death and taxes—when you're married you're going to encounter temptation. Everyone will be tempted because Satan is looking for someone to destroy. Husbands will be tempted, and so will wives, albeit in different ways.

What are some of the common ways husbands are tempted? Sexual impurity is a big one; lust is a struggle for many men. Then there's relational neglect. It's really easy to ignore our wives and avoid the time investment that's needed. Harshness and anger enter into the picture, especially when expectations are not being met or we feel out of control. Personal idolatry gets in there as well. It occurs when we begin to worship our careers, what we own, or our "toys."

Wives struggle, too. Some of them are tempted to manipulate their husbands into what they want them to be instead of relying upon God to make the changes. Some women engage in peacekeeping rather than peacemaking, but peacekeeping doesn't make the hurt disappear. Have you ever heard of simmering anger, the forerunner of resentment? It's quite common. And sometimes the way women express their anger (after it builds up) confuses their husbands. The two most common forms of expression for women who are angry, based on a national survey, are yelling and crying.

There are other temptations in marriage, but the good news is that Jesus was also tempted—and He triumphed. When temptation comes, remember that God is your answer. Temptation gives God an opportunity to demonstrate His faithfulness. It's up to you to avail yourself of it![23]

Appreciation, Empathy, and Acceptance

Bear (endure, carry) one another's burdens.
GALATIANS 6:2 AMP

How do you show appreciation in marriage? By going out of your way to notice all the positive things your partner does and letting him or her know you appreciate them. It also means focusing on the positive experiences instead of dwelling on the negative. Working toward agreement and appreciating your spouse's perspective is also important. Compliments convey appreciation, but they need to be balanced between what a person does and who he or she is. Affirmations based on the qualities of a person are rare, but highly appreciated.

Showing genuine concern for your spouse when he or she is upset builds unity and intimacy in a relationship. You may not be able to physically do anything, but sharing your desire to do so may be all that is necessary. When your partner shares a problem with you, don't relate a similar problem you once had, tell your spouse what to do, crack jokes to cheer him or her up, or ask how the problem came about in the first place. Instead, listen, put your arm around your mate, show you understand, and make it clear that it's all right to feel and act the way he or she does.

In marriage you have a choice to respond with empathy, sympathy, or apathy. Empathy is the feeling of being with another person both emotionally and intellectually. Sympathy is being overinvolved in the emotions of your spouse. Apathy means you couldn't care less. There are no in-betweens.

Accepting each other for who you are and what you say is positive. Acceptance means letting your spouse know that even though you don't agree with what he or she is saying, you are willing to hear him or her out. It means freeing your partner from being molded into the fantasy you desire. It's saying, "You and I are different in many ways. It's all right for you to be you and for me to be me. We are stronger together than we are separately as we learn to complement one another." This doesn't mean spouses won't help to change each other—that's inevitable. But the purpose for which it's done and the method used makes a world of difference.

The Security
of Commitment

Love never fails [never fades out. . .].
1 CORINTHIANS 13:8 AMP

Donald Harvey, author of *The Drifting Marriage,* said:

> Making a commitment to marriage as an institution is not meant to be a sentencing. Its intent is to offer security and stability. All couples have conflicts. Every marriage has to make adjustments. Feeling secure in a mate's commitment to the marriage allows the opportunity for dealing with conflicts and for needed adjustments to occur. This is what makes marriage resilient.
>
> A marriage can endure many affronts, whether from within or without, if the commitment to marriage as an institution is strong. It takes this kind of commitment for growth to occur.[24]

I like what Neil Warren has said about one of the advantages that commitment provides for a relationship:

> Commitment significantly eases the fear of abandonment. It is this fear that is central to so many persons. It is often the most potent fear of all.
>
> When we were young and unable to take care of ourselves, we worried about becoming lost in a crowd, forgotten while waiting to be picked up at school, or left alone by dying parents. Fears like these persist throughout our lives. We shudder at the very thought of abandonment.
>
> That's why a spouse's promise to remain devoted means so much. Your partner will be loyal through every kind of circumstance. That frees you in a radical way. It allows you to be yourself at the deepest of levels, to risk and grow, to be absolutely authentic without any fear of being abandoned.[25]

What has your spouse's commitment meant to you over the years? How has it been demonstrated? How have you demonstrated commitment to your partner?

A Husband's Love

Husbands, love your wives, as Christ loved the church.
EPHESIANS 5:25 AMP

Anne Morrow Lindbergh, the wife of Charles Lindbergh, emerged to become one of America's most popular authors, a woman highly admired for her own accomplishments.

How did this happen? She gives us a clue to the success of her career:

> To be deeply in love, of course, is a great liberating force and the most common experience that frees....Ideally, both members of a couple in love free each other to new and different worlds. I was no exception to the general rule. The sheer fact of finding myself loved was unbelievable and changed my world, my feelings about life and myself. I was given confidence, strength, and almost a new character. The man I was to marry believed in me and what I could do, and consequently I found I could do more than I realized.

Charles did believe in Anne to an extraordinary degree. He saw beneath her shy surface. He realized that down in her innermost well was a wealth of wisdom, a deep, profound, untapped reservoir of ability. Within the security of his love she was freed—released—to discover and develop her own capacity, to get in touch with her own feelings, to cultivate her own skills, and to emerge from that cocoon of shyness a beautiful, ever-delicate butterfly whose presence would enhance many lives far beyond the perimeter of her husband's shadow. He encouraged her to do her own kind of flying, and he admired her for it.

Make no mistake about it, this lady was inseparably linked in love to her man. In fact, it was within the comfort of his love that she gleaned the confidence to reach out far beyond her limited, shy world.

We're talking roots and wings. A husband's love that is strong enough to reassure yet unthreatened enough to release. Tight enough to embrace yet loose enough to enjoy. Magnetic enough to hold, yet magnanimous enough to allow for flight...with an absence of jealousy as others applaud her accomplishments and admire her competence. Charles, the secure, put away the net so Anne, the shy, could flutter and fly.[26]

Missing
Your Children

I trust in you, O LORD; I say, "You are my God."
My times are in your hands.
PSALM 31:14,15

I miss the early years with my children. I was so tied up in work at that time."

"The nest doesn't seem to empty as fast as I want. They're sure slow about moving out."

"I looked at that small chair and started to cry. It seemed like yesterday my son was sitting in it."

"I'm sure I'll be glad when they leave. But won't I feel useless?"

"That room seemed so empty when he left."

"I'm looking forward to a new job—this time for pay!"

"Now that they're gone, we sit, we don't talk, don't look at each other. Nothing!"

"Parenting is hard work and I want to get out of this job."

"We married at 20 and had the first one at 22. The last one came at 34. He left when he turned 21. Why didn't someone tell us it would take 29 years until we were alone again as a couple!"

"We're adjusted to the children being gone. I hope none of them divorce or lose a job and have to move back. I like this step!"

"I don't want to build my happiness on when they call, write, or visit. I need my own life now."

"They left too soon, married too young, and had kids too soon. I hope they realize I'm not their babysitter. I already raised one family, and I'm not going to raise another!"

"I've done what I could. They're in the Lord's hands now. And I guess they always have been, come to think of it."

Perhaps your children have already left the nest. Do you ever say any of the above statements? Who did you share these thoughts with? Or are you in the midst of raising a tribe of young ones and don't have a minute to think about what you'll say then, let alone now? Take a break and reflect for a moment. How will you feel when your children are gone? What would you like to say when they leave? What would your partner want to say? Let God guide your thoughts.

Accountability

*Reprove a wise man and he will love you. Give instruction
to a wise man and he will be still wiser.*
PROVERBS 9:8,9 NASB

Dennis Rainey offers insights on not being accountable:

I believe if there is anything that can ensure and incorpo-
rate…godly character in your life and in mine, it is through accountability. You don't have to go long before you learn of
some Christian pastor, singer, evangelist or ministry leader
who has lost his or her ministry, usually because of adultery.…

I once sat down and wrote a list of characteristics of
people who have fallen to temptation. Over and over, this is
how other people described them:

- A loose spirit with few boundaries;
- Rationalizes and justifies behavior;
- Detached, reclusive, insulated from people;
- Makes decisions without consulting others;
- A lack of authenticity and realness about his or her
  life;
- Defensive, proud, unwilling to admit mistakes and
  failure;
- Hides major areas of life from others;
- Intimidating, unapproachable, secretive.

…They are isolated, keeping people at arm's length, and
not willing to submit themselves to the scrutiny of others.

When you are isolated, you are much more susceptible to
temptation. Years ago I attended a Christian writer's confer-
ence in Minneapolis. I was walking down the stairwell in
the hotel when I looked down and saw a pornographic
magazine lying there. I walked on, but later on in the day I
saw it in the same spot.

Here I was, alone in Minneapolis. I could pick up that
magazine, carry it a few feet to my door and read it in the
privacy of my room, and nobody would ever know.

Fortunately, I made the correct decision and left the magazine alone. But I could understand the power of temptation
to a person who is alone. Isolation is one of the most powerful weapons the enemy uses to trap Christians.[1]

What Is Prayer?

The prayer of a righteous man is powerful and effective.
JAMES 5:16

How would you define prayer? Here's some help from what others have said. Perhaps your definition is similar.

Leonard Cohen: "Prayer is translation. A man translates himself into a child asking for all there is in a language he has barely mastered."

E. M. Bounds: "Prayer is no fitful, short-lived thing. It is no voice crying unheard and unheeded in the silence. It is a voice which goes into God's ear, and it lives as long as God's ear is open to holy places, as long as God's heart is alive to holy things. God shapes the world by prayer."

William Law, *A Serious Call to a Devout and Holy Life:* "Prayer is the nearest approach to God, and the highest enjoyment of Him, that we are capable of in this life."

Oswald Chambers, *My Utmost for His Highest:* "We think rightly or wrongly about prayer according to the conception we have in our minds of prayer. If we think of prayer as the breath in our lungs and the blood from our hearts, we think rightly. The blood flows ceaselessly, and breathing continues ceaselessly; we are not conscious of it, but it is always going on. We are not always conscious of Jesus keeping us in perfect joint with God, but if we are obeying Him, He always is. Prayer is not an exercise, it is the life."

Billy Graham: "Praying is simply a two-way conversation between you and God. It is not the body's posture but the heart's attitude that counts when we pray. Prayer is not our using of God; it more often puts us in a position where God can use us."

Eugene Peterson, *Working the Angels:* "Praying puts us at risk of getting involved in God's conditions. Be slow to pray. Praying most often doesn't get us what we want but what God wants, something quite at variance with what we conceive to be in our best interests. And when we realize what is going on, it is often too late to go back. Be slow to pray."[2]

Alone Is Not Good

The LORD God said, "It is not good for the man to be alone. I will make a helper suitable for him."...Then the LORD God made a woman from the rib he had taken out of the man, and he brought her to the man.
GENESIS 2:18,22

You've probably had the experience of working long and hard on some project that turned out great. You stand back and say, "I did a good job." That's not pride, it's fact. It's a good feeling to know you did a quality job. It lets you know a little about how God felt when He created the earth:

- The first daylight burst forth and He saw it was good.
- Then there was land and sea and He saw it was good.
- When the land produced trees and plants He saw it was good.
- When two great lights were formed He saw it was good.
- When the sea creatures and birds were created He saw it was good.
- When man was created He said, "It is not good for the man to be alone."

You need your spouse more than you realize. The greatest hurt in marriage today is to end up feeling like you're a married single. Isolation is the first step toward adultery. Couples need intimacy, including verbal intimacy. Talking, listening, and sharing is one of the purposes of marriage. Dr. John Baucom makes an interesting observation:

> With the appearance of the two-bathroom home, Americans forgot how to cooperate. With the appearance of the two-car family, we forgot how to associate, and with the coming of the two-television home, we will forget how to communicate.[3]

Ask your partner if there are times when he or she feels lonely and if so, what you could do to help. Whatever is said, reply with, "Thank you for letting me know. I'll begin to work on that." This answer will do wonders in curing the loneliness.[4]

Are You
Discouraged?

*I will say of the LORD, "He is my refuge
and my fortress, my God, in whom I trust."*
PSALM 91:2

Read what Charles Swindoll has to say regarding discouragement:

Discouragement. Where does it come from? Sometimes it feels like a dry, barren wind off a lonely desert. And something inside us begins to wilt. At other times it feels like chilling mist. Seeping through our pores, it numbs the spirit and fogs the path before us. What is it about discouragement that strips our lives of joy and leaves us feeling vulnerable and exposed?

I don't know all the reasons. I don't even know most of the reasons. But I do know *one* of the reasons. We don't have a refuge. Shelters are hard to come by these days…you know, people who care enough to listen. Who are good at keeping secrets. And we all need harbors to pull into when we feel weather-worn and blasted by the storm.

Where do *you* turn when the bottom drops out of *your* life? Or when you face an issue that is embarrassing…maybe even scandalous?

What do you need when circumstances puncture your fragile dikes and threaten to engulf your life with pain and confusion?

You need shelter. A listener. Someone who understands…

Discouraged people don't need critics. They hurt enough already. They don't need more guilt or piled-on distress. They need encouragement. They need a refuge.

A place to hide and heal.

A willing, caring, available someone. A confidant and comrade-at-arms. Can't find one? Why not share David's shelter? The One he called My Strength, Mighty Rock, Fortress, Stronghold, and High Tower.

David's Refuge *never* failed. Not even once. And he never regretted the times he dropped his heavy load and ran for cover.

Neither will you.[5]

Burnout

*What does the worker gain from his toil? I have seen
the burden God has laid on men.*
ECCLESIASTES 3:9,10

Burnout can happen to any of us. It impacts marriages. Consider the words of Frank Minirth:

> The crux of the consideration for Christians who don't
> want to burn out may be to consider if they are in the job
> God has for them. If you think you'll be fired if you spend
> sufficient time with family and on rest and relaxation, then
> it is unlikely that it is the job God has for you. Before quitting
> the company, however, it may be fruitful to consider if
> there is another type of position in the same company that
> would suit you better.
>
> When we put God, family and work in any other order,
> we have diminished our faithfulness to God and are saying,
> "I don't trust God to meet my needs." God would much
> rather we have less income and a more enjoyable lifestyle. If
> you quit the road to burnout, you may indeed face the possibility
> of being fired. However, you may be surprised to
> find that your rating in the company will go up instead of
> down, as you enter each day fresher and more ready to give
> your best to producing during the part of the day that
> should be allotted to work.
>
> Learning a new way of life comes hard for a workaholic,
> but it is necessary. A workaholic has to practice being relaxed,
> practice saying no to others' expectations of him,
> schedule time with God, schedule eight hours of sleep, and
> schedule time with family. The alternative is to become progressively
> less productive and of less benefit to loved ones
> and to himself as a result of burnout.[6]

Do you see any signs of burnout in yourself or your partner?
Any signs of workaholicism? If not, rejoice! If yes, what
steps can you take to reverse this process?

Thoughts for
Your Marriage

Rejoice with those who rejoice.
ROMANS 12:15

Read these thoughts out loud to each other meditatively. One of you read a point and the other make a comment. On the next idea switch roles, and so on, until you have read and commented on each idea. Conclude in prayer.

Love is what love does. To define love at rest is impossible because love never rests. If love rests it is no longer love, but indifference. Love is always doing. Love is always in motion.

Love is the glue that holds our marriages together and the oil that keeps us from rubbing each other the wrong way.

Sometimes with tenderness we must intentionally hurt each other in order to make our relationship whole. Some things just need to be said. It may hurt, even to tears, but being completely open and honest with each other is the only possible basis for a genuinely harmonious marriage.

When we get into the custom of praying for the healing of each other, we get out of the silly common-sense idea that we are bound by our circumstances. We are not. Jesus can, and will, reach down into the hubbub of human circumstances and do the supernatural—if we ask.

Share the extremes of life with one another—the embarrassing moments, the great victories, the dark temptations, the tragic failings, the ecstatic joys. Laugh, cry, sing, and dance. Make beautiful music together. Smell the flowers. Joke around; lighten up. Be real. You are stuck with each other! Enjoy it.

The strongest expression of love we can make is to sacrifice ourselves for one another. When we deny ourselves for our mates we prove by our actions that we "get it" about the true meaning of love.

At any point in time our social (and other) needs will likely not be the same as our mate's. This means that marriage partners must make compromises. One will want to talk out of *desire*. The other must be willing to talk out of *duty*.

The repetitious ignoring of the little things important to our mate is like ignoring rising flood waters against a levee. If enough pressure builds, the levee bursts. Little things left undone put pressure on a marriage.[7]

A Sensitive Prayer

*Do not merely listen to the word,
and so deceive yourselves. Do what it says.*
JAMES 1:22

Lord,

I praise You for understanding me and my struggles. I admit that I have numerous faults that still interfere with living my married life as You want. Forgive me for my conscious and purposeful acts of sin, as well as those which seem to creep in even though I'm fighting against them.

Help me not to say one thing with my words and another with my actions, especially to my partner. I realize this makes me untrustworthy.

Help me not to criticize my spouse for the same faults I see in myself.

Help me not to demand standards from my spouse which I make little or no effort to fulfill.

Help me not to play with, but to skirt around temptations that I know are my weakness. I want to protect my marriage.

Help me to deal with the inability to say yes or no and to be definite in my commitments, especially in my family.

Help me with my stubbornness and reluctance to give up habits which I know are wrong and break my relationship with You.

Help me quit trying to please both worlds; forgive me for pleasing others and myself first rather than You.

Help me to be consistent and live the week the way I live on Sunday morning.

Help me to kick out anything in my life that keeps me from giving You all of me.

Thank You for hearing, for responding, and for working in my life.

In Jesus' name.

Amen.[8]

Follow Jesus

"Come, follow me," Jesus said.
MATTHEW 4:19

Why do you follow Jesus?

Christ said to follow Him because following anyone or anything else gets us lost.

Christ said to know who we look like because drawing our self-image from any other source but God poisons our souls and spirits.

Christ said to clean the inside of the cup because that is the only way to develop true character and avoid a shallow existence.

Christ said to stop fitting in with our culture because our culture is sick, and adapting to it will make us sick, too.

Christ said to get real because wearing masks makes our lives empty and our relationships unfulfilling.

Christ said to stop blaming others because taking responsibility for our own problems is essential for true maturity and health.

Christ said to forgive others because unforgiveness is arrogant and hurts others as well as ourselves.

Christ said to live like an heir because to live like an orphan leads to settling for far too little in life.

Christ said to solve paradoxes because it is often that which seems contrary to common sense that is the healthiest route of all.

Christ said to stop worrying because worry only drains us of the energy we need to work on the things that we can do something about.

Christ said to persevere because the fruit of our labor won't ever show up if we grow tired of doing what it takes to bear it.

Everything Christ tells us is in our best interest, and it is critically important to understand that. His counsel wasn't designed to burden us, but to set us free. When He gave His counsel to us, it was aimed at meeting our deepest needs and it will if we follow it.[9] And following Him will make a difference in your marriage.

Memorize
God's Word

*How can a young man keep his way pure? By living according
to your word....I have hidden your word in my heart
that I might not sin against you.*
PSALMS 119:9,11

This is personal, from me to you. I've got a confession to
make. When I was a teenager I got into something. I got into
memorizing Scripture. And it has helped me more times than
I can remember. On several occasions when I was facing a
temptation and struggling with a decision, guess what happened? A Scripture I'd memorized just happened to "pop"
into my mind at the right moment. And usually it was 1 Corinthians 10:13: "No temptation has seized you except what is
common to man. And God is faithful; he will not let you be
tempted beyond what you can bear. But when you are tempted, he will also provide a way out so that you can stand up
under it." That passage was a lifesaver.

Over the decades of adulthood (I'm 62 as I write this), I really didn't make any consistent attempt to memorize God's
Word...until a few summers ago. A friend of mine at a family
camp shared a session based on his book *Seeking Solid Ground*.
It's all about Psalm 15 and talks about how to get the most out
of life. At the end of his talk, he gently challenged us to memorize this psalm.

I don't know why, but I decided to do it. One thing I found
was that the synapses of the brain cells at my age aren't quite
as alive as they were 40 years ago. It took more work, but just
two or three minutes each morning and it was mine. Sometimes when I wake up at night, I quote it silently. I quote it
when I'm driving. The words are reassuring. They keep me
alert and on track for God. But why not—it's His Word.

So give it a shot. You can do it. If you're not memorizing
God's Word, you're missing out. It's a great activity for a couple
to do together.

Order in
the Marriage

Everything should be done in a fitting and orderly way.
1 CORINTHIANS 14:40

Is there order in your marriage? God loves this. He lives according to order. He also puts order into everything He creates. He didn't set everything in motion and then retreat from involvement. He created, but *He also sustains*. He likes regularity, even though some of us are easily bored by such. Dr. Larry Crabb talks about the order in the creation of man and woman:

> God created Adam first, then Eve. "For man did not come from woman, but woman from man; neither was man created for woman, but woman for man" (1 Corinthians 11:8,9). Did you ever wonder why? "Ladies first" wasn't involved here. There was order to this plan. It made their relationship suitable for representing the order that marks the relationship between Christ and His church. (See Ephesians 5:21-33.)
>
> God also said Adam's existence without Eve wasn't good. So what did God have Adam do? He gave Adam the task of naming the animals. There was a purpose. Can you imagine Adam going out and looking at all the animals? He probably didn't realize how many there were. Did you ever notice that in Genesis 2:20 it says Adam didn't find a suitable companion in all those animals. He probably spent a lot of time noticing and naming and naming and noticing. Perhaps in doing this he came to realize "something is missing here." We don't even know if he was looking. But perhaps through this experience he awoke to the fact, "I don't have anyone, and I want a companion." Then it was that God created Eve. Then Adam felt complete. This was a good design. It was complete.
>
> You as a married couple are complete. God wants us to live orderly lives. How can they be expressed? Perhaps by being the best you can be as a spouse. Perhaps by following the teaching of Scripture in your marriage and being committed to making your marriage last until death do you part. That's the order God has for marriage—lasting and fulfilling.[10]

Transformed

And we, who with unveiled faces all reflect the Lord's glory,
are being transformed into his likeness with ever-increasing glory,
which comes from the Lord, who is the Spirit.
2 CORINTHIANS 3:18

Transformation. We use this word when we're serious and when we jest. Sometimes men will joke about a beauty salon being the "transformation den." They'll say, "Man, you should have seen her when she went in there compared to when she came out. What a difference! What a transformation! They're miracle workers in there." (They're careful to whom they say that!) That home was transformed from a dump to a palace. Or he was transformed once he became a Christian—and that's the way it should be, too. All of us are in the process of being transformed because, as Christians, we aren't complete yet.

How are we transformed? Consider this question: Is your thought life or pattern of thinking any different now than when you weren't a Christian? It should be. Our minds, our thoughts, are at the core of how we behave. Romans tells us: "Do not be conformed to this world, but be transformed by the *renewing of your mind*" (Romans 12:2 NASB, italics added). There's to be a change of focus and a change of mind—and it is a process. Have you ever listened to someone learning to play the piano? At first it's agony for those around. But if this person practiced an hour a day, and you listened to him at intervals of three months, six months, a year, and two years, you would have witnessed a transformation.

Are there any indications of this in your Christian life? Here are a few to consider:

- Does thinking about the Christian life become progressively easier—or do you have to work at it?
- Does the fruit of the Spirit appear more and more naturally—or is it something you work at trying to produce?

Transformation will come naturally. Take a week to reflect on what's going on in your life together. It could mean transformation.[11]

There Are
No Shortcuts

Everyone who competes in the games goes into strict training.
They do it to get a crown that will not last;
but we do it to get a crown that will last forever.
1 CORINTHIANS 9:25

For some men and women, shortcuts are a part of their lives. If they can save time or energy by eliminating some steps in the process, they'll do it. We're encouraged to take shortcuts. Listen to all the "get rich quick" schemes you hear about. Why do we get hooked into those "lose 30 pounds in 30 days" diet schemes? Would we bite if the offer was "lose 30 pounds in 90 days?" Not likely. What about "learn how to speak a foreign language fluently in just 16 easy at-home audio lessons—nothing to read either!" Why take two years of college classes when you can do it in one-tenth the time?

Perhaps you've taken a shortcut while hiking or driving only to discover it took you twice as long to get there. That's the problem with many shortcuts. They don't work. They're often longer in the long run or you bypassed or left out some essentials. Even though you got there, or finished much sooner, you weren't well equipped.

The Scripture illustrates the fact that to attain you have to train. There are no shortcuts to Christian growth. It's training, and this means work, diligence, sweat, persistence, and practice.

It's the same way in marriage. There are no shortcuts to having a fulfilling marriage. You have to put in the hours of conversation, the consistency of being attentive and sensitive to build a closeness. It won't happen overnight. And you can't read "30 days to super sex and super marriage" to substitute for training.

So when tempted to cut corners in giving time and attention to one another...don't. It's a good way to get lost in your marriage.[12]

What Builds
a Relationship?

*But everyone who hears these words of mine and does not put them
into practice is like a foolish man who built his house on sand.*
MATTHEW 7:26

It's time for a marital quiz. Relax—this is not a final exam or
an IQ test or anything of the sort. It's more like an opinion poll
(with some information coming later).

There are certain elements that go into the building of any
relationship for it to succeed. If any of them are absent, neglected, or adversely treated, the relationship is in trouble and
could break apart. We're going to look at four of them. Instead
of identifying each one right away, here are the characteristics
of each. Without looking ahead, see if you can identify them.

1. _____ the most enduring (the word begins with the
   letter L).

2. _____ the most fragile (the word begins with the
   letter T).

3. _____ the most neglected (the word begins with the
   letter R or H).

4. _____ the one that takes the longest (sorry, no help
   here).

So, what did you come up with? Hopefully you figured out
the first three.

Of course the one that is the most enduring is love. It has a
lasting quality. And as believers, we are able to love because
God first loved us. But it needs to have the "S & S" quality to
it—shown and said.

The most fragile is trust. It's easily broken and not easily restored. Respect or honor is the most neglected. The last one,
the one that takes the longest is understanding or knowledge.

You may be thinking, "Hey, that's not bad. I'm really strong
in three of them. That ought to make up for the absent one." It
doesn't work that way. You can't say you don't trust the other,
but still love that person. Love doesn't make up for distrust. It
won't work to say, "I've lost respect for my partner, but I understand him (her)." Understanding does not fill the void for
disrespect. A relationship is built on four legs. If one is weak, it
wobbles. If two are weak, it could collapse. How are the four
pillars in your relationship today?[13]

Do You
Need Approval?

Am I now trying to win the approval of men, or of God?
Or am I trying to please men? If I were still trying to please men,
I would not be a servant of Christ.
GALATIANS 1:10

How badly do you need other people's approval? Can you live without it or is it a consuming drive? Some like approval more than others. Those who have a high need for approval also wither under criticism more than others.

When we live for approval, we work harder to make an impression even in marriage. We wonder, "Do others *really* like me? Do they really think I'm all right?" We're looking for others to give us the "thumbs-up sign," and do it constantly.

John Ortberg likened this problem to a kind of mental jury box in which resides all the people of our lives who rate us like judges at a major ice skating event. Do you have one of those boxes in your mind? What about your partner? Who's in the box? It could be parents (even at your age). For some it's teachers, our bosses, our pastors, our peer group, and others in our professions. If they're all still there, it's kind of crowded, isn't it? How many times do you really know what others are thinking about you? We never know for sure. All we know is what we think they're thinking—and that's a lot of guesswork, isn't it?

Sure, we want to be seen as sharp, secure, and successful. Does it really matter what others think? God wants us to live another way—to live to please Him. The more we do that, the greater our security becomes and the less we need other people's approval. Of course, we never really *need* it. We just think we do.[14]

Love Is. . .

1 CORINTHIANS 13
New International Reader's Version

Suppose I speak in the languages of human beings and of angels. If I don't have love, I am only a loud gong or a noisy cymbal. Suppose I have the gift of prophecy. Suppose I can understand all the secret things of God and know everything about him. And suppose I have enough faith to move mountains. If I don't have love, I am nothing at all. Suppose I give everything I have to poor people. And suppose I give my body to be burned. If I don't have love, I get nothing at all.

Love is patient. Love is kind. It does not want what belongs to others. It does not brag. It is not proud. It is not rude. It does not look out for its own interests. It does not easily become angry. It does not keep track of other people's wrongs.

Love is not happy with evil. But it is full of joy when the truth is spoken. It always protects. It always trusts. It always hopes. It never gives up.

Love never fails....

When I was a child, I talked like a child. I thought like a child, I had the understanding of a child. When I became an adult, I put childish ways behind me.

Now we see only a dim likeness of things. It is as if we were seeing them in a mirror. But someday we will see clearly. We will see face to face. What I know now is not complete. But someday I will know completely, just as God knows me completely.

The three most important things to have: faith, hope and love. But the greatest of them is love.[15]

Morph?...Me?

...until Christ is formed in you.
GALATIANS 4:19

How would you describe yourself five years ago? Go ahead and do it. Now, describe yourself today. Were the words the same or were some different?

Now describe your marriage five years ago. What words would you use? Now describe your marriage at the present time. Were the words the same? Is your marriage changing? If so, which direction is it going?

You see, as believers we change. That's our calling—to be different, to grow, to be refined in a positive way.

A number of years ago the main interest of young children was a TV show produced in Japan. It was the adventures of a group of teenage superheroes called The Mighty Morphin' Power Rangers. Children loved the show because the characters had the ability to "morph." The Power Rangers were a group of ordinary teenagers, but when needed they could use a power beyond what they ordinarily would have to become martial arts heroes to defeat the evil forces. They'd cry out and say, "It's morphing time!" And with that they'd be transformed with the ability to do amazing things. And thus the word "morph" has become part of our everyday vocabulary.

Most of us would like to morph—and we can. Do you know where this word comes from? *Morphoo* (Greek) means "the inward and real formation of the essential character of a person." It's used to describe the formation and growth of an embryo in a mother's body. Look at today's Scripture. The word "formed" is the word "morph" in the original Greek. Do you know what this means? Paul wanted the Galatians not only to have Christ born in them, but to also reflect Jesus in every aspect of their lives.

Think of this—we're in a spiritual gestation process. Jesus is being formed in us. And the more this happens, the more we reflect Him and the more our marriages can change. So get ready to morph![16]

Is Depression
Wrong?

Why are you so downcast, O my soul?
Why so disturbed within me? Put your hope in God,
for I will yet praise him, my Savior and my God.
PSALM 42:11

One of the most common questions Christians ask about depression concerns sin. "Is depression a sin? Is it a sin for a Christian to be depressed?" In and of itself depression is not a sin. Depression is sometimes a *consequence* of sin, but not always. When it's a symptom of sin, it serves as a warning to us.

There has always been depression, and there always will be. Many people God used mightily in the Old Testament were so depressed they wanted to die—Moses, for example, plus Job, Elijah, Jonah, and certain writers of the psalms (see especially Psalms 42 and 43). Great men and women throughout history have struggled with depression, so don't let anyone tell you that it's abnormal to be depressed, that it's a sin to be depressed, or that Christians don't experience depression. Depression is a normal response to what is occurring in life.

Many people are surprised to read the account of Jesus' depression in the Garden of Gethsemane. Jesus was a perfect man and free from all sin, yet complete in His humanity and tempted as we are. Look at the account in Matthew 26:36-38:

> Then Jesus went with them to a place called Gethsemane, and He told His disciples, "Sit down here while I go over yonder and pray." And taking with Him Peter and the two sons of Zebedee, He began to show grief and distress of mind and was deeply depressed. Then He said to them, "My soul is very sad and deeply grieved, so that I am almost dying of sorrow. Stay here and keep awake and watch with Me" (AMP).

Jesus knew what was about to happen to Him, and it caused Him to be depressed. Jesus did not feel guilty over being depressed, and neither should we.

Depression?

Singing to a person who is depressed is like taking off
a person's clothes on a cold day or like rubbing salt in a wound.[17]
PROVERBS 25:20

Have you ever shared with one another the times in your lives that you've been depressed? If not, it could be an interesting discussion. Depression is a part of life. It's a normal response when we have certain experiences or even when changes occur within our bodies. You and your partner will be depressed at some time in your marriage. Will you know how to respond to one another at that time?

Let's consider depression. This may be a time when we're called upon to minister to our partners. We'll need to listen to them, encourage them, and support them. Telling them to snap out of it, cheer up, things could be worse, get a life, or avoiding them will not be helpful.

You probably already know what it's like to be depressed. It's that feeling of overall gloom—hopelessness, despair, sadness, apathy. Depression is not like a sense of sadness in which there is a "down" feeling from a disappointment or loss. Depression is different: It lasts longer and is more intense. It can linger and linger with its immobilizing intensity making it difficult to carry on life activities. Depression slams down the window of hope, and sometimes it even draws down a darkened shade.

If you think of the literal meaning of the word "depression," it means to move something from a higher position to a lower level. Frequently a depressed person, when asked how he or she is feeling, will say "quite low."

Depression is a message telling us that something is wrong in our lives. If it happens to you or your spouse, listen to its message, and then seek the help needed. Above all, stand by one another during this time.

What's Driving You?

He is before all things, and in him all things hold together.
COLOSSIANS 1:17

Who is at the center of your life? Who is at the center of your marriage? Consider what Tim Riter has to say:

On my Honda Gold Wing motorcycle, power comes to the rear wheel through the hub. The hub at the center of the wheel receives the power and transmits it through the spokes to the rim. The wheel then moves. Think of our lives as that wheel. The hub is the center of our lives, what motivates and drives us. The spokes are the specific areas, such as our personality, character and activities. The rim is the outer part of our lives that shows action. If our spokes aren't firmly connected to God at the hub of our lives, we won't move.

We may have action. The hub moves; the spokes may even flop around. But the rim doesn't move. Despite the activity, little is accomplished. However, when all the pieces of our lives are connected to God, we can have peace and harmony. Our lives may never slow down; we may not be able to escape the pace of life. But we can unify everything under Christ.

Anxiety over paying the mortgage doesn't possess our thoughts. We trust in God's promise to meet our needs when we put him first. We're not in constant fear over health issues. Either we die, which brings us directly to the love of our life, or we live and serve God here on earth. If our health improves, we're pleased; but if it doesn't, we know that God's power is made perfect in our weakness. Concern over government officials and school boards doesn't bring depression; what person can oppose what God truly wants done?

Instead of worrying or feeling rushed, we focus on pleasing him. By relying on God as the center of our lives, all the pieces of our existence connect. We have completeness. We have peace. We trust in God's love and power and yield responsibility for how things develop.[18]

God's Plan

He who conceals his sins does not prosper,
but whoever confesses and renounces them finds mercy.
PROVERBS 28:13

Charles Stanley has a suggestion for all couples.

God gave the husband and wife to each other to make them more than they could be singly. The completion of each cannot take place until they learn to share their innermost being and work for the good of the other. The personal areas that are kept private have no opportunity for growth. Why not try God's plan?

Marriage, love, and communication cannot be separated from God without shriveling them. There may be numerous areas of your life that you mark "off limits" to God as well as to your spouse. Could they include fear of inadequacy, deeply rooted bitterness, feigned love, or a spirit of revenge? These are poisons in the soul that God and your mate can help dispel—if you seek help.

God seeks to develop your soul as well as your body. Many personable people are not using all their God-given gifts because their emotional life is constricted. They refuse to allow their emotions to be exposed and to be brought to maturity. Examine yourself for a moment; are you courageous enough to look inward to see what is really there? Then are you willing to talk to God and your spouse about your hidden self? Little by little, you may be strengthened until you will care to say: "Honey, tell me exactly what you feel about me, about yourself, everything" and not say a word until the other finishes!

Open your heart to the light of God and the sympathy of your mate, and you will see the enemy retreating. The fullness of emotional development and interrelationships can be yours.[19]

What Do
You Do?

For you created my inmost being; you knit me together in
my mother's womb. I praise you because I am fearfully and
wonderfully made; your works are wonderful, I know that full well.
PSALM 139:13,14

Tim Stafford, in *Knowing the Face of God*, shares keen insights
on God and His creation:

> The first question we ask someone after learning his
> name is, "What do you do?" In getting to know God, then,
> we must ask that question. He may hide his face, but he has
> not hidden his work.
>
> What does God do? He makes flowers and mountains
> and starry nights, the severity of the desert and the lushness
> of the forest meadow. In these he reveals himself as an artist
> of incomparable imagination.
>
> But God's work is more than nature. He barely began
> there. People generally concede that you can know some-
> thing about God through the universe he has made: "The
> heavens are telling the glory of God." But to know someone
> through his work you ought to concentrate on the work he
> loves best. God does not love stars as he loves me. The heav-
> ens, for all their splendor, will outlive their usefulness; they
> will be rolled up and taken away. So will the world we live
> in, for all its sensual glory and intricate ecology. They are
> like scaffolding that Michelangelo designed for painting the
> Sistine Chapel—marvelous in its own right, but dismantled
> at the proper time so that the great work could be more
> clearly seen. When God had created everything else he went
> on to man and woman, creatures who sat up and talked to
> each other, who talked to him. He has been working to com-
> plete these creatures ever since. He even became one. His
> people are God's great work, to be displayed in an entirely
> new setting—a new heaven and a new earth.
>
> To marvel at yourself is not far from marveling at God.
> This is the logic of the familiar Psalm 139: "You knit me to-
> gether in my mother's womb. I praise you because I am fear-
> fully and wonderfully made; your works are wonderful"
> (13-14).[20]

God created each of you. You are a great work made in the
image of God. Treat one another as such!

Take Out
the Plug

Do not put out the Spirit's fire.
1 THESSALONIANS 5:1

Out in Colorado there's a little town nestled down at the foot of some hills—it's sort of a Sleepy Hollow village. There's not much rainfall out there, and they depend on irrigation. But some enterprising citizens ran a pipe up the hills to a lake of clear, sweet water. As a result the town had plenty of water. The population increased and the place had become quite a boomtown.

One morning the housewives turned on the water spigots. There was no water. There was some sputtering. So the men climbed the hill. The lake was as full as ever. They couldn't find a cause for the stoppage. And as days grew into weeks, people started moving away again, the prosperous town was reverting back to its old condition. One day one of the town officials received a note. It was poorly written, with bad spelling and grammar. It said, "Ef you'll jes pull the plug out of the pipe about eight inches from the top you'll get all the water you want." So the men went back up to the top of the hill, they examined the pipe, found the plug which someone had inserted. Not a very big plug—just big enough to fill the pipe. It is surprising how large a reservoir of water can be held back by one small plug. Out came the plug and down came the water.

Why is there such a lack of power in our lives? After all, we have a reservoir of life-giving water. The problem is that all around us the earth is dry, thirsty, and cracked open. We have connecting pipes between the reservoir and ourselves. Why aren't the refreshing waters rushing down? The answer is plain. *There is a plug in the pipe.*

Is there anything hindering your marriage relationship from growing at this time? If so, find that plug![21]

How Can We
Build Trust?

His master replied, "Well done, good and faithful servant!
You have been faithful with a few things; I will put you in charge of
many things. Come and share your master's happiness!"
MATTHEW 25:21

Perhaps you've had a difficult time trusting others. Life experiences can make us gun-shy. Or perhaps someone you know has a struggle in trusting. Often people ask, "How can I build my trust in another but also build their trustworthiness?" That's a good question. Tom Marshall has some helpful suggestions.

Trust costs. You have to run the risk of being hurt. Every time you place yourself in another's hands you're being vulnerable. That's the risk. When you trust your partner, trust him or her to do the things he or she is good at doing. Why put both of you at risk by trusting in an area that a person isn't likely to succeed at? Discover one another's strengths. Concentrate on those.

When your partner comes through with what you've asked, never, never take it for granted. Let him or her know how much you appreciate what occurred. That's what today's passage is all about.

Are you a trustworthy person? That's the big question. Modeling this quality encourages others, especially your spouse. When both partners can be fully trusted there's a sense of feeling safe. You don't have to be a "checker upper" like you frequently do with children.

So what happens, though, *if* (this is a big if) your spouse lets you down in some area? That's a good question. What's wrong with giving him or her another opportunity? Why not go back to where your mate succeeded last time and start again? Gradually rebuild. There are some phrases to avoid like the plague that could cripple future trust. Some are: "It will be a long time before I'll ever depend on you again"; "I should have known not to trust you." These are wedge-building statements. They divide. They don't draw couples close together.

Hopefully your trust of one another will never be broken. If it is, remember that it can be rebuilt. The Holy Spirit can do wonders for us as individuals and as couples.[22]

The Pillar
of Love

We love because he first loved us.
1 JOHN 4:19

Tom Marshall shares some wonderful insights on how to love. Here is an adaption from his book *Right Relationships.*

It's true. You've heard about the pillar before. Probably many times. But very possibly not in the following way. You were made for love—divine love. We have a need to be loved in such a way that only God can meet that need. And when we experience His love for us and we love Him, then and only then can we freely love others in a way that it makes a difference. And there are many expressions of this love.

One of these is *care*. This is love in action. Care is not a matter of having warm feelings for your spouse. Care means we attend to our partners' welfare and their best interests in a consistent way. We look out for the other person.

Another expression of love is *kindness*. When you are kind to the other person, you know that you're responding in a way that you'd like them to respond in a similar situation.

Love is also *liking* the other. It's a pleasurable part of life. What's this all about? It involves attraction, interest, fondness, and other favorable responses. You like to be with and do things with your spouse.

Another expression of love is *tenderness*. This is an expression of gentleness and is a healing response when your partner is hurting and vulnerable. It is given out of your strength.

When you love you're also *generous*, especially with your time, attention, assistance, and encouragement. The model for this comes from God's generous nature.

Compassion is the calling to all Christians, but the ideal place for its expression is within marriage. It's the feeling of pity or being distressed at what your partner is experiencing. It's hurting with him or her but with a desire to help.

Forgiveness is the survival kit for a marriage. Forgiveness says, "No more blame. No more keeping score." It's a non-deserved gift. There are no records kept.[23]

When Did
It End?

Lean on, trust and be confident in the Lord with all your heart and mind, and do not rely on your own insight or understanding.
PROVERBS 3:5 AMP

So when did it end? It usually does. For some, it ends almost immediately. For others it lasts for weeks or months or in some cases a few years. But it does come to an end at some point—it's the honeymoon. This is supposed to be an idyllic time in which everything is perfect for the couple. Actually, the dictionary simply states it's a vacation or trip for a newly married couple. But this cannot go on forever. When we say the "honeymoon ended," it usually means the romantic idealism has diminished and the reality of who the other person is and what marriage is all about has sunk in to the couple. What wasn't apparent before or what wasn't noticed is now very obvious. Couples have three choices at this time, and the selection determines the future course of their life together.

One choice is to focus on the apparent flaws of the other person and embark upon a crusade with the sole purpose of changing one's spouse.

A second response is harmony—but achieved only through a sense of toleration and distance. "If you don't bother me about that, then I won't bother you about this issue." It's actually an acceptance of the selfishness of one another by avoiding any confrontation that leads to an emotional separation. This can last for 50 years. We all have seen marriages of toleration. This couple ends up as a pair of married singles.

A third style is where husbands and wives notice flaws, but in this case they notice their own more than those of their spouses. They ask Jesus Christ to refine them and their focus is becoming all He wants them to become, especially in marriage.

Where are you in these three scenarios? Where would you like to be?

Honeymoons do end and thankfully so. Then there's an opportunity for the real growth of marriage to begin. And perhaps, just perhaps, a new honeymoon can begin.[24]

Relationship Change

*Call to me and I will answer you, and I will tell you great
and mighty things, which you do not know.*
JEREMIAH 33:3 NASB

Building new and solid relationships requires change, and
change can be frightening. Yet we can transform any relationship when we make a decision and a commitment to live our
lives according to the Word of God. But to live and reflect
something in our lives, we not only have to *know* it, but we
also have to give it time to seep into our lives and become part
of our thoughts and values.

If someone tells you, "You're too old to change and to learn
a new way of responding after all these years," that is *not true!*
If someone tells you it is easy to change if you set your mind
to it, that, too, is *not true!* Change is difficult, but possible. It
takes energy, effort, and time, but it is possible. The essence of
our Christian faith is hope. In counseling situations, I have
seen married couples change, although sometimes I honestly
did not believe it was possible.

We are creatures of habit, but the presence of Jesus Christ in
our lives can override the habit patterns that have been constantly reinforced over the years.

Here are three proven steps to change: 1) Select a behavior
you would like to change; 2) decide how you would like to respond differently (base it upon God's Word); 3) memorize a related Scripture and repeat it 15 to 20 times a day.

Because our thoughts are such a critical factor in how we respond to others and to ourselves, some of our relational habits
may need radical reconstruction. Visualize yourself responding in a new way in several varied situations. Do this 15 to 20
times a day. If necessary, role-play the situation with a friend.
Commit this new way of responding to God, and thank Him
for what He will be doing in your life.

Measure your growth with new criteria. Instead of focusing
on the 90 percent of the time you reverted to the old pattern,
dwell on the 10 percent when you came through with flying
colors.

The Dream

*We were like men who dreamed. Our mouths were filled
with laughter, our tongues with songs of joy.*
PSALMS 126:1,2

Walter Wangerin shares this story:

I had a dream. It was a simple dream, more feeling than
detail, but it seemed to last a long while.

Simply, a friend of mine was coming to see me, and I was
excited by the prospect. I didn't know who the friend was.
That didn't seem odd. I suppose I didn't occupy myself with
the question *who?* Just with the anticipation and with the
certainty that he would come.

As the time for his arrival drew nearer and nearer, my excitement increased. I felt more and more like a child, beam-
ing with my pleasure, distracted from all other pursuits,
thinking of this one thing only. I wanted to stand on the
porch and bellow to the neighborhood, *My friend is coming!*

Well, it was clear that I hadn't seen this friend for years.
Even in the intensity of excitement, I didn't picture him to
myself. Perhaps I didn't know what he looked like. Is that
possible? I could scarcely stand the waiting. Strangely, I think
I expected to recognize him by his scent, by a certain smell I
remembered, rich and steadfast, fleshy, warm, enveloping—
like the strong declaration of a stallion's flank after galloping.
It wasn't so much my eyes I strained, then, but my nostrils
and the fullness of my mouth.

A wild kind of music attended my waiting. And the
closer he came, the more exquisite grew this music.

And he came.

Then I put my hands to my cheeks and cried and laughed
at once.

He was looking directly at me, with mortal affection—and
I grew so strong within his gaze. And I knew at once who he
was. I was a perfect flame of the knowledge of his name. It
was Jesus. He had come exactly as he said he would.

I cherish this dream and think of it often. I was a full
grown man when I dreamt it.[25]

Do you dream of Jesus? Share with one another what He
means to each of you.

The Little Things

Now his master saw that the LORD was with [Joseph].
GENESIS 39:3

How do you follow through on the small things of life? Do they get done, postponed, or forgotten? A biblical example of someone who was faithful in little things is in the last chapters of Genesis. As you look at the story of Joseph, you see a man who was dependable and trustworthy:

- He was given responsibility to shepherd his father's flocks "while he was still a youth" (Genesis 37:2).

- After he was sold into slavery by his brothers, he ended up in the house of Potiphar, where he performed his duties well enough to be appointed overseer of all that Potiphar owned (see 39:5). Scripture doesn't say why he was elevated, but he probably had to fulfill some basic menial and unpleasant tasks to earn the trust of his master.

- He refused the amorous advances of Potiphar's wife. Unfortunately, he was thrown into prison when she lied and said he had tried to seduce her (see verses 7-18).

- His character in prison was so strong that the chief jailer placed him in charge of all the prisoners (see verses 21-23).

- After interpreting Pharaoh's dream, he was taken from prison and made a ruler in Egypt, second in power only to Pharaoh (see 41:38-41).

Did Joseph try to move up in responsibility? Not really. He was faithful to fulfill his responsibilities and content to allow God to give him more. Even his words to Potiphar's wife tell something of his character: "Behold, with me here, my master does not concern himself with anything in the house, and he has put all that he owns in my charge....He has withheld nothing from me except you, because you are his wife. How then could I do this great evil and sin against God?" (Genesis 39:8,9).

We all have ambitions, but sometimes are our ambitions in the right areas? Jesus said the greatest ambition is to be the slave of all—a servant (see Mark 10:42-45).

If you want to be a leader, then you've got to be a servant. Who in your marriage follows through on the "little things"?[26]

Help from
the Holy Spirit

We do not know how to pray worthily,
but his Spirit within us is actually praying for us
in those agonizing longings which cannot find words.
ROMANS 8:26,27 PHILLIPS

I just don't know what to say when I pray." Have you ever felt like this when it comes to prayer? "Sometimes I'm at a loss for words." You're not alone; we've all felt like this. As we sit down to pray our minds wander. Every few minutes we sneak a look at the clock to see if we've prayed long enough. Does that happen to you when you pray alone? Interestingly, when couples pray together that happens less often.

The Holy Spirit is God's answer when we don't know how to pray, when we are crippled in our prayer lives. That's where the work of the Holy Spirit really comes into play. He helps us by showing us *what* we should pray for and *how* we ought to pray. That's quite a promise—and the Holy Spirit delivers! There are several specific ways He helps us:

- *The Spirit intercedes* for you when you are oppressed by problems in your life.

- *The Spirit guides* you by directing your thoughts to the promises of God's Word that are best suited to your needs.

- *The Spirit helps* you pray in the right way.

One of your callings in marriage is to assist your partner when he or she needs help. You are always to be listening for a call for assistance. When you are having difficulty praying, remember that you can pray for your mate and you have someone to draw on for strength—the Holy Spirit.

How Determined
Are You?

Recalling your tears, I long to see you, so that I may be filled with joy.
2 TIMOTHY 1:4

Stubborn, dogged determination. That's what it takes to persevere. Just keep trying again and again and again." That's the message that's been given to children, groups, communities, and even nations: Keep at it.

When Robert the First (1274–1329) was the king of Scotland, the English were trying to invade his small kingdom. "Robert the Bruce" tried to protect Scotland, but a time came when he had to retreat from his castle to avoid capture and death. He escaped to a cave and struggled with depression and the uncertainty of what to do next.

Do you ever feel uncertain what to do next?

Then he noticed a very small spider spinning its web. It kept working and working, adding one new strand at a time. Sometimes the spider failed, but it kept at its task, and finally, there was a web inviting some careless fly to come and be captured.

The king observed that the spider's perseverence reflected two qualities—patience and tolerance. The spider never gave thought to giving up. As Robert reflected on the spider, he began to evict his anxious thoughts.

Are there some anxious thoughts which need evicting from your life?

Looking at his problems more objectively and logically, the king saw them in a different light.

Could you take a different perspective of issues facing you?

The king then made a decision that he would be like the spider and never give up. He came up with some new ideas and put them into practice, kicking the depression out of his life. Finally, in the year 1328, he was successful and the English recognized Scotland's independence.

Do you ever feel that other people conspire against you much like the English did against Robert? Are there obstacles blocking what you would like for your life? Whatever you're facing, instead of hitting it head-on with a direct onslaught, why not go over it, around it, or under it? Try a new approach: calm down, kick out the confusing depressing thoughts and—like the spider— persevere. It's possible with your Lord as your partner.[27]

Take the
First Step

Therefore, treat people the same way you want them to treat you,
for this is the Law and the Prophets.
MATTHEW 7:12

Have you ever sat back and waited for your spouse to take the first step toward you when there's been a disagreement? Have you ever felt that you both did something wrong or said something you know you shouldn't have said, but you're determined not to admit it first? Could it be that if you admit you're wrong your spouse will say, "You're right" rather than admitting his or her part in the problem? Joy Davidson said:

> We hesitate to be the first to apply the Golden Rule; we feel that it isn't safe, that we must wait until the whole world is ready to apply it with us. But that is why the whole world is never ready—they're all leaving it to the other fellow to start. Of course it isn't safe. We shall lose many worldly advantages if we love our neighbors as ourselves; we may even lose our lives. But then, that is what we were told to do.
>
> Christ never offered us security. He left that to the politicians—Caiaphas probably offered lots of it. Christ told us to expect poverty, humiliation, persecution, and pain, and to know ourselves blessed through accepting them. The good news out of Nazareth was never reassuring news by this world's standards; reassuring news has a way of coming from the devil. For a long time we have been trying to make the best of both worlds, to accept Christianity as an ideal and materialism as a practice, and in consequence we have reached a spiritual bankruptcy....

O God, help me to forgive others as I want them to forgive me. May I try to understand them as I in turn would like to be understood. May I see with their eyes, think with their minds, feel with their hearts. Then let me ask myself whether I should judge them or judge myself and accept them as children, like me, of one heavenly Father.[1]

Do You Remember?

Remember, dear brothers and sisters...
1 Corinthians 1:26 NLT

Do you remember?" It's a question you'll say to one another for the life of your marriage. Do you remember...

The first time you saw one another.

The first time you went out together.

The first kiss. The first disagreement? The first making up? Do you remember exactly what your vows were at the wedding ceremony? Do you remember the best times in your marriage or the worst? (That may not be a fair question among all the others, but what you remember the most can set the tone for your marriage.)

Remember. Do you know what it means? Literally speaking, it means to bring the picture back to your mind so you relive it, see it, and do it again. Videos and photographs are so important because they help us remember. Life is full of memories. Unfortunately, many of them fade too quickly or are crowded out by the immediate—even the good ones.

Remembering is an important part of your present and future. Woodrow Wilson said, "A nation which does not remember what it was yesterday does not know what it is today, nor what it is trying to do. We are trying to do a futile thing if we do not know where we came from or what we have been about."

Moses reminded the children of Israel who and what they were: "Remember that you were a servant in the land of Egypt and that the Lord your God brought you out from there with a mighty hand and an outstretched arm" (Deuteronomy 5:15 AMP).

It's important to remember the significant events of your marriage. It's even more critical to remember your calling and who you were before Christ came into your life. Always remember what God has done for you—not each month or each week, but daily. It's the greatest gift you've ever received.

Just remember...[2]

A Word
to Husbands

Husbands, love your wives and do not be embittered against them.
Colossians 3:19 NASB

Today's message is for husbands, but it's all right for wives to follow along, but only on these conditions: You don't make references back to this—"Remember what Norm said." You don't say, "See, I've been telling you that all along. I was right." And you consider if this applies in any way to you. Agreed?

Now, this verse is like many in the Scriptures. It tells husbands what to do and what not to do. The word embittered is an interesting one. Have you ever cooked something and the instructions said, "Bring it to a boil and then let it simmer for 10 minutes?" Embittered is anger that simmers. It may stay just inside of a person, eating a hole in the lining of his or her stomach and keeping that person awake, or it may be expressed verbally or even in nonverbal ways like glaring or scowling.

It usually develops because you've been hurt or frustrated since something didn't go your way. Too often a man will spend hours going over the issue in his mind again and again and again. It's as though he has an anger video and every now and then he says to himself, "Okay, it's time to put that disc in the DVD and hit the play button." Playing it once may not be so bad, but each time he replays it, he actually feels the experience all over again. And each time he feels it he deepens the wound of resentment. It sears into his brain just a little deeper. Some hurts even seem to be tattooed on the memory banks of the brain.

God's Word says to get rid of bitterness. It has no place in a husband's life. There's a much better way for couples to live. It's called forgiveness. Your spouse can't earn it. She doesn't have to. After all, we were forgiven by God. We didn't earn it, because we couldn't. We didn't deserve it; it was a gift. That's the pattern for us to follow.

How Does
He Know?

For the ways of a man are before the eyes of the LORD,
and He watches all his paths.
PROVERBS 5:21 NASB

Have you ever tried to keep something from your spouse? You know, like you forgot to pay a bill and the bill collector called or sent you a letter… and you just neglected to share this experience. Were you successful in keeping this to yourself? It could have been for a brief period of time or even forever. You may be capable of keeping something from one another. But don't try doing that with God. It's a lost cause. He knows everything; He sees everything. He can't be surprised by anything.

Do you really know your spouse? *Somewhat.*

Does your spouse really know you? *Somewhat.*

There is no somewhat with God. It's complete. And it's a personal knowing.

> O Lord, you have examined my heart and know everything about me. You know when I sit or stand. When far away you know my every thought. You chart the path ahead of me and tell me where to stop and rest. Every moment you know where I am. You know what I am going to say before I even say it. You both precede and follow me and place your hand of blessing on my head. This is too glorious, too wonderful to believe! I can *never* be lost to your Spirit! I can never get away from my God! If I go up to heaven, you are there; if I go down to the place of the dead, you are there (Psalm 139:1-8 TLB).

Is this something to be terrified about? *No.*

Is this something to be concerned over? *No.*

Is this something to rejoice over? *Yes—yes—yes!*

Why? God knows you, accepts you, and loves you. He's a model for the way we're to love and accept one another. Often the love, respect, and acceptance diminishes the more a person knows about his or her spouse. That's not the way it's supposed to be. God's plan is for you to know as much as possible about one another. It gives you more to love—not less. When you have difficulty with this, remember God loves you and He knows all about you.

Holy Living
Is Possible!

The fear of the LORD is the beginning of wisdom,
and knowledge of the Holy One is understanding.
PROVERBS 9:10

Let's bottom line this discussion. What does it mean to live a holy life? God wants us to turn our backs on evil. We don't have to look for evil because it's all around us. Can we avoid all sin? No, we will sin. But there's a way to get rid of it: "Under this new plan we have been forgiven and made clean by Christ's dying for us once and for all....For by that one offering he made forever perfect in the sight of God all those whom he is making holy" (Hebrews 10:10,14 TLB).

God wants us to serve Him. What would happen if each morning you asked God to show you how you could serve Him in a new way? If you live a holy lifestyle, it means you're not the controller or decision maker of your life. Jesus is the Lord. By consulting God you're adopting His perspective and mind-set for your life.

God also wants you to get rid of idols in your life. The idols we worship today may be a bit different than those of other centuries, but perhaps some of these will hit home.

God does not want us to worship the god of affluence—wealth doesn't equate with happiness. We're to trust in God rather than CDs, money-market accounts, or stocks.

There's also the god of pleasure, which comes in many forms. Entertainment is great, but who's in charge—it or us?

There's the god of achievement—title and status are other words for pride.

There's the god of self-worship—there are more people than we realize today who have fallen into the trap of narcissism. Good looks, fit bodies, and looking good are all right, but not as a preoccupation.

God doesn't want us chasing after these other gods. If we do, we're not worshiping Him as the Holy God, nor are we living a holy life. Yes, it does take some refining. But in the long run, what's going to last?[3]

A Sacred Canopy

He has taken me to the banquet hall, and his banner over me is love.
SONG OF SONGS 2:4

Good marriages and spirituality should go hand in hand. Spiritual commitment improves the quality of our marriages. Faith in God should make a radical difference in our relationships with our spouses; it should enhance our love for each other. But something is terribly wrong if commitment to God is the only thing holding a marriage together. Then marriage becomes a prison for dissatisfied mates instead of an oasis of love and acceptance and a place of refreshment and restoration.

In his book *Spheres of Love*, Stephen G. Post, Ph.D., suggests that the high esteem marriage once enjoyed has been difficult to sustain because it lacks what he defines as "a sacred canopy"—an affirmation of the significant foundational beliefs concerning the holy state of marriage. Post writes: "The full dignity of marriage must be newly articulated." This means we must restate, in a way others can understand, the seriousness and status of marriage. Marriage is a solemn state taken too lightly by the world. Marriage was part of God's original natural order. Marriage transcends cultures. It is a serious commitment intended to be a permanent tie and is the foundation of the family unit. Dr. Post adds: "Marriage is an essentially mysterious union like the mystical one between Christ and the church, should be entered reverently with the exchange of vows, and is a place where God dwells."

Henri Nouwen, in *Seeds of Hope*, expands on the concept of marriage being a dwelling place for God:

> Marriage is not a lifelong attraction of two individuals to each other but a call for two people to witness together God's love....The real mystery of marriage is not that husband and wife love each other so much that they can find God in each other's lives but that God loves them so much that they can discover each other more and more as living reminders of God's presence. They are brought together, indeed, as two prayerful hands extended toward God and forming in this way a home for God in this world.[4]

Following Jesus

Only conduct yourselves in a manner worthy of the gospel of Christ.
PHILIPPIANS 1:27 NASB

As a follower of Jesus Christ, are you doing what today's verse says in your marriage? Are you following Him in what you do and how you respond to your spouse? Consider these examples from Jesus' life.

Jesus had compassion. We see His compassion expressed in Mark 8:2: "I feel compassion for the people because they have remained with Me now three days and have nothing to eat" (NASB). His concern was to alleviate suffering and meet the needs of the people. In what way can you demonstrate compassion to your spouse?

Jesus accepted people. When Jesus first met people, He accepted them as they were. In other words, He believed in them and what they would become. The characteristic of acceptance is seen in John 4, John 8, and Luke 19. When Jesus met the woman at the well, He accepted her as she was without condemning her. He accepted the woman caught in adultery, as He also did with Zacchaeus, the dishonest tax collector. How can you accept your spouse more?

Jesus gave people worth. People were Jesus' top priority. He established this priority and gave them worth by putting their needs before the rules and regulations the religious leaders had constructed. He involved Himself in the lives of people who were considered the worst of sinners, and He met them where they had a need. In so doing, He helped elevate their sense of self-worth.

One of the ways Jesus gave worth to people was by showing them their value in God's eyes, by comparing God's care for other creatures with God's care for them: "Are not two sparrows sold for a cent? And yet not one of them will fall to the ground apart from your Father" (Matthew 10:29 NASB). How can you help your partner feel more valuable today?

Watch Your Mouth

The tongue of the wise commends knowledge,
but the mouth of the fool gushes folly.
PROVERBS 15:2

Trivia question: How many times are the words "tongue," "mouth," "lips," and "words" mentioned in Proverbs? The answer is coming later, but suffice it to say that Proverbs is the finest guide we have on how to communicate. In practical advice it surpasses all the other books in the Bible. Consider the following insights on what not to say:

- How about boasting? "Like clouds and wind without rain is a man who boasts of gifts he does not give" (Proverbs 25:14). It's talk that is useless and ridiculous. Paul talked about this, too: "Do not let any unwholesome talk come out of your mouths, but only what is helpful for building others up according to their needs, that it may benefit those who listen" (Ephesians 4:29).

- How about flattery? "He who rebukes a man will in the end gain more favor than he who has a flattering tongue" (Proverbs 28:23). We know how to butter up someone, especially when we want something. This doesn't help a marriage relationship.

- How about being verbose and running off at the mouth? Look at Proverbs 10:19 (TLB): "Don't talk so much. You keep putting your foot in your mouth. Be sensible and turn off the flow!" That's graphic! You've met people like this; they fill the air with words—empty words of no significance especially for married couples.

- One last thing to avoid—angry, argumentative words. "An angry man stirs up dissension, and a hot-tempered one commits many sins" (Proverbs 29:22). Strife implies rigidity, stubbornness, and unhealthy anger. Purposeful, constructive, resolvable arguments are healthy, but many arguments are not conducted in this spirit.

If you would like to read some other powerful passages in Proverbs on communication and anger, look up 14:16,17; 15:4; 17:14,22,24,25. And these are just for starters. As you read, which verses do you think would strengthen your life if you applied them?

Would you believe the answer to the trivia question is more than 150 times!

Time—
Friend or Foe?

There is...a time to be silent and a time to speak.
ECCLESIASTES 3:1,7

I'd just like to pass the time away."

"I just can't afford to waste my time."

"Soon my time restraints will be lifted, and I can spend more time with my spouse."

"I'm going to find time this year to date my spouse."

"Someday, when I get time, I'm going to talk with my partner. Really I am."

These are common, well-intended phrases. Phrases meant to correct, simplify, streamline. Words designed to ease out tension and give us hope. But they all too often remain empty dreams in marriage.

How do you "get time" or "find time" or "restrain time" or "waste time"? Have you ever thought about some of the phrases we use when we talk about how we use time? We stretch it (I didn't know it was elastic!). We juggle it (does time come in balls, hoops, or pins?). And we schedule it (do we use a timer for time?).

In fact, how do you define the word "time"? Did you ever stop to wonder whether Adam and Eve had a sense of time? Did they have some sort of clock to mark the passing of the hours? Probably not. Is your life dominated by the clock? Does your watch tell you when to start work, when to play, when to eat or sleep, or even when to make love? Do you ever say, "It's too early to go to sleep" or "It's not time for dinner" or "It's too late to nap"? Do you even say, "I don't have time to talk now"? If you do, who's in control of your life? Is it you or your clock?

The more refined our time-saving methods have become, the greater our struggle with time. Time is supposed to be our servant, not our master. We need time to enrich our marriages. Is the time you allot to other events taking away from your marriage? Perhaps it's time to talk about the use of time with your partner.[5]

What's Dwelling in You?

Let the word of Christ richly dwell within you.
COLOSSIANS 3:16 NASB

Have you ever opened up a peach or an apple and found something living in it that you weren't pleased to see? You know what your reaction would be, especially if you had already taken a bite out of it!

At a family gathering one time, my adult daughter came in and saw a bowl of the biggest, ripest, juiciest strawberries she'd ever seen. She proceeded to sit down and eat a bowl of them one by one. She bit one in half so when she took what was left out of her mouth and held it in front of her she could see inside the strawberry. There was a little hollowed out place there. She noticed a number of little specks like miniature eggs, as well as half of an earwig wiggling. It dawned on her where the other half was and with that she ran to the bathroom to spit out the strawberry and crushed remains of the rest of the earwig! That bug had been dwelling, making itself at home, inside the strawberry.

We all have different things dwelling in us. It could be germs. It could be an infection. It could be thoughts and fantasies that hurt our marriage. Paul said there is something that needs to be at home in a husband and wife's life. It's called the Word of God.

How comfortable are you with Scripture being not only in your mind but also directing your life? It may be a new experience, but it can become very comfortable. A lot of people know Ephesians 4:32, "Be kind and compassionate to one another, forgiving each other, just as in Christ God forgave you." But living it out is another step. If this passage is really living in a husband and wife, it means it's at home there. It's comfortable. It means each looks at the other and thinks, "How can I be kind and tenderhearted to you today?"

Does Scripture live in your marriage? What can you do for your lifemate today?

Companionship—A Necessity

Let us therefore make every effort to do
what leads to peace and to mutual edification.
ROMANS 14:19

How's your friendship with one another? Marriage works so much better when friendship is involved. Sometimes this is called "companionship" or even "companioning." Ron Hawkins has some helpful thoughts on this subject:

Good companioning involves our free choice of our partner as a companion and our unconditional acceptance of his or her unique personality.

Good companioning rests on the conviction that we are completely loved by our mate. We need change nothing to win or retain that love.

Good companioning requires a commitment to majoring on the positive while in the presence of the companion.

Good companioning involves our free choice to spend the bulk of leisure time with the companion of choice.

Good companioning results from our willingness to allow for and support individual differences. Good companions don't try to make each other over to fit some predetermined mold.

Good companioning involves a willingness to speak to a partner in a language of love that communicates.

Good companions do not try to meet every need that partners have. We meet those we have the resources to meet. Only Jesus Christ can meet some of our mate's needs.

Spend time together. We give the gift of time.

Have fun together. We give the gift of laughter.

Share feelings and thoughts. We give the gift of sharing.

Like being together. We give the gift of appreciation.

Discuss issues. We give the gift of confidence.

Survive crises together. We give the gift of dependability.

Discuss fears. We give the gift of vulnerability.

Cover our partners' weaknesses. We give the gift of protection.

Celebrate our individual values together. We give the gift of respect.

Encourage a life separate from our life together. We give the gift of separateness.

Speak the truth together. We give the gift of honesty.

Handle conflict together. We give the gift of surfaced anger.

Practice forgiveness. We give the gift of forgiveness.

Practice unconditional acceptance. We give the gift of love.[6]

What Does Commitment Mean?

For this reason a man will leave his father and mother
and be united to his wife, and the two will become one flesh.
MATTHEW 19:5

The word "commitment" is not used in the Bible, but its derivatives "committed" and "commit" are. Commitment has two meanings in the Greek: "doing or practicing something" and "delivering or entrusting something to a person." Commitment involves the binding or pledging of oneself to a particular course of action. It also implies a choice based on reasoning. The act of entrusting oneself to another should be supported by sound reasoning. Men and women should be able to offer themselves and others sound, rational arguments for why their marriages are healthy relationships and should be expected to flourish. Commitment also involves consent; persons will themselves into relationships. When the will to relate to another person is supported by reasons that validate the goodness or the fit, then we may reasonably expect to see a stable, long-term relationship.

Commitment implies a pledge by each spouse to fidelity for life. When commitment is present, a couple enters into an irrevocable covenant. They pledge their faithfulness, regardless of circumstances. It has something of the spirit of Hernando Cortez when, in 1519, he landed his troops at Vera Cruz, Mexico. The more than 6,000 men were irrevocably committed to their task of conquering the new land for the mother country. When Cortez set fire to the vessels that brought them, there was no retreat. That kind of "no retreat" commitment in marriage is indicated in the verse for today.

Commitment is the unconditional acceptance of the other partner. Commitment is the surrender of personal pleasure and comfort.

Commitment costs something; dependability has a price tag. Consistently encouraging a partner, giving the gift of sympathetic understanding, and saying no to personal desires cuts against the grain of the selfish nature. Commitment means organizing one's time, thoughts, and resources for the benefit of others. It means the surrender of a measure of personal freedom and rights.[7]

Trust in Whom?

Let us acknowledge the LORD; *let us press on to acknowledge him.*
HOSEA 6:3

Trust in the LORD *with all your heart and lean not on your own
understanding; in all your ways acknowledge him, and he
will make your paths straight....The* LORD's *curse is on the
house of the wicked, but he blesses the home of the righteous.*
PROVERBS 3:5,6,33

When you think about holding a marriage together for 60
years, through good times and bad, and wonder what it really
takes...

Or when you boil down the whole gargantuan project of
raising children to its core, looking for the one secret of success, the key that allows you to turn out respectable adults instead of serial killers...

It's not just common sense.

It's not just following the traditions of your parents and
grandparents.

It's not luck.

It's not reading all the worthy advice of experts.

It is, rather, all the worthy advice of experts.

It is, rather, to "trust in the Lord" (Proverbs 3:5).

That familiar Scripture does not rule out the usefulness of
human understanding. Go ahead and read all the books, it
seems to say. Talk to older, wiser generations about what they
did right. Gather all the advice you can, *but don't lean on it.* It's
not strong enough to carry you the distance.

Imagine that you're standing on the South Rim of the Grand
Canyon, viewing the chasm below. There's a fence at the edge
of the precipice and various signs that tell you to be careful.
Good advice. But don't go *leaning* on the fence or the signs.
They might not be as sturdy as they look. Keep your weight
firmly planted on the rock beneath your feet.

So it is with dodging the many pitfalls of family life. Human
signs and warnings have their place, but the only real safety is
to remain anchored to the Rock.[8]

The Cost
of Success

Young men, in the same way be submissive to those who are older.
All of you, clothe yourselves with humility toward
one another, because, "God opposes the proud but gives grace
to the humble." Humble yourselves, therefore, under God's mighty
hand, that he may lift you up in due time. Cast all your
anxiety on him because he cares for you.
1 PETER 5:5-7

Most of us want to be successful. In fact, all of us want to succeed in some way. It's much better than tasting the fruits of failure. We live in a success-saturated society. There are books, classes, videos, cassettes, and seminars all promising to teach us some new approach that will enable us to taste success. The problem with success is the cost. Who counts it in advance? A comment in *The Executive Digest* read, "The trouble with success is the formula is the same as the one for a nervous breakdown." That's sobering, uncomfortable, and too often true.

There's another way to gain success rather than by pushing, striving, promoting, being slick and aggressive. It's a simple way. It's God's way. You read it in today's passage. It involves authority, attitude, and anxiety. Read it again. First of all, submit yourself to those who know more than you. Listen to their advice, their wisdom, the lessons they've learned, their guidance. On some occasions your partner is in this role.

Next, be humble, especially before God. Let Him bring the success to you in His way and in His time. It will happen. We can choose to pull strings and manipulate, or we can let God work. A humble attitude doesn't offend or repulse other people, but attracts them because you are different. How do you demonstrate humility in your marriage?

Finally, take the anxieties that will definitely come into your life and throw them, cast them, relinquish them to God. Let Him deal with them.

Success is there waiting for you. So is God's plan. They do go hand in hand![9]

Love Is...

1 CORINTHIANS 13
Translation by J.B. Phillips

If I speak with the eloquence of men and of angels, but have no love, I become no more than blaring brass or crashing cymbal. If I have the gift of foretelling the future and hold in my mind not only all human knowledge but the very secrets of God, and if I also have that absolute faith which can move mountains, but have no love, I amount to nothing at all. If I dispose of all that I possess, yes, even if I give my own body to be burned, but have no love, I achieve precisely nothing.

This love of which I speak is slow to lose patience—it looks for a way of being constructive. It is not possessive: it is neither anxious to impress nor does it cherish inflated ideas of its own importance.

Love has good manners and does not pursue selfish advantage. It is not touchy. It does not keep account of evil or gloat over the wickedness of other people. On the contrary, it shares the joy of those who live by the truth.

Love knows no limit to its endurance, no end to its trust, no fading of its hope; it can outlast anything. Love never fails....

When I was a little child I talked and felt and thought like a little child. Now that I am a man I have finished with childish things.

At present we are men looking at puzzling reflections in a mirror. The time will come when we shall see reality whole and face to face! At present all I know is a little fraction of the truth, but the time will come when I shall know it as fully as God has known me!

In this life we have three great lasting qualities—faith, hope and love. But the greatest of them is love.

A Prayer for
Your Marriage

*Therefore, I urge you, brothers, in view of God's mercy,
to offer your bodies as living sacrifices, holy and pleasing to God—
this is your spiritual act of worship.*
ROMANS 12:1

Dear God,

I'm praying today for wisdom to know what I need to be doing in my marriage.

Help me to overcome my not wanting to face the truth, which I need to face. Sometimes it's hard to hear the truth from my spouse.

I need help in overcoming my laziness that keeps me from learning the truth.

Help me to overcome my stubbornness that keeps me from accepting the truth, especially in my own family.

I really need strength to overcome pride that keeps me from looking for and accepting the truth.

Keep my eyes and ears open so I can hear You speak to my conscience.

Take away any arrogance in my life which would keep me from accepting advice.

Open my locked-up mind, which resists what my partner suggests and even resists the Holy Spirit, the Spirit of truth.

Give me the grace and power to do what I know I ought to do in my marriage.

Lord, keep me from getting off course. Help me with my lack of resistance which gives into temptation all too easily.

Help me to overcome my procrastination of the things I know are needed.

Give me the perseverance to complete the tasks that are important to my spouse.

So now once again I ask for wisdom to know Your will and do it.

In Jesus' name, amen.[10]

He's in Charge

Truly my soul silently waits for God; from Him comes my salvation.
He only is my rock and my salvation; He is my defense;
I shall not be greatly moved.
PSALM 62:1,2 NKJV

It's so important that as a couple you both seek God's will for your decisions as well as discuss how you feel God is speaking and leading you. Remember these facts about God's will.

God has something for you to do for Him in this life. He has a pattern for the way you are to live your life. He also has something else for you—the right time for you to do what He wants you to do. Timing is a big part of His will. It's difficult for some individuals and couples to wait. Their personalities are wired in such a way that waiting is not part of their vocabularies. There is a restlessness to their lives. This can cause a person to act before God says it is the time to act.

How are you about waiting in your life? It could be simple things like eating most of your dessert before dinner because you "couldn't wait to taste it," opening your birthday or Christmas present before the appointed day because you "couldn't wait to see it," spending your paycheck before you received it because you "couldn't wait to get that new item."

"Couldn't wait" is not a part of the vocabulary God instills within us. It goes contrary to His Word. Listen to these words and notice the benefits of waiting:

> Let integrity and uprightness preserve me, for I wait for You (Psalm 25:21 NASB).

> Wait on the LORD; be of good courage, and He shall strengthen your heart; wait, I say, on the LORD! (Psalm 27:14 NKJV).

> Wait on the LORD, and keep His way, and He shall exalt you to inherit the land; when the wicked are cut off, you shall see it (Psalm 37:34 NKJV).

> I will wait for You, O You his Strength; for God is my defense (Psalm 59:9 NKJV).

Remember: God has all the time in the world. God has an order and rhythm for our lives. Experience it.

You Can
Be Content!

I am not saying this because I am in need,
for I have learned to be content whatever the circumstances.
PHILIPPIANS 4:11

Many couples are discontented. You can see it in their faces and hear it in their voices. In fact, many times they'll tell you why if you give them a chance.

Many couples are contented. You can see it in their faces and hear it in their voices. In fact, they'll tell you why if you give them a chance.

What's the difference? The contented couples have discovered what the apostles discovered. Take Paul, for example. What did he do? He learned to focus on God's sovereignty rather than on the advice and opinions of other people. He learned to praise and thank God rather than focus on what he didn't have. He learned to trust in God to make things right and to give him strength rather than what our world has to offer. He learned to look to Jesus and away from those who were a pain in the neck. By doing that he gained strength rather than being drained.

Paul was content. The dictionary defines "content" as happy enough with what one has. Have you been around a cat after it stuffed itself on a big bowl of cat food? It's sitting there purring, eyes barely open. That's a sign of contentment. You may have pushed yourself away from the table some evening, patted your stomach, smiled, and said, "Now, I'm content."

In the midst of a rising and falling stock market, uncertainty about our jobs, life-threatening diseases, the threat of wars, terrorism, and natural disasters, it's still possible to be content. How? Do as Paul did. He trusted in Jesus. We, too, can trust Him for strength, shelter, wisdom, and peace.

"Peace I leave with you, My peace I give to you; not as the world gives do I give to you. Let not your heart be troubled, neither let it be afraid" (John 18:27 NKJV).[11]

Are You Holy
or Wholly?

Be holy, because I am holy.
1 PETER 1:16

Would you say that you and your spouse are holy? Is this a strange question? How would you answer that question, especially in light of today's Scripture?

What comes to mind when you think of being a holy person? Usually we think of it as living in such a way that there's no sin or foul-ups in our lives. Perhaps you were told that the idea behind biblical holiness comes from words that mean "to be separate." Is your idea of being holy "don't do this or that" and "avoid all this kind of stuff"? You may have a negative perspective on what it means to be holy. You may think it is supposed to be uncomfortable and you've got to be different and unattractive, to be odd like a hermit or extreme like a martyr.

Being unholy seems a lot easier than being holy. For many, holiness is not a lifestyle but a certain time selected. The hymn "Take Time to be Holy" perpetuates this belief, but it really makes little sense. How do you take time to be holy? Does it mean we take time not to be holy?

To live a holy life as an individual or as a married couple involves simply making choices—choices that transform you to positive goodness. *Holiness is positive.* You and your spouse have been commanded to be holy. How? One way is an active, consistent prayer life. Prayer and holiness go hand in hand: "Therefore, confess your sins to one another, and pray for one another so that you may be healed. The effective prayer of a righteous man can accomplish much" (James 5:16 NASB).

Perhaps it starts by realizing that *you can be holy.* How? Remember what God's Word says about you: "For we are God's workmanship, created in Christ Jesus to do good works, which God prepared in advance for us to do" (Ephesians 2:10).

Sure, you'll have your ups and downs. Just start and keep on. It's possible. "Flee the evil desires of youth, and pursue righteousness, faith, love and peace, along with those who call on the Lord out of a pure heart" (2 Timothy 2:22).[12]

Temptation

I made a covenant with my eyes not to look lustfully at a girl.
JOB 31:1

Myth or fact? Once a man or woman is married the problem of sexual temptation disappears. If you believe that, you'll find salespeople lining up at your door ready to sell you some Florida swampland.

Now and then you do run into people who are so naive they actually believe they'll never notice the attractiveness of other people of the opposite sex after they marry. They also believe they'll never be tempted sexually. It just isn't so.

We suffer under the consequences of the fall. Our minds have been affected in many ways—and the mind is our main sexual organ. Our thoughts, fantasies, and intentions create struggles and tension. The other problem we encounter is living in our promiscuous, sexually blatant society. Sex is all around us and available.

What can a Christian husband or wife do to deal with temptation?

Follow God's Word. First, make the same decision Job made. He decided not to allow himself to give in to the lust of his eyes. We've got to watch what we see. If we don't, we capture the image and replay it time and time again in our minds. Soon it becomes more real and exciting than our spouses.

Then follow 1 Corinthians 6:18: "Flee from sexual immorality." Get away from sexual temptation, whether it be another person, movies, or the internet.

Proverbs 5:15-19 gives a great principle: stay at home and get your sexual satisfaction there. That's the place to invest time and effort. If your sex life is kind of stale, warm it up. Romance one another. When was the last time you read a Christian book on sex? They're out there.

Remember, temptations are always lurking around the corner. But they're not as tempting when your marriage is alive and growing and you ask the Lord to help you combat them.[13]

God Told Me

For where your treasure is, there your heart will be also.
MATTHEW 6:21

Has your spouse ever come to you and said, "God told me that this is what we are to do"? If so, perhaps your response was, "How do you know it was God speaking to you?" That's a good question. When you're married, does God reveal His plans to just one person or to both? How can we know when God is speaking? Scripture gives us some great insights.

God spoke audibly to Moses, Samuel, and Elijah (see Exodus 3:4,5; 1 Samuel 3:1-4; 1 Kings 19:13,14). Some people say they've "heard" God's voice inaudibly while they're praying. He has also spoken during dreams (see Acts 16:9). God has also used angels, visions, and third parties. Most of us today don't experience these types of responses.

God may speak to us during our prayer times by causing us to remember a forgotten passage of Scripture. But we have to read the Scripture first for that to occur! God also can speak to us through speakers or discussions with other people. God speaks to us by changing our circumstances as well. You've probably heard of open and shut doors, and this, too, could be the Lord speaking.

But there's something more important than what's been said.

First, do you *want* God to speak to you, to direct your life as a couple? His ways aren't going to be your ways and His answers and timing will probably be different than you expect.

Second, in order to hear Him you need to spend time with Him, individually and as a couple.

And finally, when you're married you're a team. Both of you need to seek the Lord in prayer. If you each get a different answer, something's amiss. Wait until you're in agreement—then it's more likely to be God directing you.[14]

What's Going
on at Work?

*A man can do nothing better than to eat and drink and find
satisfaction in his work. This too, I see, is from the hand of God.*
ECCLESIASTES 2:24

On a scale of zero to ten, how do you feel about your job?
Do you love it, like it, or would you like to leave it? Too many
people today don't like what they do or they don't find it fulfilling. For some work is a chore, and others dread the thought
of going to work. That's what some would call a "bummer."
There's nothing worse than having a job you detest—but some
people have experienced this for 40 years! They only put in
their time to get a paycheck.

It's true that some jobs are less than exciting or challenging.
It's true that some jobs put you in contact with people you'd
rather have never known existed, let alone work with.

Perhaps you're in a job like that, and you can't change. You
have too many bills and responsibilities or the money is too
good. There is a way out. There is something you can change.
You can change the way you look at your work. You can
change your orientation or your attitude. You see, God wants
you to find meaning in your work. Have you ever asked God
to help you feel fulfilled by your work? Have you ever asked
Him to help you develop the ability to enjoy your work? To
see the significance of your work? Have you considered that
your work is something you can do for the glory of God?

It's true. This may be a brand-new way of looking at work,
but why not? How we feel about our jobs and the attitudes we
have about work (at the office and at home) will affect our
marriages. A bad day at the office or running the household
can infect our marriage relationships. It doesn't have to; it's a
choice. It's attitude. It's perspective.

Thank God for whatever work you have right now. There
are many who don't have any job. They'd love to have yours![15]

How's Your
Appetite?

*Blessed are those who hunger and thirst for
righteousness, for they will be filled.*
MATTHEW 5:6

Appetites come in various sizes—small, medium, large, and gigantic. Sometimes you tell the size of a person's appetite by the size of their girth. What's consumed expands their width—sometimes. There are some people who can eat like a horse and never put on an ounce. That's almost immoral!

We have a fascination with food and appetite in this country. The trend is to be skinny, and yet we're admonished to have a healthy appetite. How's your appetite toward food? Do you look forward to eating and choosing the right kinds of foods?

"Appetite" is used for other needs and desires, too. We talk about sexual appetites. Sometimes this can be a conflict in marriage since appetites vary. One person's drive may be excessive (or so it seems to the other spouse), and the other's appetite may seem not to exist.

There's yet another appetite—spiritual. A healthy spiritual appetite is evident when a person desires to read and learn the Scriptures, pray on a deeper level, spend time fellowshiping with other believers, and worship the Lord. The psalmist gives a very visual description of a strong desire for God: As the deer pants for the water brooks, so my soul pants for You, O God (Psalm 42:1 NASB). Have you ever been so thirsty for water that you're panting like a dog? Have you ever desired God's presence in your life so much that you're almost panting?

Fat isn't in vogue in our society, but it's better to be spiritually fat than to be spiritually skinny. When we hunger and thirst, God responds. He speaks. And He fills us up.[16]

Which One
Are You?

Blessed are the merciful, for they will be shown mercy.
MATTHEW 5:7

You've probably heard the term "empathy." You've probably experienced empathy because you're married. You feel with the other person and experience what that person has experienced. You're with your partner in his or her emotional experiences. It's the practical expression of two becoming one in marriage. It's a way of helping your mate carry the load. Any burden is easier with four hands carrying it rather than just two.

Jesus talked about another way of responding that is similar and just as crucial for the health of a marriage. It's called mercy. We all have our own definition of this word, so share yours with your spouse right now.

Webster's dictionary helps us understand the depths of this word. One meaning is "refraining from harming or punishing offenders." Let's stop there. When your partner offends you, is there a repayment plan ready to slap on him or her, or does forgiveness come into play? Forgiveness from God's perspective means the offense never happened. God does not remember it at all. He doesn't have a giant scorecard, and He doesn't want us to keep tabs either.

Mercy also means kindness in *excess* of what may be expected or demanded by fairness. It's not just doing enough to get by; it's not just giving enough to meet the basic expectation. It's going a second, third, and fourth mile. It means searching for ways to surprise your spouse.

There was a man in Luke 10 who did this—the Good Samaritan. We aren't sure why because he didn't know the stranger. There was no obligation. But he reached out, put himself out, changed his plans, delayed his journey, made sure the man would be helped when he wasn't around, and never complained.

How could you be more merciful toward one another this week? Read today's verse once again.

Who Do You
Love More?

Everyone who competes in the games goes into strict training.
1 CORINTHIANS 9:25

Jim Ryun, the runner, shared a personal story about his wife. It may cause you to look at each other differently.

> One night [my wife] Anne and I were lying in bed challenging one another on this very piece of Scripture. What does it mean to discipline our bodies? How do we bring them into subjection to do the things they ought to do (spending time alone with God and His Word, loving and helping those who are naturally abhorrent to us) and not the things we want to do?
>
> At one point Anne turned to me and exclaimed, "You know what? I love Jesus more than I love you. Yes, that's the way He intended it to be. That we would first love Him with all of our heart, and soul, and mind, and strength."
>
> Wham! I felt like I'd been socked in the belly with a baseball bat. It may have been a revelation to Anne, but for me it was devastating to hear those words spoken out of my wife's mouth! From my wife, who loved me and had stood by me through thick and thin. The pain must have shown all over my face. Yet once I recovered and could see what Anne really meant, it proved to be an awakening of where we as a family were headed. We were moving into a love relationship with the Lord of our lives. After the initial shock, I could see that her words represented my heart's attitude as well.
>
> We were becoming one just as the Bible said we were meant to be, fitting our strengths and weaknesses together.
>
> We had grown to the point where we loved the Lord with everything that was in us. And nothing—not even each other—could take the place of the Lord being first in our lives. And because we loved Him so much, we loved each other all the more.
>
> Everywhere our spiritual horizons are being expanded. We are allowing God to map our own destinies in Christ Jesus. We are in the hold of God's Spirit, moving with Him wherever He takes us.[17]

What Our
Work Says

The LORD *will fulfill [his purpose] for me; your love,*
O LORD, *endures forever—do not abandon the works of your hands.*
PSALM 138:8

Our work is meant to be an expression of who we are as God's handiwork. Because of who God is and how He sees us, as evidenced in the gift of His Son, Jesus Christ, we must be worth something. We have value, worth, dignity, and adequacy because God has declared that we have them—not because of our work

The *way* of the level of our work is an expression of the high value God has ascribed to us.

The *proficiency* of the level of our work is an expression of the high value God has ascribed to us.

We bring *dignity* to our work because God gives us a sense of dignity. As believers, we have the opportunity to do a job out of the sense of *adequacy* we have because of God's declaration that we are adequate. We should not be using our work to make us feel fulfilled. If we search the Scriptures, we discover that we are special and worthwhile only because of God.

Over the centuries, people have used many means to feel worthwhile, but they are all temporary. None are permanent except God's declaration. This is the initial step in preventing or lessening our sense of loss when our work is no longer available to us. It is the same step in preventing or lessening our sense of loss when our abilities, looks, or positions in life are no longer part of our lives.

What would happen to you and the quality of your work if your attitude was, "My work is an expression of me and the presence of God in my life"? It would be the beginning of feeling good about yourself in spite of what is going on at your job.

Fear and Faith

*Ignoring what they said, Jesus told the synagogue ruler,
"Don't be afraid; just believe."*
MARK 5:36

Remember the movie *Chariots of Fire?* Eric Liddell, the man whose life was the theme of this film, wrote the following words:

> Fear paralyzes all our powers. We fail because we fear. If you feel afraid, stop, and quietly in God's presence ask yourself why. Be honest in giving the reason. Do not let your feeling or fear dictate your action. When convinced something should be done, go ahead and do it despite the feeling of fear. God's power is at your disposal. Paul said, "I can do all things [all things God wants me to do] through Christ which strengtheneth me" (Philippians 4:13 [KJV]). He learned to appropriate the strength and power God had put at his disposal.
>
> When a decision is made, do not be anxious or doubtful as the result. Trust absolutely: remember God asks [for] faithfulness; the rest can be left in his hands.
>
> Each person has his own fears. Common ones are fear of what others will think or say; fear of making restitution; fear of apologizing, due to the loss of face it brings; fear of being different from others; timidity, or distrust of oneself; fear of the future.
>
> Fear comes by looking at oneself or others instead of looking at Jesus. Jesus said, "Be not afraid [of what the crowd thinks or does], only believe" (Mark 5:36 [KJV]).
>
> Are you afraid in any situation? Stop a moment. Surrender the feeling to God, *make a decision which fully satisfies your conscience,* and act quietly but firmly on it. This act is faith, the faith that overcomes the world of fear. God in this way will teach you to overcome all kinds of fear. *He can do this only with your trustful cooperation.*[18]

What is the greatest fear in your life? What is the greatest fear of your spouse? Discuss how you can help each other handle these fears.

Sharing Jesus

He reached down from on high and took hold of me;
he drew me out of deep waters.
PSALM 18:16

We've heard much about the *Titanic*. Reverend Newell Hillis relates a story about Colonel Archibald Gracie, one of the survivors.

> When Colonel Gracie came up, after the sinking of the *Titanic*, he says that he made his way to a sunken raft. The submerged little raft was under water often, but every man, without regard to nationality, broke into instant prayer. The night was black and the grave where the *Titanic* lay was silent under them, and the stars were silent over them! But as they prayed, each man by that inner light saw an invisible Friend walking across the waves. Henceforth, these need no books on Apologetics to prove there is a God. This man who has written his story tells us that God heard the prayers of some by giving them death, and heard the prayers of all others equally in keeping them in life; but God alone is great!

An anonymous writer told of his experience:

> Four years after the *Titanic* went down, a young Scotsman rose in a meeting in Hamilton, Canada, and said, "I am a survivor of the *Titanic*. When I was drifting alone on a spar on that awful night, the tide brought Mr. John Harper, of Glasgow, also on a piece of wreck, near me. 'Man,' he said, 'are you saved?' 'No,' I said, 'I am not.' He replied, 'Believe on the Lord Jesus Christ, and thou shalt be saved.'
>
> "The waves bore him away; but, strange to say, brought him back a little later, and he said, 'Are you saved now?' 'No,' I said, 'I cannot honestly say that I am.' He said again, 'Believe on the Lord Jesus Christ, and thou shalt be saved'; and shortly after, he went down. There, alone in the night and with two miles of water under me, I believed. I am John Harper's last convert."[19]

In the midst of tragedy people came to know Jesus. Who can you share Jesus with this week?

Journey
of Prayer

But when you pray, go into your room, close the door
and pray to your Father, who is unseen. Then your Father,
who sees what is done in secret, will reward you.
MATTHEW 6:6

Fred Littauer shares his journey of prayer:

Six years ago I began, at the Lord's direction, to write down my daily prayers. I've done it almost every day since then. I simply write a letter to my Father in heaven, sometimes addressing Him as "Dear Lord Jesus," other times as "Dear Heavenly Father." There are times when I don't address Him at all; I just start writing to Him. The words and the form are not important. What is important is that I come into His presence to talk to Him, praise Him, worship Him, confess to Him, ask of Him, and to intercede before Him for someone else.

Writing your prayers does many things for you. In my life, the most obvious thing it has done is bring me the healing power of the Lord. All the old issues I struggled with for so many years have been cleansed away.

Writing your prayers is also an important discipline; by dating your prayers you can see very quickly if you have missed any days. Second, it helps you focus your mind on the Lord and prevents your thoughts from wandering.

Perhaps the most significant benefit of daily written prayer is the totally changed life! For verification that it has changed *my* life, you could ask my wife. She lives with me. She sees that the suppressed anger that once raged within me is gone. She no longer sees a critical spirit in me. Now she not only enjoys being with me, she misses me deeply on those few occasions when we're apart. Jesus said, "I have come to heal the brokenhearted, to set the captive free" (paraphrase of Luke 4:18). He has done that for me through written prayer simply because I was obedient to His offer to "come unto me, all ye that labour and are heavy laden, and I will give you rest" (Matthew 11:28 [KJV]).[20]

Sex Is Sacred

Flee from sexual immorality. All other sins a man commits are outside
his body, but he who sins sexually sins against his own body.
Do you not know that your body is a temple of the Holy Spirit,
who is in you, whom you have received from God? You are not your
own; you were bought at a price. Therefore honor God with your body.
1 CORINTHIANS 6:18-20

William Kirk Kilpatrick, in *Psychological Seduction*, has some
very insightful thoughts on sexuality and today's culture.

> If one says nowadays that sex is sacred, one runs the risk
> of being ridiculed. But that is only because the job of de-
> mystification has been done so well. If someone managed to
> kidnap a princess, dressed her in rags and knocked her
> about the head so her speech was slurred, and then told his
> fellow thugs that this woman was a princess, they would
> likely not believe him.
>
> Our society is in a similar situation with regard to sexual
> love. We find it difficult to see how anything that can be
> found in low places can also be found in the highest. Given
> the common and easily available state to which sex has
> fallen, it is not to be wondered at that the medical and psy-
> chological estimate would prevail; sex is not sacred at all. It
> is a natural thing, one more biological process among many.
> So let us eat and drink and sleep and have sex and be
> healthy.
>
> Unless you understand that Christianity considers sexual
> love to be a sacred thing, you can never fully understand
> why it insists that sex be set apart with exclusions and re-
> strictions. All sacred things are. It is not that it thinks sex is
> a bad thing, but a high thing. Like other high things, it de-
> serves to be bounded by objective rules and not wafted
> about by gusts of changing emotion. The Christian position
> on this is quite clear. Sexual love is too important to be left
> up to spontaneity. The correctness of our sexual conduct
> must not turn on the intensity of the moment's feelings but
> rather on objective criteria: Whether we have made a vow
> and to whom. How else can it be?[1]

Commitment
Through Change

Love bears up under anything and everything that comes.
1 CORINTHIANS 13:7 AMP

There will be ups and downs throughout the life of your marriage. There will be massive changes, some predictable and others intrusive. They hold the potential for growth, but they are risky at the same time. Many marriages die because too many couples choose to ignore the inescapable fact that relationships and people change. A wife shared the following with the congregation at her son's church.

> Since we have been married 50 years, you can just imagine how much change we have gone through: 3 wars, 11 presidents, 5 recessions, going from the model A to the moon, from country road to the information superhighway. While these changes around us have been great, the personal changes that God has enacted within us through each other have been even greater. Although we often couldn't see how God was working in our lives at that time, we look back now and realize that our marriage has been a school of character development. God has used my husband in my life, and he's used me in his life to make us more like Christ. So what are the lessons that we've learned about how God uses marriage to change us? There are many. Through 50 years of marriage we've learned that differences develop us, that crises cultivate us, and that ministry melts us together.
>
> First, God has used our differences to help us grow. There have been many, many crises that God has used to develop us and to grow us. The first one was the big, big one—the crisis of being separated as soon as we got married. Ours was a wartime romance. We met at church, dated two months, got married after three weeks of engagement, and just after two months of marriage, we didn't see each other for the next two years, for Jimmy was shipped to the South Pacific during World War II. When he returned two years later, we were total strangers, but we were married to each other!

How would you have handled that situation?

The Carpenter

Isn't this the carpenter?
MARK 6:3

Most of us don't spend much time thinking about Jesus as a carpenter. It doesn't seem very significant…and yet maybe it does at that. A carpenter is one who fashions and creates. Jesus did this both in the expression of His divinity and in His humanity. He created the universe: "Through him all things were made; without him nothing was made that has been made" (John 1:3).

But He also fashioned simple pieces of furniture for people. If anyone knew about hard work it was Jesus. This was not a "Home Improvement" set with drills, electric saws, and the latest gadgetry. It was muscle-pushing rough tools that were very basic and produced calluses. His hands were probably bruised with numerous cuts from handling the wood and the crude saw or hammer. You would not believe the amount of time and energy spent then to make a simple chair or table.

But what does Jesus being a carpenter have to do with us? Consider these thoughts from one of the officers in the Salvation Army.

> As the Carpenter, Christ forever sanctified human toil. We are all members of the corporate society. As we derive many benefits, so must we be contributive to the community. Our tasks are given dignity by the One who worked amid the wood shavings at the carpenter's bench for the greater part of His life. His labor enabled the oxen to plow without being chafed by their yokes, children to take delight in the hand-carved toys, families to live in the comfort of a home built by the Carpenter.
>
> Today, the Carpenter of Nazareth, who once smoothed yokes in His skillful hands, would take a life that is yielded to Him and fashion it into a beautiful and useful instrument of God's eternal kingdom.[2]

All your efforts and toil in your marriage has purpose and merit. As Jesus is fashioning your life, let Him work through you to fashion a marriage that reflects His influence and presence.

Are You
the Lone Ranger?

I can do everything through him who gives me strength.
PHILIPPIANS 4:13

It's been one of those days—a bad day, a fur-ball day, a rotten day. The kind of day where nothing seems to go well: your spouse was late, she or he didn't follow through, dinner is cold, everyone wants something from you, the expressway is a joke, and nothing you do seems to turn out right! You're irritated and discouraged. You snap at your partner or won't say anything. You may even be a bit depressed.

When days like this occur, sometimes we compound the problem by making one major mistake—we try to fix everything by ourselves. We take on the role of the "Lone Ranger" and tough it alone. But even the Lone Ranger was smart enough to have a partner—"Tonto."

This is the time to say, "God, help me"—and He will. One of the best ways to handle these days is to dwell on God's Word. Read these passages out loud during your dark days. Reflect on what each one is saying, and then note the differences.

> I have set the LORD continually before me; because He is at my right hand, I will not be shaken (Psalm 16:8 NASB).

> You, O LORD, keep my lamp burning; my God turns my darkness into light (Psalm 18:28).

> The LORD is my light and my salvation; whom shall I fear? The LORD is the defense of my life; whom shall I dread? (Psalm 27:1 NASB).

> God is our refuge and strength, an ever-present help in trouble (Psalm 46:1).

> Create in me a pure heart, O God, and renew a steadfast spirit within me (Psalm 51:10).

> Cast your cares on the LORD and he will sustain you; he will never let the righteous fall (Psalm 55:22).

> My soul finds rest in God alone; my salvation comes from him (Psalm 62:1).

Sometimes God uses your partner to give you the help and support you need. Be open to what he or she has to offer.

Laws or Suggestions?

The law of the LORD is perfect, reviving the soul. The statutes of the LORD are trustworthy, making wise the simple. The precepts of the LORD are right, giving joy to the heart. The commands of the LORD are radiant, giving light to the eyes. The fear of the LORD is pure, enduring forever. The ordinances of the LORD are sure and altogether righteous. They are more precious than gold, than much pure gold; they are sweeter than honey, than honey from the comb. By them is your servant warned; in keeping them there is great reward.
PSALM 19:7-11

Rules...and more rules. Have you ever read the section of the newspaper that tells you what laws were passed in your state capital that day? We live in a culture that wants as much freedom as possible, yet we enact so many rules. It's unnerving at times. Sometimes it seems like there are rules for the rules.

Rules and laws are there for a reason. We need boundaries. Granted, sometimes some of our laws are ridiculous, but God's laws never are. What are some of God's rules or laws that you resist? Some of us resist only in our minds, some of us flagrantly break God's laws, while others of us devise clever schemes to get around them, believing that we'll never get caught. But God's laws are not given to restrict our lives and freedom. Their purpose is to give us a better life.

Television newscaster Ted Koppel shocked a number of people in his address to a graduating class at Duke University some years ago when he said:

> We have actually convinced ourselves that slogans will save us. Shoot up if you must, but use a clean needle. Enjoy sex whenever and with whomever you wish, but wear a condom. No! The answer is no! Not because it isn't cool or smart or because you might end up in jail or dying in an AIDS ward....In its purest form, truth is not a polite tap on the shoulder. It is a howling reproach. What Moses brought down from Mount Sinai were not the Ten Suggestions.[3]

Are you treating some of God's laws as suggestions, or do you see that He has given them to us for our benefit?

Stress Fractures

The LORD is my shepherd, I shall not be in want. He makes me
lie down in green pastures, he leads me beside quiet waters.
PSALM 23:1,2

Have you ever watched a marathon race? Better yet, have you ever experienced running those 26 miles under a hot, baking sun or even in a cold, driving rain? Mile after mile the runners lift one foot, slam it down on the concrete, and do the same with the other foot. Have you ever wondered how many times each foot slams into that unyielding surface? Thousands upon thousands of times.

Sometimes microscopic cracks begin to appear in the outer layers of bone in the feet or legs. If the running continues and the lower body continues to sustain the same degree of punishment, those tiny crevices enlarge. Soon they're large enough to create pain. There's a name for this: stress fracture.

You may think stress fractures are limited to the bones, but they're not. We pound our bodies in other ways. Our schedule begins to pile up, as do the bills, we take on a coaching job, learn to eat on the run (usually junk food), try to satisfy the boss, volunteer at church, and then there are the responsibilities of marriage as well. Before long our nerves have these microscopic cracks beginning. We're on edge like a tightly wound rubber band ready to snap at whatever gets in our way. Sometimes stress fractures are evident in our marriage relationships.

Your spirit and your heart can be stress fractured as well. It comes from taking on and doing too much by yourself. Whoever said you were called to go through life alone? That approach will fracture your life. There's a Shepherd waiting to help you and your spouse. Why don't you let Him?

> He refreshes and restores my life (my self); He leads me in the paths of righteousness [uprightness and right standing with Him—not for my earning it, but] for His name's sake (Psalm 23:3 AMP).

Read Psalm 23 aloud each day for a month. Then check your stress level.

The Hug

His left arm is under my head, and his right arm embraces me.
SONG OF SONGS 2:6

Willard Harley shares that to most women affection symbolizes security, protection, comfort, and approval, vitally important commodities in their eyes. When a husband shows his wife affection, he sends the following messages:

- I'll take care of you and protect you. You are important to me, and I don't want anything to happen to you.
- I'm concerned about the problems you face, and I am with you.
- I think you've done a good job, and I'm so proud of you.

A hug can say any and all of the above. Men need to understand how strongly women need these affirmations. *For the typical wife, there can hardly be enough of them.*

Most women love to hug. They hug each other, they hug children, animals, relatives—even stuffed animals.

Obviously a man can display affection in other ways that can be equally important to a woman. A greeting card or a note expressing love and care can simply but effectively communicate the same emotions. Don't forget that all-time favorite—a bouquet of flowers. Women, almost universally, love to receive flowers. For most women flowers send a powerful message of love and concern.

An invitation to dinner also signals affection. It is a way of saying to one's wife, "You don't need to do what you do ordinarily for me. I'll treat you instead. You are special to me, and I want to show you how much I love and care for you."

Holding hands is a time-honored and effective sign of affection. Walks after dinner, back rubs, phone calls, and conversations with thoughtful and loving expressions all add units to the Love Banks.

From a woman's point of view, affection is the essential cement of her relationship with a man. With it she becomes tightly bonded to him.[4]

An Example
for Us

*I have brought you glory on earth
by completing the work you gave me to do.*
JOHN 17:4

Let's consider Jesus. Why was He so effective in dealing with people? His ministry was involved in helping people achieve fullness of life, and assisting them in developing their abilities to deal with the problems, conflicts, and burdens of life. We too have been called to minister in this way—especially to our spouses.

Foremost in Jesus' personal life was obedience to God. There was a definite relationship between His Father and Him: "For I did not speak on My own initiative, but the Father Himself who sent Me has given Me a commandment as to what to say and what to speak" (John 12:49 NASB).

Jesus lived a life of faith. Because of this He was able to put things in proper perspective. He saw life through God's eyes. *In what way does your faith need to be strengthened? Your spouse's?*

Jesus lived a life of prayer. "But the news about Him was spreading even farther, and large crowds were gathering to hear Him and to be healed of their sicknesses. But Jesus Himself would often slip away to the wilderness and pray" (Luke 5:15,16). *Is prayer a daily event for you? Do you pray together as a couple?*

Jesus spoke with authority: "He was teaching them as one having authority, and not as their scribes" (Matthew 7:29 NASB). When we realize the authority that we have in Jesus we can become more effective in talking about Him.

Jesus was personally involved. He wasn't aloof; He was personal, sensitive, and caring. *Are these qualities seen in your marriage?*

The power of the Holy Spirit enabled Jesus to be effective. We see how His ministry began when He received the power of the Holy Spirit in Luke 3:21,22: "Now when all the people were baptized, Jesus was also baptized, and while He was praying, heaven was opened, and the Holy Spirit descended upon Him in bodily form like a dove, and a voice came out of heaven, 'You are My beloved Son, in You I am well-pleased.' "

What a difference it makes when you experience this power in your life.

Time Robbers

Be very careful, then, how you live—not as unwise but as wise,
making the most of every opportunity, because the days are evil.
EPHESIANS 5:15,16

You're probably being robbed each day, and you may not be aware of it. Who's the thief? The time bandit. How does he operate? He shackles you to your clock. He misplaces your car keys, creates interruptions, double-books activities, and makes you forget that you already have too many activities for that day. This bandit steals not only your time but also your energy. He does this by convincing you to buy into outmoded beliefs, rules, "shoulds," and myths. His greatest delight is to see you spin your wheels and lose your joy, spontaneity, satisfaction, creativity, and productivity.[5]

Most of our top time robbers are imposed on us by other people; the other time robbers are self-inflicted. What are the time thieves in your life? Unless you identify them, they'll continue to pick your pocket. Perhaps you recognize this one: You know what interruptions are, especially if you have children. The interruption could be a phone call, someone at the door, a business associate who comes to your office and says, "This will only take a minute." Some interruptions are necessary. Most aren't. Sometimes we interrupt ourselves by allowing ourselves to be distracted or even by creating a distraction. Some people are wired this way, and they love the variety that interruptions bring. To them interruptions are merely possibilities![6]

Think about the interruptions in your life. Do they control you or do you control them? How do you feel when you're interrupted? How do interruptions contribute to your marriage? You may not be able to control whether or not you're interrupted, but you can control how you handle it when you are. Even a marriage relationship can be interrupted if we fail to control our time. During this next week, say no to interruptions. You may discover a whole new way of living.

How Not
to Comfort

Then Job replied: "I have heard many things like these; miserable comforters are you all! Will your long-winded speeches never end?"
JOB 16:1-3

You're having a rotten, lousy day. Nothing has gone right. One thing after another seems to pile up on you. How could anyone have so much difficulty at one time? It's like your world is crumbling around you. Yes, this does happen when you're married!

Fortunately, you have some friends who are around to comfort you. Or at least you thought they were your friends. At first, they didn't say anything. They were just there silently in their support of you, and it helped. Then they began to talk, and you wished they hadn't. One of them told you to remember the advice you gave to others in the past. That didn't help too much, but this friend went on with the clincher. He had the audacity to tell you that he'd had a vision showing him that your suffering was the result of some sin. Imagine a friend (or your spouse) telling you your problems were caused because of some sin you committed! Isn't that great? Then he told you that you sounded like a fool and what you needed to do was repent. To make matters worse, he said these problems were blessings in disguise. Great! Just when you needed comfort, empathy, and support, what do you get? Theology. And as you argue with your friends, their insensitivity grows. It's as though you need to argue with their theology. If this has happened to you, you're not alone. Remember Job? You can read about it in Job 4 and 5.

When someone is hurting he or she needs comfort, not theology. He or she needs you to listen, not give advice: "Understand [this], my beloved brethren. Let every man be quick to hear [a ready listener], slow to speak" (James 1:19 AMP). Your spouse doesn't need criticism, he or she needs encouragement. Be there, be silent, be available, be sensitive.

A Prayer
for Your Marriage

*The LORD, the God of heaven...will send his angel before you
so that you can get a wife for my son from there.*
GENESIS 24:7

O "Matchmaker of Heaven,"

What a delight to call You by the name of Matchmaker, Lord God! You care about crushes and first loves and soul mates. You send Your angels to bring a man and woman together—as You did for a lonely Isaac and a distant Rebekah. You work through wise mothers-in-law—as You did through Naomi for the dutiful young widow Ruth (Ruth 2–4).

Matchmaker, we see clues of Your affection and involvement in so many of the love stories You told us in Your Word. In the faithful devotion of Elkanah for his barren wife, Hannah (1 Samuel 1–2). In the sacrificial forgiveness of Hosea for wandering Gomer (Hosea 3). In the brave loyalty of beautiful young Esther for brash King Xerxes (Esther 5).

And yet, Matchmaker, we also hear Your voice from the wings even when Your love stories seem to falter.

When everything on the stage of love is a mess: "Then David comforted his wife Bathsheba, and he went to her and lay with her" (2 Samuel 12:24).

When believing in love requires extraordinary faith: "Joseph...did what the angel of the Lord had commanded and took Mary home as his wife" (Matthew 1:24).

And yes, Lord, even when a match "made in heaven" is tested by deep differences: "Isaac, who had a taste for wild game, loved Esau, but Rebekah loved Jacob" (Genesis 25:28).

Thank You, Lord, that we don't have to be "made for each other" to be *meant* for each other! Thank You, Lord, that You are not only a matchmaker, You are a marriage maker! Regardless of how we come together, as soon as we marry You become our "witness"—and the champion of our union (Malachi 2:14). Now we belong to You (verse 5).

Today we rest in the sweet knowledge that our love story is precious in Your eyes. And we pray that You will continue to make us into a match that will proclaim Your glory.

Amen.[7]

A Balanced
Lifestyle

Be still before the LORD *and wait patiently for him.*
PSALM 37:7

Would you like to hear some suggestions for living a balanced lifestyle? If so read on.

Begin your day 15 minutes early, and do something you enjoy. If you tend to skip breakfast or eat standing up, sit down and take your time eating. Look around the house or outside and fix your interest upon something pleasant you have been overlooking.

Think about what your values are. Where did they come from? How do they fit into the teachings of Scripture?

Each day try to spend a bit of time alone. Whatever you do at this time, do it slowly in a relaxed manner.

Begin to develop some interests and hobbies that are totally different from what you do for a living. Experiment a bit.

Periodically decorate your office or work area with something new. Take pride in what you do to express yourself and run the risk of being different.

As you play games or engage in sports, do it for the enjoyment of it and do not make it competition (this could be a struggle for some). Begin to look for the enjoyment of a good run, and the good feelings that come with recreation, which you may have been overlooking.

Allow yourself more time than you need for your work. Schedule ahead of time and for longer intervals. If you usually take a half hour for a task, allow 45 minutes. You may see an increase in the quality of your work.

Evaluate what you do and why you do it.

In one of his sermons, Dr. Lloyd Ogilvie, chaplain of the U.S. Senate, raised two interesting questions that relate to what we are doing and how we are doing it: "What are you doing with your life that you couldn't do without the *power of God?*" and "Are you living life out of your own *adequacy* or out of the abundance of the riches of Christ?" Both questions are something to think and talk about with your lifemate.

Failure

I do not understand what I do.
For what I want to do I do not do, but what I hate I do.
ROMANS 7:15

Failure! The word we dread. Some of us don't allow it into our vocabulary. Failure is what happens to others, or so we hope, but it hits all of us at times.

The word "failure" means "to deceive or disappoint." The words *fallacy* and *fallible* come from the same source. Webster's dictionary says failure is "the condition or fact of not achieving the desired end."[8] But is failure just the absence of success? Is it simply a matter of bombing out, of not completing what we set out to attain? Perhaps not.

Many men and women have achieved significant goals but found no satisfaction in them. They really didn't matter after all. This is a side of failure. It's like climbing a path up a mountain and making it to the top, only to find out you climbed the wrong mountain! Failure is not just the pain of loss but the pain of a new beginning as well.

When you experience failure, do you judge yourself as having failed or what you did as having failed? The difference is crucial. We will fail in many ways as husbands or wives. We can let failure devastate and cripple us, or we can look at Scripture and see how God used people who failed, such as Noah, Abraham, Jacob, and Moses, to accomplish His purposes.

How do you handle failure? How does your spouse? Do you ever talk about your failures or feelings of being a failure? Why or why not?

What can you do to reconstruct the way you view failure? Talk about this together. Share how you would like your spouse to support you when you fail.

The Wake-Up
Call

But you, lazybones, how long will you sleep? When will you wake up?
PROVERBS 6:9 NLT

Who wakes up first in the morning—you or your spouse?
And how do you wake up? Some people are able to come
awake without the benefit of any type of alarm clock. It's as
though they have some kind of internal clock that activates
them at a precise moment. Others, though, may need not only
an alarm clock but also a cattle prod. Without ever opening
their eyes they can find the snooze button. And when they
arise, even though they're walking around, they still may not
be alert. The body is moving; the mind isn't. It may take two
tankards of coffee before everything works.

And if one of you wakes up alert, cheery, talkative and your
spouse is just the opposite, you're in for some big adjustments.
It usually takes the alert, talking one to make the adjustments
by backing off and quieting down until his or her partner becomes fully awake.

Most of us do need some kind of wake-up call, and not just
when we're sleeping. Wake-up calls are part of life. They alert
us to something significant in our lives that we need to be
more aware of. God uses wake-up calls to get our attention
and alert us to what He has in store for us.

Sometimes it takes a personal crisis to get our attention.
Wake-up calls often come at a time of transition in life. This is
a time to stop, listen, and reflect. It's a time to realize that
you're at a crossroads in your life, and you have some choices
to make.

Throughout the journey of marriage, you may receive a
number of wake-up calls. Listen to them. They're opportunities to grow—and they just might be coming from someone
else's alarm clock...such as God's. He may be trying to get
your attention. He could be saying, "Wake up! Come alive! It's
time to get with it!"

Love Is. . .

1 CORINTHIANS 13
Basic Bible Translation

If I make use of the tongues of men and of angels, and have not love, I am like sounding brass, or a loud-tongued bell. And if I have a prophet's power, and have knowledge of all secret things; and if I have all faith, by which mountains may be moved from their place, but have not love, I am nothing.

And if I give all my goods to the poor, and if I give my body to be burned, but have not love, it is of no profit to me.

Love is never tired of waiting; love is kind; love has no envy; love has no high opinion of itself; love has no pride;

Love's ways are ever fair, it takes no thought for itself; it is not quickly made angry, it takes no account of evil;

It takes no pleasure in wrongdoing, but has joy in what is true;

Love has the power of undergoing all things, having faith in all things, hoping all things....

When I was a child, I made use of a child's language, I had a child's feelings and a child's thoughts: now that I am a man, I have put away the things of a child.

For now we see things in a glass, darkly; but then face to face: now my knowledge is in part; then it will be complete, even as God's knowledge of me.

But now we still have faith, hope, love, these three; and the greatest of these is love.[9]

Nothing Hidden

O Lord, you have examined my heart and know everything
about me. You know when I sit or stand. When far away you
know my every thought. You chart the path ahead of me and tell me
where to stop and rest. Every moment you know where I am.
You know what I am going to say before I even say it.
PSALM 139:1-4 TLB

Who knows you the best of all? Who is it that knows every secret part of you? Naturally God knows everything. Nothing, absolutely nothing, can be hidden from Him. In fact, it's kind of scary to realize that He knows what you're going to say before you say it. Sometimes we don't even know that! There is absolutely no way we can hide anything from God, but not so with people. It takes a secure person to reveal him- or herself to others. Yes, to a degree we do this with some close relatives or friends and hopefully we do this with our partners.

We all have some traits that are less than desirable. After all, we're all sinners saved by the grace of God. Some of these traits will change dramatically over time; some may change just a small amount. What is amazing is that whether they change a lot, a little, or not at all, it has no impact on God's love for us.

There are probably some traits or behaviors that you'd like your spouse to change. For most couples, there are. The longer you're married, the more you learn about each other. You may know what the other person is thinking or what they're going to say. Those who are married come the closest to knowing the most about one another. And you discover some traits you'd like to see changed.

Here's the big question: What if your partner doesn't change as much as you want? What if he or she doesn't change at all? Can you accept the way he or she is? God may have created your mate with some of those "bad" traits. Think about it.

Different?
You Bet!

For this reason a man will leave his father and mother and be united to his wife, and the two will become one flesh. This is a profound mystery—but I am talking about Christ and the church.
EPHESIANS 5:31,32

Remember when you were dating? You were aware that the other person wasn't a replica of you. Now, you probably didn't go so far as to say, "You're really different than I am." At least not then. You probably looked into your future spouse's eyes and said, "You are so unique." Then you married and discovered just how unique the other was. But now you used a new word—"different."

Wouldn't it have been better if both of you were exactly alike? Wouldn't marriage be a lot easier and smoother? Maybe, maybe not.

It's interesting to note that God has compared marriage to another union—His own relationship with the church. Look at how God created woman. For a woman to be intimate there must be relationship. If she could be intimate sexually without the emotional, social, intellectual, and spiritual, why would a man have to pursue the "getting to know you" process? The relationship is what adds depth and meaning to marriage. Getting to really know one another is what marriage is all about.

God wants a relationship with us as well. He wants to know us, and we'll spend the rest of our lives getting to know Him. Do you enjoy the "getting to know God" journey? Some people do, some don't. What the latter want from God is for Him to just fulfill their requests and meet their needs. Unfortunately, there are some marriage relationships like that.

God wants a relationship with us forever. He wants us to have a relationship with our spouse that lasts as well. His model of loving us is the model for our marriage. It's "I love you while we're getting to know one another." It's not "I'll love you when..." It's simply "I love you." It works for Him. And it can work for you.[10]

Worship

God is spirit, and his worshipers must worship in spirit and in truth.
JOHN 4:24

Let's start with some discussion. Take a moment and share with one another the first time you can remember being in a worship service. Now that you've done that, share with one another the first time you can remember *experiencing* worship. But wait a minute—aren't these questions the same? Not at all. You can be in a worship service and still not worship. We've all done this. Our bodies are there, but our hearts and minds are elsewhere, such as the golf course, with a sick child, or anticipating the guests coming to Sunday dinner.

Worship really has nothing to do with a place. Sure it's important to come together with other Christians, but it's more than that. In Jesus' time, Jews had to go to the temple to worship. The Samaritans had their own place of worship in a temple on a mountain called Gerizim. That was the old pattern, the old system. Worship was tied to where people were. In John 14:21, Jesus told the Samaritan woman that a day was coming when the issue in worship would no longer be *where* they worshiped.

The new basis for worship was not where people were, but who they were. First Corinthians 6:19 says, "Do you not know that your body is a temple of the Holy Spirit, who is in you, whom you have received from God? You are not your own." God's presence is not in a temple. He lives inside His people. We're all a temple of the Holy Spirit. When you're driving in a car on the freeway, or eating breakfast with four noisy kids, or raking the lawn, you could worship there.

The keys to worship are "Spirit and truth." When you worship the focus is not on you and what you're experiencing. When you worship the focus is on God. The next time you go to church together why not say, "Let's really worship. Let's concentrate on what God has for us and praise Him. Let's not be so concerned over what we get out of the service.[11]

Private Prayers

And when you pray, do not be like the hypocrites, for they love to pray standing in the synagogues and on the street corners to be seen by men. I tell you the truth, they have received their reward in full.
MATTHEW 6:5

Archibald Hart offers some valuable advice regarding prayer.

> One reason I believe prayer is so difficult for us is that private prayer is usually carried out silently. Silent praying, as with silent reading, is a modern phenomenon—the by-product of living close together in urban settings. In New Testament times, praying and reading was always done out loud. In fact, Jesus' admonition to his followers to go into a closet (off by ourselves) to pray was *not* an admonition to pray silently; it was a criticism of the hypocrites who prayed standing in public places....We need a "closet" for prayers because our prayers make noise—or at least they ought to. Speaking your prayers out loud can be a refreshing and meaningful experience. You'll have to find a private place to do it, but I commend it as a helpful encouragement.
>
> There are many books available to help you in your prayer life, so I won't attempt an exhaustive summary of help here. I will simply make a few suggestions for how you can improve your prayer life.
>
> 1. *Simplify your praying as much as possible.* Prayer takes many forms—contemplative, thanksgiving, requesting. It should also include waiting quietly so that you can be instructed by God.
>
> 2. *The attitude of prayer should always be the same:* a simple waiting upon God and an experiencing of his presence in humility.
>
> 3. *You should develop the prayer of "being" in addition to the prayer of "asking."* The prayer of "being" is the prayer that only asks to experience God's presence. Such a prayer is receptive rather than expressive....It asks for no benefit. It appreciates God for who he is, not for what he can give. This kind of prayer is a habit we neglect to our detriment. We are the losers for not being in communion with God.[12]

How do you feel about praying out loud with your spouse? Why not talk about it and try it?

Memorizing Scripture
for Your Marriage

I have hidden your word in my heart that I might not sin against you.
PSALM 119:11

In *The Heart of the King,* Ron Auch shares the true meaning of hiding the Word in our hearts.

> To hide the Word in our heart is to do more than just read the Bible or to memorize it. To memorize or read the Word puts it in our head. However, everything must get from the head to the heart before it transforms us. The heart is who we are. When we allow the Word of God to get deep within our heart, we are allowing it to shape the very essence of who we are.
>
> The Word of God is hidden deep within the heart through the practice of prayer. God speaks to us in many different ways and at many different times. However, if we will take the Word that God speaks to us into the prayer closet, and talk to Him intimately concerning that Word, we will rise as new beings. In the secret place of prayer, the spoken Word of God becomes our sustenance. It becomes the very thing that gives us life and liberty. Prayer takes the Word of God and brings life to us. That new life becomes the very thing that keeps us from going back to the old way of sin.
>
> Equally powerful is that of praying the written Word of God. When we pray the written Word of God, we express things we do not ordinarily express. Praying the Word of God teaches us to say the things the Holy Spirit wants us to say. The value of it is that it brings us into the knowledge of God while increasing our desire for God. This knowledge and desire keeps us from sin.
>
> David said, "But his delight is in the law of the Lord, and on his law he meditates." God has always intended for His children to hide the Word in their hearts. Meditation accomplishes this in a most effective way. Meditation is done through running a particular verse over and over in your mind.[13]

How could you pray God's Word for your marriage? What effect might this have upon it?

Faithfulness Under Fire

Greater love has no one than this,
that he lay down his life for his friends.
JOHN 15:13

This story from World War II, shared by Fred Hartley in *Men and Marriage*, is reportedly true.

> The fighting was heavy. A platoon of U.S. troops was driven back, and one of their infantrymen was wounded in gunfire. As he lay on the battlefield, a friend and fellow soldier asked his sergeant in the foxhole, "Can I go get 'im?"
>
> "There's no use. He's probably dead," the sergeant answered. "And even if he isn't dead, you'd never make it back alive. But if you want to..." Those last few words were all the friend needed to hear. Off he ran, dodging bullets. Crawling on elbows and knees, he reached the bleeding infantryman, hoisted him to his shoulders, and hobbled back. As he neared the foxhole, the heroic friend was hit in the chest with a bullet and the two friends collapsed in a heap. The sergeant tried to find the pulse of the infantryman and there was none. Dead. Then he told the soldier, "I told you it would be senseless. Your friend is dead, and now you've been shot." Fighting for air, the friend painfully explained, "No, I have no regrets. You see, when I first got to my friend he was alive. He recognized me and said, 'Thanks, Jack. I knew you'd come.' " With those words the soldier friend died.

That is friendship. Friendship says, "I knew you'd come"—*I knew if I needed you, you'd be there for me. I knew I could count on you.*

That is what makes a good marriage—not heroics but faithfulness under fire.

Faithfulness under fire is what every man longs for. It is love that keeps its word even when it hurts. It is the integrity that is just as loyal on a business trip halfway around the world as it is sitting at the breakfast table with our spouse. It is the inner sense of equilibrium that knows how to fight off the molesting demands of an overloaded schedule in order to maintain a man's commitments. This is the kind of love that has sticking power.

Faithfulness under fire is what separates a great marriage from a mediocre one. It is what every man and woman deep down longs for, but which very few seem to enjoy.[14]

A Talent
from God

May the favor of the Lord our God rest upon us; establish the work of our hands for us—yes, establish the work of our hands.
PSALM 90:17

You know you have *some* talent because God gave it to you. What you need to do is offer it back to Him, dedicate your talent to Jesus. World renowned musician Dino Kartsonakis tells us what comes after that:

> After dedication comes discipline—the hard grind to sharpen this tool that God has given you to work for Him. I learned very early that God had given me a very special talent. But I had to do the practicing. The Holy Spirit doesn't do this for you. What He does, though, is to give you a confidence, a poise when you really do your part. He helps you to feel inside, "I can do it. I *can*, for God, for his glory." [To maximize your opportunities:]
>
> - Recognize that you do have a God-given talent. Remember everybody does!
> - Dedicate the talent *and yourself* to the Lord.
> - Discipline yourself to train to be the best in your field, *for God*.
> - Believe you can do it.
> - Take every opportunity, no matter how seemingly small. It might be the very door God is unlocking for some future big work for Him.
>
> *As we walk with the Lord in the light of His Word* and try to be our very best for Him, it's exciting! We never know what God has in store for us. I just can't wait to see what He's going to do next!
>
> Talent? Yes, it's important. But it's just one piece of the picture. We have to be on the alert to take and make opportunities to use this talent to glorify Jesus Christ.
>
> Then—be ready for life with a capital L.[15]

What is your talent? What do you see as your spouse's talent? How can you use these to enhance your marriage and glorify God?

Guard Your Heart

So, if you think you are standing firm, be careful that you don't fall!
1 CORINTHIANS 10:12

Years ago the television audience was captivated by the cop show *Hill Street Blues*. After their morning briefing and just before they hit the streets, the sergeant would say to the officers, "Let's be careful out there." He was warning them to keep their guard up because the unpredictable could and would happen.

That was good advice for those police officers.

It's good advice for us who are married as well.

You are faced with a number of issues in the world that are just begging you to leave behind your Christian values and standards, especially in marriage. Some of the temptations are very enticing. Scripture warns us again and again: "Be on your guard." Jesus tells us to be on our guard against hypocrisy (see Matthew 16:6-12), against greed (see Luke 12:15), against persecution from others (see Matthew 10:17), against false teaching (see Mark 13:22,23), and above all, against spiritual slackness and unreadiness for the Lord's return (see Mark 13:32-37). "Be careful," He said in Luke 21:34, "or your hearts will be weighed down with dissipation, drunkenness and the anxieties of life."

The same caution is repeated throughout the Scriptures. Listen to these warnings: "Be careful to do what is right" (Romans 12:17). "Be careful, then, how you live" (Ephesians 5:15). "Be careful that none of you be found to have fallen short" (Hebrews 4:1). "Only be careful, and watch yourselves" (Deuteronomy 4:9). "Be careful to do what the LORD your God has commanded you" (Deuteronomy 5:32). "Be careful that you do not forget the LORD" (Deuteronomy 6:12). "Be careful to obey all that is written in the Book [of the Law of Moses]" (Joshua 23:6). "Give careful thought to your ways" (Haggai 1:5).

There's a reason for all the warnings. We need to be reminded of them constantly. Read these passages out loud every morning for a month. Read them as a couple. Before long you'll know them from memory. That's the best safeguard.[16]

Power—
What a Feeling!

You are awesome, O God, in your sanctuary;
the God of Israel gives power and strength to his people.
PSALM 68:35

We come into the world looking for power. One of our first experiences in life is a power struggle between ourselves and our parents. One of our first words, if not *the* first one, is: *No!* Why should we be surprised at that? The first couple here on earth engaged in a power struggle with God. God created humanity with free will—the ability to choose. Well, Adam did choose. And he messed it up for the rest of us because of his failure to follow God's way.

We equate power with security and control. Books are written in the leadership arena telling us how to gain power, retain power, and use power. In the Christian world we even have a group of men called the "Power Team," men with bulging muscles and the strength of Hercules who go around bursting chains strapped to their bodies and giving their Christian testimonies. The feeling of power can be addictive; it gives an adrenaline rush. Notice the abundance of ads that appeal to our desire for power. We buy into whatever they're selling because they promise to give us power.

The misuse of power in marriage usually manifests itself as domination. In fact, some men demand that their wives be submissive to them because Scripture says wives are supposed to do this. How sad because any time a man demands submission, he's lost it. He's failed. Instead of bringing up what his wife is supposed to do, all a man really needs to do is follow God's instructions for *him*—love his wife as Christ loves the church. Power isn't the problem unless we make it our god. Power isn't the problem unless we misuse it. David gives perspective to this issue: "It is God who arms me with strength and makes my way perfect" (Psalm 18:32); "The LORD is my light and my salvation—whom shall I fear? The LORD is the stronghold of my life—of whom shall I be afraid?" (Psalm 27:1).

Me? Angry?

A wise man controls his temper. He knows that anger causes mistakes.
PROVERBS 14:29 TLB

*If you are angry, don't sin by nursing your grudge. Don't let
the sun go down with you still angry—get over it quickly;
for when you are angry, you give a mighty foothold to the devil.*
EPHESIANS 4:26,27 TLB

*My dear brothers, take note of this: Everyone should be quick to listen,
slow to speak and slow to become angry, for man's anger does not
bring about the righteous life that God desires.*
JAMES 1:19,20

How do today's passages make you feel? Upset, angry, or...?
Did you notice that the Bible doesn't declare anger totally out
of bounds? Paul says in Ephesians that if you get steamed, try
to get over it quickly. James advises being *"slow* to become angry." Even God Himself, according to the prophet Joel, is not
easily angered" (see Joel 2:13 TLB).

That means He does get ticked off sometimes.

Sometimes we do feel a surge of irritation when our partners do something that bothers us. Sometimes we want to say,
"What is the matter with you?" "If you had half a brain..." And
soon our temples are pounding, and the other person is cring-
ing or ready to throw something.

At such a moment, it helps to remember the words of Scripture that teach *responding in anger usually doesn't achieve what
we want.* It's counterproductive. It only aggravates an already
tense situation. It "causes mistakes," says Proverbs 14:29 TLB.
Every sports coach knows that an angry player can't think
straight and ends up committing fouls or errors. So do angry
spouses.

While our ancestors sometimes stifled anger too much, our
modern generation has swung to the opposite side, popping
off about every little thing in the name of being honest about
our feelings. Scripture doesn't seem to be terribly worried that
we'll harm ourselves by stuffing our fury. It leans in the direction of self-control, of letting offenses pass without rebuttal, of
leaving vengeance to God.

What will you do with your anger today? Share with one
another how it will be different.[17]

The Evidence
of Love

Dear friends, let us love one another, for love comes from God....
This is how God showed his love among us: He sent his one
and only Son into the world that we might live through him.
1 JOHN 4:7,9

Wh   hat word is the opposite of love? It's "apathy." It's the attitude that says, "I don't care—do what you want—I'll take care of my life, and you take care of yours." "Who wants to work on a marriage? Let it take care of itself."

In today's passage, how did God show that He loved? He became *involved*. He sent His Son into a messed-up world. The apostle John says that if we claim to love a spouse, or anyone else, we will get involved, too.

When a family member whom we say we love turns stubborn, or chooses the wrong activity, or strays toward sloppiness, it's hard to act. After all, we don't want to cause a big fuss. It's easier to tell ourselves, "Oh, well, it's not that big of a deal....Maybe I've misunderstood the facts. I'm beat tonight anyway."

Loving correction is part of love, but there is another side as well. The same principle of involvement is true when a family member does something *positive* and a warm affirmation is in order. The loving person says, "You were great! I appreciate you." The apathetic person gives a faint smile and turns back to the TV program. No response.

So what's the evidence of love? Involvement? Yes. Involvement in the other person's life, engagement with what's *really* going on inside his or her mind and heart, caring enough to take the other person seriously. And every married person wants to be taken seriously by his or her partner. That's what God did with us. That's how we show that His love has invaded us.[18]

Me or We?

Wives, fit in with your husbands' plans....Don't be concerned about
the outward beauty that depends on jewelry, or beautiful clothes, or
hair arrangement. Be beautiful inside, in your hearts, with the lasting
charm of a gentle and quiet spirit that is so precious to God....You
husbands must be careful of your wives, being thoughtful of their
needs and honoring them as the weaker sex. Remember that you and
your wife are partners in receiving God's blessings, and if you don't
treat her as you should, your prayers will not get ready answers.
1 PETER 3:1,3,4,7 TLB

There's enough in this short passage to make everybody
squirm. It challenges our cherished images of being independent, self-assured, unencumbered, and captains of our own
fate.

What the apostle has in mind is marriage as an invisible
province, a commonwealth of two minds and wills ready to
bend and flex for one another. The phrase "partners in receiving God's blessings" (verse 7) is translated in the Revised Standard Version as "joint heirs of the grace of life." What does that
mean? It means procreation, for one thing: New life is born
only from the joining of male and female. And therein lies a
model for a thousand other endeavors in marriage. When husband and wife blend their unique efforts in willing cooperation with each other, wondrous results occur.

Just as a husband and wife are a single unit in financial matters, so they are to God. The mortgage company and the Internal Revenue Service think of us as John *and* Susan Smith,
facing all liabilities together. God sees us as inseparable partners awaiting His blessing.

We are like a medieval castle with one bold flagstaff. Prior
to the wedding, our individual pennants used to read "Me."
But now the initial letter has been turned upside-down so that
it reads "We." *We* are a unit. *We* are a team. *We* look out for
each other. *We* are joint (and joined) heirs.[19]

You Have a
Peace-Keeping Mission

When others are happy, be happy with them. If they are sad,
share their sorrow. Work happily together....Never pay back evil
for evil.... Dear friends, never avenge yourselves.
ROMANS 12:15-17,19

Diplomacy is the art of letting the other person have it your
way. It is an art sorely needed not only in the United Nations
and the halls of Congress, but also at our kitchen tables and in
the halls of our homes.

A step beyond diplomacy (negotiation, compromise) lies
peacemaking. What marriage couldn't use more of that? Today's passage gives us some keys to developing this priceless
skill.

1. *Empathize with your spouse* (Romans 12:15). Feel what he
or she is feeling; see the situation from behind your mate's
eyes for a change. Think of more than just your own agenda.

2. *Stop keeping score, remembering who did what to whom, carrying grudges.* Jesus didn't. His attitude was basically, "Let it
go; let the Father take care of My persecutors, whenever He
gets around to it. It's not My job." Remember, it takes two to
argue. A one-sided quarrel doesn't go anywhere.

3. *The final key is in Romans 12:20—surprise your antagonist
with a gift!* "Heaping coals of fire on his head" makes no sense
to us today, but in ancient Palestine it did. Most homes used
wood or charcoal for heating and cooking. If your fire went
out overnight, there were no matches to use. You had to get
live coals from somebody else. And you carried them in a
bucket on your head, like you carried everything else!

What this Scripture says is that if your enemy comes looking for warm coals don't slam the door in his face. Be generous with him; heap the glowing coals into his bucket and send
him on his way with kindness.

Do this and you will have established a new reputation for
peacemaking.

The standard atmosphere in our marriages does *not* have to
be contentious and argumentative. We *can* let the peace of God
prevail. It starts in our own hearts.[20]

Who Are the
Two of You?

*"Haven't you read," [Jesus] replied, "that at the beginning
the Creator 'made them male and female,' and said, 'for this reason a
man will leave his father and mother and be united to his wife, and the
two will become one flesh'? So they are no longer two, but one."*
MATTHEW 19:4,6

What words do you use to refer to the two of you? You
might say...

- We are the...(your last name).
- We are Mr. and Mrs. ...
- You probably use the word "we" to refer to the two of you.
- How often do you refer to the two of you as "us"? Yes, us!
  You are an "us," you know. You became an "us" when you
  married. So what can you learn about "us" from this prayer
  for the two of you?

Lord of married lovers,

Only You could defy the law of mathematics to make one
plus one equal one. And that "one" is not even two halves that
add up to a whole but two drastically different people who
add up to an entirely new creation: Us!

We come before You in prayer on behalf of Us—a husband
and wife who long to reflect Your beautiful likeness (Genesis
5:1,2) and experience the amazing oneness You promise: "Has
not the Lord made them one? In flesh and spirit they are his"
(Malachi 2:15).

Yet, You hear the voices, Lord, that attempt to separate Us:
"Are you sure you did the right thing?" "You deserve more
than this." "What if you get bored?" "Well, as long as you're
happy..."

But You've shown us "the most excellent way" (1 Corinthians 12:31)—cherishing our commitment as we cleave to one
another (Genesis 2:24), nurturing mutual respect as we submit
to each other (Ephesians 5:21), finding our lives as we surrender them to You (Luke 9:24).

And this way of love will never fail (1 Corinthians 13:8).

Lord of married lovers, bind us together in an everlasting
covenant.

We dedicate Us to You. Amen.[21]

Are You Fun
to Be Around?

A glad heart makes a cheerful countenance,
but by sorrow of heart the spirit is broken.
PROVERBS 15:13 AMP

Being around some people is a downer. They're just not much fun. They're full of gloom; there's no joy, no laughter, no life. Sure, life's tough, but there is also a lot to smile about, a lot to laugh over. Do you ever wonder what made Jesus laugh? Probably a lot of the same humorous things that we enjoy, and quite possibly there are some things we laugh at that He wouldn't.

Humor is everywhere. Look at the misprints in church bulletins or on signs, such as "This being Easter Sunday, we will ask Mrs. Jones to come forward and lay an egg on the church altar" or "Due to the Rector's illness, this week's healing services will be discontinued until further notice."

What about some of the rules and regulations that are outdated but still on the books? In Seattle it's illegal "to carry a concealed weapon of more than six feet in length." In the state of Oklahoma there's a law that says, "Any vehicle involved in an accident which results in the death of another person shall stop and give his name and address to the person struck." How would you like to see these enforced?[22]

How do other people view you? What about your partner? Are you someone who can laugh easily, who exudes joy in your marriage? Or are you a gloom machine? God is the author of smiles, joy, and laughter. He wants us to experience these gifts, express them, and infect other people with their positive potential. It's one of His prescriptions designed to make life bearable. Think about the words of Elton Trueblood:

> The Christian is joyful, not because he is blind to injustice and suffering, but because he is convinced that these, in the light of the divine sovereignty, are never ultimate....The humor of the Christian is not a way of denying the tears, but rather a way of affirming something which is deeper than tears.[23]

A person of strength has a cheerful heart.

Waffles and Spaghetti

And become useful and helpful and kind to one another.
EPHESIANS 4:32 AMP

Bill Farrel offers an interesting take on differences.

The way I see it, *Men are like waffles and women are like spaghetti.* Let's deal with us guys first. If you look at a waffle, you see a lot of individual boxes with walls between them. Each box is separate and does not interact with the other boxes. We deal with life as if there were a waffle in our brain. We take one issue and put it in a box. We take the next issue and put it in another box. If we do an MRI on our thinking, it would look just like a waffle—little boxes, each holding one area of life. We deal with one thing at a time and one thing only. When we are fishing, we are fishing. When we are at work, we are at work. When we are doing yard work, we are doing yard work. And when we are having sex with our wives, we are thinking *only* about sex.

Our wives, on the other hand, approach life like spaghetti. If you look at a plate of spaghetti, you immediately notice that everything is touching everything else. That is the way women process life. They connect everything! They have this incredible ability to deal with multiple things at the same time. Since it is impossible to fix everything and have it all under control at once, our wives process life by connecting everything emotionally.

A woman will travel through a conversation, emotionally connecting with each thing on her mind until she has "felt" something about each issue in her life. She may experience positive emotions like sentimentality, joy, and enthusiasm or she may experience negative emotions like anger, depression, or frustration, but the key for her is *to experience some emotion.* Once she has emotionally connected with each issue in her life, she will relax and begin to thoroughly enjoy the people around her.[1]

What do you think? Is this your style? Talk about it a while.

Reaffirmation

All who keep His commandments abide in Him.
1 JOHN 3:24 AMP

Do you remember your wedding vows? What were they specifically? What did you commit yourself to for the rest of your life? Most of us don't remember; if we don't remember how can we follow through and live up to them? God's Word tells us we are faithful when we keep His commandments. We are faithful in marriage when we keep the promises we made way back when.

Perhaps that's why more and more couples are having reaffirmation ceremonies. It's a positive step for any couple. It's saying, "We've made it for 25 years or 50 years, and we want to renew the step we took ages ago." If the wedding ceremony is the celebration of falling in love and starting a marriage, then a reaffirmation ceremony could be considered the celebration of still being in love and staying married.

What can it do for you?

It's an opportunity to redefine your marriage, rededicate yourselves, celebrate what you've accomplished, and look ahead.

But what is reaffirmation? In a sense it's the opposite of divorce. It's rejoicing over the fact that you've been able to make your marriage work, to make it fulfilling, to weather the storms, and to fully experience your marriage. Reaffirmation is the public demonstration of renewing your commitment to one another.

Reaffirmation is making a new choice. The reasons for doing this are probably much different than the reasons you originally had for wanting to marry your spouse. Instead of basing it on a hope of future dreams fulfilled, it is based on a history of what has occurred as well as hope for the future.

Why not consider this possibility? If you do, you *will* remember these promises. It could be a life-changing experience.

Resolved

Clothe yourselves with compassion,
kindness, humility, gentleness and patience.
COLOSSIANS 3:12

You've probably heard of Jonathan Edwards. But have you read anything he wrote? Consider his words:

Resolved, That I will do whatsoever I think to be most to God's glory, and for my own good, profit and pleasure, in the whole of my duration.

Resolved, To do whatever I think to be my duty, and most for the good and advantage of mankind in general.

Resolved, Never to lose one moment of time, but improve it the most profitable way I possibly can.

Resolved, Never to do anything which I should be afraid to do if it were the last hour of my life.

Resolved, Never to do anything out of revenge.

Resolved, To maintain the strictest temperance in eating and drinking.

Resolved, Never to do anything which, if I should see in another, I should count a just occasion to despise him for, or to think any way the more meanly of him.

Resolved, To study the Scriptures so steadily, constantly and frequently, as that I may find, and plainly perceive myself to grow in the knowledge of the same.

Resolved, To ask myself at the end of every day, week, month and year, wherein I could possibly in any respect have done better.

Resolved, Never hence-forward, till I die, to act as if I were any way my own, but entirely and altogether God's.

Resolved, I will act so as I think I shall judge would have been best and most prudent when I come into the future world.

Resolved, Never to...in the least to slacken my fight with my corruptions, however unsuccessful I may be.

Resolved, After afflictions, to inquire, what I am the better for them, what good I have got by them, and what I might have got by them.[2]

He probably didn't write these words for married couples, but consider how they might apply to your marriage.

A Prayer
for Others

The effective prayer of a righteous man can accomplish much.
JAMES 5:16 NASB

Here is a prayer by John Baillie to help you live this day being concerned for others.

Lord,

I thank you for pursuing me with your love even when I wasn't interested. I thank you that you give me thoughts to guide me and that you strengthen my will through your Holy Spirit. Sometimes I think some things happen by chance, but I am learning that with you there is no "chance" or "accident." Thank you for the way your Spirit leads. Keep me from being blind to your Spirit's direction. I pray that each day I would grow more into the person that you would have me to be. I pray that I would become more like your son, Jesus.

But I want to pray for more than just myself. There are so many others in need and I tend to overlook them.

I pray for those struggling with temptations right at this moment.

I pray for strength for the people who have tasks that are overwhelming them.

I pray for wisdom for the men and women who are struggling with decisions difficult to make.

For those overcome by debt or poverty;

For those experiencing the consequences of behavior done a long time ago and forgiven by you;

For those who at an early age were abused or never had a chance to experience life;

For families torn apart by divorce or death;

For those serving you in countries I don't even know about.

I pray that the concerns of my prayers would be less focused on me and more on the others you love, as well.

In Jesus' name, Amen.[3]

Money Lifestyle

What good is it for a man to gain the whole world, yet forfeit his soul?
MARK 8:36

Most of us have never thought about, let alone developed, a "money lifestyle" in marriage. We all have four choices regarding that lifestyle. Some choices have better consequences than others.

Living above your means—that's easy. Anyone can do it. We look rich to other people. We accumulate as much as we want in goods...and pay more than we should in high interest rates. We indulge our insecurities with material goods. The problem is, it's never enough. It takes more...and more...and more. Question: How does this lifestyle glorify God?

Living at your means is a better choice, but still not a good one. It comes in one hand and goes out the other at the same rate. At least there's not much debt. But there are no savings, either. The focus is still on gathering rather than on planning for the future. Things occupy our thoughts. The problem is there's not much room left for God. Question: How does this lifestyle glorify God?

Living within your means follows the scriptural teaching of being a good steward of what God has entrusted to you. The couple who lives within their means thinks about today and the future. But more than that, they look at how their money can be used for the kingdom of God. Tithing is a part of this couple's life, even when they can't afford it. Question: How does this lifestyle glorify God?

Living below your means is not a typical choice. It requires unusual self-discipline and a deliberate choice not to move up. The gift of giving rather than acquiring is this couple's joy. They simply use only what's necessary.

Which of these four styles describes your life? And is it by choice?[4]

Making Wise
Use of Time

Teach us to make the most of our time,
so that we may grow in wisdom.
PSALM 90:12 NLT

Are you interested in a look at how you possibly will spend your time in the future? Time analysts are now able to tell in advance how we make use of the time allotted to us. I wonder what we would do differently if we knew at an early age that we would spend 1,086 days "sick." The average person does. And some of our illnesses are preventable. Do you want to spend 1,086 days sick? Not likely.

You may be surprised to discover that you will spend 8 months of your life opening junk mail. Do you want to spend 2 years of your life on the telephone? Do you want to spend 5 years waiting in line or 9 months waiting in traffic? Just the basic necessities of life consume a large quantity of time. You'll spend 4 years cooking and eating. (You can't live on McDonald's, Burger King, and Taco Bell all the time.) You'll spend 1.5 years dressing, 1.5 years grooming, and (get this) 7 years in bathrooms! Finally, the time experts tell us we'll spend 24 years sleeping and 3 years shopping.[5]

Who knows if all of these calculations are accurate. But even if they are close, we need to ask whether this is the way we want to use our time.

Years ago someone wrote an article with this attention-getting title: "If You Are 35, You Have 500 Days to Live." Your first reaction might be, "Wait a minute, that couldn't be true!" Consider what the author said, though. When you take away all the time spent sleeping, working, doing odd chores, taking care of personal hygiene, taking care of personal matters, eating, and traveling—you end up with only 500 days in the next 36 years to spend as you want. Isn't that sobering? It sheds new light on what the psalmist said: "Teach us to make the most of our time, so that we may grow in wisdom" (Psalm 90:12 NLT).

How will you make wise use of your time? How will you take the investment God gives you and use it with purpose and meaning?

Distractions

But one thing I do: Forgetting what is behind and straining toward
what is ahead, I press on toward the goal to win the prize for which
God has called me heavenward in Christ Jesus.
PHILIPPIANS 3:13,14

In *Developing the Leader Within You*, John Maxwell raises an important focus point for marriage.

Pay attention! Those words echo in my mind from childhood. Teachers, piano teachers, and parents gave me that message time and time again. Perhaps you heard it, too. Sometimes we get distracted trying to listen, when we're praying, or trying to accomplish some goal. Some distractions can be fatal. It's possible to allow activities or commitments to distract us from our marriage. Sometimes we paralyze our progress by trying to accomplish several things at the same time or else we put our energy into doing a task that isn't very important and neglect something that's vital.

A number of years ago an Eastern Airlines jumbo jet crashed in the Florida Everglades. You may remember the story of flight 401. It carried a full load of passengers and had taken off from New York bound for Miami. As the plane came closer to the Miami airport and began its approach to land, the pilots noticed that the light which indicates the landing gear is down failed to come down. The pilots flew in a large looping circle over the Everglade swamps while they worked on the problem. It could have been that the landing gear wasn't properly deployed or it could have been a defective light bulb.

The flight engineer tried to remove the light bulb but it was stuck. The other members in the cockpit tried to help him loosen the bulb. While they were distracted with trying to get the bulb out, they all failed to notice that the plane was losing altitude, and it flew right into the swamp. Dozens of passengers were killed. The cockpit crew had a job to do, but they were distracted by a stuck 75-cent light bulb. This was a fatal distraction.

What distracts you from your marriage? What distracts you from responding to your spouse's requests? And what distracts you from your relationship with God? That's the major question.[6]

Opposition

*We do not want you to be uninformed, brothers, about the hardships
we suffered in the province of Asia. We were under great pressure, far
beyond our ability to endure, so that we despaired even of life. Indeed,
in our hearts we felt the sentence of death. But this happened that we
might not rely on ourselves but on God, who raises the dead.*

2 CORINTHIANS 1:8,9

There are days when you feel like throwing in the towel.
You're wiped out, exhausted, crushed, and devastated. Even
the apostle Paul felt this way.

Perhaps you've felt that kind of weariness. It could be the
tasks of parenting or even your marriage. It could be experiencing opposition from other people at work, at church, or in
your family. When you have to face opposition from others
over a period of time, your defenses and resolve slowly erode
until nothing is left.

Paul wasn't the only one to face this. David had his time,
too. His son Absalom literally "stole the hearts of the men of
Israel" (2 Samuel 15:6 RSV) and created conditions that were so
bad that David had to leave Jerusalem. He had to evacuate his
home, his throne, and the city he built. Then a distant relative
of Saul came by and proceeded to attack, curse, and stone
David. That was like salt in the wound. It was not a fun trip.
He was bone-weary when they arrived at their destination.
"The king, and all the people who were with him, arrived
weary at the Jordan; and there he refreshed himself" (2 Samuel
16:14 RSV).

Opposition exhausts. What do you do at a time like this?
May I suggest that you put into practice the three Rs.

Remember. You're not alone. There is One who is with you.
When you're married you can gain support from your partner.

Rest. There is no substitute for allowing your body and
mind to heal. Look to the One who gives you rest.

Resolve. When your strength is back, as much as possible try
to resolve the differences between you and those opposing
you. Your adversaries may not change, but at least you went
the extra mile.

Change Can Happen

*Love bears up under anything and everything that comes,
is ever ready to believe the best of every person,
its hopes are fadeless under all circumstances.*
1 Corinthians 13:7 amp

Have you ever thought that "nothing can change or improve your relationship"? If so, don't believe it. If you do it will become a self-fulfilling prophecy. If you or anyone else believes that nothing can improve your marriage, test this belief. Challenge it. Look at, define, and clarify some of the problems, then select one that appears to be the easiest to change.

One husband just wanted to be able to have discussions with his wife without defensive arguments that seemed to erupt constantly. He learned some ways he could stay out of the argument and eliminate his defensiveness. This is what he did:

1. He chose to believe that his wife wasn't out to get him or simply to argue with him out of spite. She might have some good ideas.

2. He committed himself not to interrupt her, not to argue or debate, and not to walk out on her.

3. He would respond to what she said by making such statements as: "Really," "That's interesting," "I hadn't considered that," "Tell me more," and "I'd like to think about that."

4. He chose to think the following: *Even if this doesn't work the first time, I'll try it at least five times.*

5. He determined to thank her for each discussion, and when her response was even five percent less defensive, to compliment her for the way she responded.

Five weeks later he said, "The fourth discussion was totally different. My belief that nothing can improve our relationship is destroyed. There's a bit of hope now."

To counter your negative and hopeless beliefs, focus upon passages from God's Word that are future-oriented and filled with hope. For example, in Jeremiah we read, "'For I know the plans that I have for you,' declares the Lord, 'plans for welfare and not for calamity to give you a future and a hope'" (29:11 nasb).

What about you? What would you like to change? The first step may be to change your beliefs.[7]

Oops—
I Made a Mistake

A man who refuses to admit his mistakes can never be successful. But
if he confesses and forsakes them, he gets another chance.
PROVERBS 28:13 TLB

Well, that's the first mistake I've made in 15 years of marriage. Guess I'm not perfect after all." We sometimes joke about the errors we make, although some people don't admit their mistakes all that readily—especially to their spouses. Perhaps we're afraid it will be used against us or be brought up in the future (again and again) or we're afraid of losing some of our power and control. Whatever the reason, we're not quick to do so even though Scripture tells us to. Too often we bring out our repertoire of devices we've perfected over the years to cover up our mistakes rather than admit them.

We plead ignorance: "Did you ask me to do that? I don't remember hearing you. Are you sure you asked me?"

We use blame: "Oh, no, I didn't do that. I think the dog came in and knocked all that stuff off the table and left it there."

We don't always admit our mistakes readily, even though we know the other person knows and they know that we know they know. (Did you follow that?)

We all make mistakes. That's a fact. We all sin. That, too, is a fact. But there's a difference between the two. Do you know what it is? A sin is a *willful* act. We know it's against God's will; it's calculated, thought out, anticipated, deliberate. A mistake is usually unintended, unplanned, sometimes spur of the moment, and the consequences never enter our minds. We miscalculate. It could be a lapse of judgment or planning. That happens.

So, what can we do? Give our mistakes to God. Admit them. It's not the end of the world. Learn from them so we don't repeat them. And if we sin, confess it.

We're all going to do both—make mistakes and sin. Thank God that He's given us a provision for both. God doesn't hold either against us—and that's our model for the way to respond to our spouses.[8]

304

Accommodating

*Don't push your way to the front; don't sweet-talk your way
to the top. Put yourself aside, and help others get ahead.
Don't be obsessed with getting your own advantage.*
PHILIPPIANS 2:3,4 MSG

Accommodation is such a nice sounding word. There's another variation of it that can be used in a sentence. It's not an easily answered sentence, though. Here it comes: "In your marriage, who does the most accommodating?" Now, many couples would say they both accommodate the other. Some may even say, "That's easy. I do the most accommodating!" Some couples actually keep a scorecard. They want to make sure their marriage really is equal.

But think about it. Who gets up to take care of something when you're both exhausted? Who goes out in the rain to get the paper? Who answers the phone when neither of you wants to talk? Who gets up to walk the crying baby at 3:00 A.M.?

Who is most accommodated in your marriage? Another way of putting this question is, Who gets center stage and calls most of the shots? Unfortunately, there are far too many Christian marriages that reflect one-way accommodation. One bends and flexes to the other person most of the time. The "shared" life really isn't. Another more blunt way of describing it is one person is a "taker" and the other a "giver." This may be the way it is, but it's not a biblical pattern. The Word of God teaches a pattern of mutual servanthood. Accommodation is a part of marriage, not just something to think about. It's a reflection of the presence of Jesus in us—and what better place for it to be manifested than in marriage. How can you accommodate your partner in a new way this week?[9]

What Is Spiritual?

Blessed are those who hunger and thirst for
righteousness, for they will be filled.
Matthew 5:6

Are you a spiritual person? That's a rather blunt question, but are you? Is your spouse? If you answered "yes" to the first question, what do you mean by it?

The answer should actually be quite simple. If you have a desire to know and to serve God and want a deeper relationship with Him, that's sufficient. To help you move forward in your spiritual walk, especially as a couple, here are some thoughts for you to consider and discuss together.

Share with each other some of your first experiences of knowing and feeling that God loved you. Tell some of the details of your spiritual journey since that time.

Share what you are doing at the present time to grow more in your Christian walk. What are your struggles in this area?

What do you think God has been saying to you these past few months as an individual? As a couple?

To whom do you usually pray? God the Father, Jesus, or the Holy Spirit? Is it easier to relate to one person of the Trinity more than the others?

What is your picture of God? How would you describe Him?

If you were to see God face-to-face as a couple, what would He say to you about your relationship? What suggestions would He have for you?

How would your spouse want you to pray for him or her for the next week? Discuss this together.

These topics and questions could be difficult, but discussing them will draw you closer to God, and to one another.[10]

Temptations

Then Jesus was led by the Spirit
into the desert to be tempted by the devil.
MATTHEW 4:1

Life is full of temptations. And once you marry they don't go away. If anything, there may be more. Jesus understands our temptations because He was tempted as well. It may help you to stop for a moment and read Matthew 4:1-11 to gain a clearer picture of His trials. Now, before you proceed, take a look at 2 Corinthians 4:1-7. Do you see the correlation between the three temptations Jesus faced and the three observations Paul mentions?

So what are these temptations and how do they relate to marriage? The first one is to be self-sufficient and self-reliant. People who try this are attempting to live their lives without the Lord. And when this happens in marriage it violates the "we" principle. Not only that, but they miss out on the wisdom and knowledge of their partners. The attitude of "I can do it myself; I don't need to consult with you or inform you" is an invitation to disaster in marriage. Ask one another for advice. Rely upon one another. Rely upon the Lord together.

A second temptation is to be spectacular, to be a celebrity, to have life revolve around us. In marriage, if we're going to draw attention or look for praise or recognition, we should do it as couples or, better yet, direct it toward our partners. Build them up rather than ourselves.

A third temptation encouraged in our society is to be in charge—in control and powerful. Remember, Paul said in 2 Corinthians 4:5: "We do not preach ourselves, but Christ Jesus as Lord, and ourselves as your servants for Jesus' sake." In marriage someone needs to lead. At times both of you will give leadership. But to dominate or push or control, there's no place for this in a Christian marriage.

There is a place for something else, though. It's called servanthood. It's the model Jesus gave to us. It's what He taught, and it's the best way to run a marriage.

Refining Fire

Who among the gods is like you, O LORD? Who is like you—
majestic in holiness, awesome in glory, working wonders?
EXODUS 15:11

They were called the "Great Fires of 1988." That was the year the huge lumberyard, known as Yellowstone National Park, ignited. It was overloaded with lodgepole pines, close together, within inches of pine needles and dead twigs on the ground. A fire started near Old Faithful, while 25 miles away a fire storm erupted. Tornado-type winds fanned the flames through the forest, devouring everything in its path. What used to be trees became piles of white ash and small charred sticks.

When it was over the devastation was seen for miles. It would take years to recover, or so they thought. Within a few months, however, the forest was growing again. The intense heat did something amazing. It split open the hulls of pine cones and the seeds spread. A forest of little saplings was on its way. The dead underbrush was gone so grass and wild flowers sprung up everywhere. The fire was really a cleansing and refining process. Wild fires can bring new growth and regeneration.

Sometimes God's holiness is pictured as a fire. One example is when God came at Pentecost as a fiery flame (see Acts 2:1-4). And God's holiness has even greater power than a forest fire. Do you understand what "God's holiness" means? God's character is pure in every way—totally pure. It can't increase, nor can it diminish. What does this mean for all of us? First Peter says, "You must be holy because I am holy" (1:16 NLT).

How can you as a couple be holy? Be different. Be careful what you spend your time watching. Perhaps it's seen in what you laugh at, talk about, kid about—the possibilities are endless. In what ways are you living a holy lifestyle?[11]

Love Is...

1 Corinthians 13
The Living Bible

If I had the gift of being able to speak in other languages without learning them, and could speak in every language there is in all of heaven and earth, but didn't love others, I would only be making noise. If I had the gift of prophecy and knew all about what is going to happen in the future, knew everything about everything, but didn't love others, what good would it do? Even if I had the gift of faith so that I could speak to a mountain and make it move, I would still be worth nothing at all without love. If I gave everything I have to poor people, and if I were burned alive for preaching the Gospel but didn't love others, it would be of no value whatever.

Love is very patient and kind, never jealous or envious, never boastful or proud, never haughty or selfish or rude. Love does not demand its own way. It is not irritable or touchy. It does not hold grudges and will hardly even notice when others do it wrong. It is never glad about injustice, but rejoices whenever truth wins out. If you love someone you will be loyal to him no matter what the cost. You will always believe in him, always expect the best of him, and always stand your ground in defending him.

All the special gifts and powers from God will someday come to an end, but love goes on forever....

We can see and understand only a little about God now, as if we were peering at his reflection in a poor mirror; but some-day we are going to see him in his completeness, face to face. Now all that I know is hazy and blurred, but then I will see everything clearly, just as clearly as God sees into my heart right now.

There are three things that remain—faith, hope, and love—the greatest of these is love.

I Will Go
with You

Don't urge me to leave you or to turn back from you.
Where you go I will go, and where you stay I will stay.
Your people will be my people and your God my God. Where you die I
will die, and there I will be buried. May the LORD deal with me, be it
ever so severely, if anything but death separates you and me.
RUTH 1:16,17

Imagine you have traveled back in time. From a great distance, looking out across the sweep of the treeless plateau, you notice a dirt road cutting the scene east to west, and on the road, three black dots. The dots are people, you can tell, moving west. They are dressed in black, and yes, it's clear they are women. As unlikely as it seems, you decide you're watching a migration of widows.

Take your imaginary viewpoint closer. Now you're beside the road, up to your chin in ripening wheat. Insects whir and sing. The widows approach, stopping and starting. Their conversation seems agitated. Another stop. One throws her arms around the other, wails, then returns the way she has come.

The remaining two keep talking and gesturing as they come closer. You see that the face of one is craggy, sunburned. The face of the other is flushed but smooth, too young by far to be wearing widows' black.

When you can finally hear what the younger one is saying, your jaw drops. They're exchanging...*wedding vows?*

Kind of a shock to modern readers! But Ruth's speech on that road to nowhere has become one of the best-known declarations of married love in the Christian world. It's a wedding favorite, even though it was delivered by one widow to another, each of whom had put away hopes for marriage.

Some distance back on the road you're traveling, you and your spouse made promises to share your lives until death. Friends and family and God, Himself, were watching. Those vows can still be wings to help you soar today.[12]

A Comfort
that Comforts

Whenever Hannah went up to the house of the LORD,
her rival provoked her till she wept and would not eat.
Elkanah her husband would say to her, "Hannah, why are
you weeping? Why don't you eat? Why are you downhearted?
Don't I mean more to you than ten sons?"
1 SAMUEL 1:7,8

One of the most touching scenes in Hannah's story is when Elkanah tries to comfort her. He was obviously in earnest. The Bible doesn't tell us to what extent he was successful, but we can learn something from studying his approach.

What did Elkanah do right? First, he noticed his wife's unhappiness. This means that Elkanah was paying attention to Hannah and was sensitive to her moods. And when he noticed her unhappiness, he responded by expressing concern for her. Most important of all, Elkanah let Hannah know that he valued their love relationship despite all the disappointments life had brought to their marriage.

We can also learn from the mistakes Elkanah may have made. Some people read Elkanah's comments, "Why are you weeping? Why don't you eat?" as a failure to identify with her feelings of sadness.

How many of us have ever said to our mate, "Hey, it's not that bad. Look at what you still have."

In a similar way, Elkanah's statement, "Don't I mean more to you than ten sons?"—while affirming his desire for relationship with Hannah—could also be interpreted as, "Hey, if you really loved me I'd be enough to make you happy! Come on and perk up!" Another easy, but unhelpful approach.

So what can we do to best comfort a troubled spouse?

Paul wrote to the Galatians, "Carry each other's burdens" (Galatians 6:2). To comfort our mates, we must also *share*—enter into—their griefs. When our mates are depressed, sad, or confused, we help best when we listen, affirm, and allow them the time they need to think.

The art of comforting takes time and patience. But to be met in our grief by one who cares, by the one closest to us, is to feel the compassion and healing touch of Jesus Christ.[13]

What Does
God Get?

Offer to God a sacrifice of thanksgiving,
and pay your vows to the Most High.
PSALM 50:14 NASB

Listen to the words of Tony and Lois Evans:

> Lois and I made a basic commitment when we got married and established our home, and God has enabled us to honor this vow we made to Him. The rule we agreed on is this: At no time would any money come into our home for which God did not get the minimum tithe of 10 percent—and He would get His portion first.

Today's verse is a powerful reminder that God is the source of our blessings and that we owe our thanks to Him for what we have.

What happens when we honor God? Here's the promise God makes in Psalm 50:15: "Call upon Me in the day of trouble; I shall rescue you, and you will honor Me" (NASB). When you honor God, when you make His glory and His work your priority, He becomes your greatest helper in your time of need, whether it's a financial crisis or a spiritual need.

"If you give Me what's Mine," God says, "then when you call upon Me about a problem with what is yours, because you brought Me into the equation by honoring Me, I will hear you when you have need of Me."

Now, I'm not talking about making a deal in which you say, "Okay, God, I'll give Your portion to You, and You fill my bank account." God doesn't make deals, but He does honor those who honor Him.

You and your spouse may say, "We trust God." That's great. But remember, trusting God involves taking a step of faith. A farmer cannot say, "I trust that I'm going to have a good harvest" and then never plant any seed. Neither can a Christian say, "I trust God to supply my needs" and then never give to Him. Honor God and watch Him work.[14]

What Do
You Choose?

But the fruit of the Spirit is love, joy, peace, patience,
kindness, goodness, faithfulness, gentleness and self-control.
Against such things there is no law.
GALATIANS 5:22,23

Max Lucado writes:

It's quiet. It's early. My coffee is hot. The sky is still black. The world is still asleep. The day is coming.

For the next 12 hours I will be exposed to the day's demands. It is now that I must make a choice. Because of Calvary, I'm free to choose. And so I choose.

I choose love…

No occasion justifies hatred; no injustice warrants bitterness. I choose love. Today I will love God and what God loves.

I choose joy…

I will invite my God to be the God of circumstances. I will refuse the temptation to be cynical…the tool of the lazy thinker. I will refuse to see any problem as anything less than an opportunity to see God.

I choose peace…

I will live forgiven. I will forgive so that I may live.

I choose patience…

I will overlook the inconveniences of the world. Instead of cursing the one who takes my place, I'll invite him to do so.

I choose kindness…

I will be kind to the poor, for they are alone. Kind to the rich, for they are afraid. And kind to the unkind, for such is how God has treated me.

I choose goodness…

I will go without a dollar before I take a dishonest one. I will be overlooked before I will boast. I will confess before I will accuse.

I choose self-control…

Love, joy, peace, patience, kindness, goodness, faithfulness, gentleness, and self-control. To these I commit my day. If I succeed, I will give thanks. If I fail, I will seek his grace. And then, when this day is done, I will place my head on my pillow and rest.

What will you choose today?[15]

Fly—
Don't Walk in Circles

[The woman of folly calls…] Who are making
their paths straight:… let him turn here.
PROVERBS 9:15 NASB

A bazaar was held in a village in northern India. Everyone brought his wares to trade and sell. One old farmer brought in a whole covey of quail. He had tied a string around one leg of each bird. The other ends of all the strings were tied to a ring which fit loosely over a central stick. He had taught the quail to walk dolefully in a circle, around and around, like mules at a sugar-cane mill. Nobody seemed interested in buying the birds until a devout Brahman came along. He believed in the Hindu idea of respect for all life, so his heart of compassion went out to those poor little creatures walking in their monotonous circles.

"I want to buy them all," he told the merchant, who was elated. After receiving the money, he was surprised to hear the buyer say, "Now, I want you to set them all free."

"What's that, sir?"

"You heard me. Cut the strings from their legs and turn them loose. Set them all free!"

With a shrug, the old farmer bent down and snipped the strings off the quail. They were free at last. What happened? The birds simply continued marching around and around in a circle. Finally, the man had to shoo them off. But even when they landed some distance away, they resumed their pre-dictable march. Free, unfettered, released, yet they kept going around in circles as if still tied.

Until you give yourself permission to be the unique person God made you to be—and to do the unpredictable things grace allows you to do—you will be like that covey of quail, march-ing around in vicious circles of fear, timidity, and boredom.

Since the strings have been cut, it's time to stop marching and start flying.[16]

Have you ever found yourself going in circles in your mar-riage? Do you have the freedom to be who you really are in your relationship or do you hold back? Think about it. And while you're at it, consider how you can, as a couple, fly rather than march in circles.

Praying for
Each Other

*Far be it from me that I should sin
against the LORD by failing to pray for you.*
1 SAMUEL 12:23

Does the Scripture give any example of couples praying for one another? Genesis 25:21 reads, "Isaac prayed to the LORD on behalf of his wife, because she was barren. The LORD answered his prayer, and his wife Rebekah became pregnant." God answered, and He blessed them in a unique way. Rebekah gave birth to Jacob and Esau.

Is prayer in the context of marriage just another aspect of living out a faithful Christian life? Or do the prayers of husbands or wives for their spouses have special meaning or effectiveness? The answer seems to be both. Marriage partners who pray draw on some key spiritual principles for blessing:

1. *In marriage we can pray with the power of oneness.* A married couple has become—and will always be in the process of becoming—"one flesh" (Genesis 2:23,24). When we pray as part of this mysterious union, we invite God to accomplish His original purpose to bless and complete us through the relationship.

2. *In marriage we can pray with the power of His presence.* Jesus said He is present in a special way when two or three of His own meet in His name (Matthew 18:20). When we pray and agree together as a couple, we obey Christ's invitation, and we experience the "power of three" (see Ecclesiastes 4:12).

3. *In marriage we can pray with the power of insight that comes from intimacy.* No one can pray for us with as much understanding and sincerity as our lifelong partners. When we know and love each other completely, our requests are more likely to be in line with God's purposes. And our thanks for our spouses will flow more naturally (Philippians 1:3-11).

4. *In marriage we can pray with the power of true love.* The effectiveness of every spiritual ministry in the lives of others begins in love; anything else is just a waste of effort, Paul wrote (1 Corinthians 13:1-8). When husbands or wives pray in love, they pray with a power that God promises cannot fail.[17]

Who's the Most Important?

For by the grace given me I say to every one of you:
Do not think of yourself more highly than you ought,
but rather think of yourself with sober judgment,
in accordance with the measure of faith God has given you.
ROMANS 12:3

Love each other with brotherly affection
and take delight in honoring each other.
ROMANS 12:10 TLB

Who is the most important person in your marriage? Is it:

- The one who brings home the most money?
- The person who does the majority of the cooking?
- The person who does the laundry?
- The person with the happiest attitude, who lifts everyone else's spirits?
- The one who spends the most time in prayer?

Couldn't a case be made for any of these? Sure. We're all good at framing ourselves as the "Truly Indispensable Spouse." My partner really can't get along without me.

Paul throws cold water on that notion. He addresses both spouses—*"to every one of you."* Not just the wives; not just the husbands. *Everybody.*

Each member of a marriage has a role to play. None of us is the whole stage troupe, even though we may like to think so.

Romans 12:10 is about learning to appreciate each other. Beyond the perfunctory "I love you," Paul calls us to genuine affection and enthusiasm about our partners' worth. There's no hint here of competition or power struggle. This is a home where each person is the other's cheerleader.

Read all of Romans 12. Some people think this chapter is unrealistic; life just doesn't work out that way. But wouldn't we like to live in such an atmosphere? Wouldn't it be great? If you as a couple set this ideal before you, could you match up to it for one evening? What about a full day? Then maybe a full weekend? Try it!

If you think a lifestyle of focusing on the other is impossible, it will be. If you think God just might help you make your marriage more of a delight than a headache, you may be in for a pleasant surprise.

It's His way. It's got to be better than our way.[18]

Loving and
Praying Together

*As for me, far be it from me that I should sin
against the LORD by failing to pray for you.
And I will teach you the way that is good and right.*
1 SAMUEL 12:23

Roberta Bondi likens prayer to falling in love:

> Living in an intentional relationship with God in prayer is like living in a happy marriage. When a person is first in love, the beloved is constantly on the mind, and time spent in the other person's presence can have an almost hallucinatory quality. The one in love has a heightened sense of the self and the lover in which every minute counts, and the other's every word and gesture seem full of meaning. It is magical while it lasts, and it is always remembered. If this initial love is to grow into the nourishing and long-term love of a good marriage, however, the way lovers come to be together on a day-to-day basis has to change. The intensely focused times continue but the two come to spend far more time together when nothing productive appears to be happening: They read the paper together, do the dishes, eat a meal, and this shared, very ordinary, everyday time becomes a fundamental and very necessary part of the precious foundation of the marriage, in which love infuses all that the lovers do together.
>
> For many people, beginning to pray regularly is like falling in love, and prayer for them often also has a very focused, very intense quality to it. Like first falling in love, it is wonderful. Nevertheless, if you believe that what you "get out of" prayer depends on having an intense experience in prayer, when that focused quality begins to fall away, you may come to believe that you are no longer truly praying when just the opposite is probably true: You are entering into the deep and solid life of everyday prayer that is equivalent to the precious ordinary time in marriage.[19]

When do you pray together as a couple? What's the result of praying together for you? How does it affect how you feel toward one another?

Thanksgiving

Give thanks to the LORD, for he is good; his love endures forever.
PSALM 107:1

*Let us come before him with thanksgiving
and extol him with music and song*
PSALM 95:2

Platters of food, mouth-watering aromas, everyone waiting for the first servings. Few holiday celebrations match the culinary art presented on Thanksgiving. You probably even sample the food while it's in the kitchen, don't you? Here's a different suggestion for you: When you serve the dinner, just put five kernels of corn on each plate and nothing else. Can you imagine what everyone's reaction would be? That's what the pilgrims did when they celebrated the first Thanksgiving. It was done to remind them of the difficult year they had experienced. After prayers of gratitude were offered, the rest of the meal was served.

Think back to the first Thanksgiving you can remember. Try to capture the sights, the sounds, the food, and who was there. Have you ever asked your spouse what he or she remembers about past Thanksgivings? What a great experience it would be for you to talk to someone who experienced Thanksgiving during the depression years or World War II. It was a completely different time and culture then.

How can you make your Thanksgiving memorable and different this year? How can you reflect the true meaning of the occasion? Some couples make it a point each year to provide for a homeless or less fortunate family as much as they provide for themselves.

Thanksgiving reminds us that we can't run our own lives. We need God; we're dependent upon Him. He desires our gratitude. Perhaps the best way is to say "God, thank You for being God. May I be a vessel of gratitude and loving in how I respond to other people."[20]

Pull the Plug

Finally, brothers, whatever is true, whatever is noble, whatever is right, whatever is pure, whatever is lovely, whatever is admirable— if anything is excellent or praiseworthy—think about such things.
PHILIPPIANS 4:8

I feel wonderful. Last night I watched TV from 6:00 until 1:00 A.M. I started with the evening news, went to sitcoms, to a violence-filled mystery, to the talk shows, and back to news. I'm feeling restored, renewed, refreshed. Oh, it was a great evening. It filled my life. I'm so thankful for the gift of television." Have you ever heard anyone say this? It's doubtful. TV desensitizes us and takes time away from relationships and conversation. It's addictive. It has created phrases that are heard constantly: "What's on?" "Move!" "Where's the *TV Guide?*" "Who took the remote?"

There's actually nothing wrong with watching TV. It's our use of it both in time and content that creates problems.

Research shows that sets are turned on an average of six hours a day. In the 80s, a Detroit newspaper offered 120 families 500 dollars apiece if they would keep the TV off for a month. Guess what? Ninety-three families turned the offer down! What would your response be to that offer?

The Scriptures talk about people fasting, and perhaps you've fasted before. But what about from television? Why not fast from television? Pull the plug. Let it stand unused. Let those circuits have a rest. Don't even discuss with others what's on TV. Don't look at the *TV Guide* either. You may go through withdrawal. You may wonder, "What do we do now? Stare at each other?" You may even have more marital conflict. You see, TV is used for more than entertainment. It's used to numb us, to overcome boredom, and to avoid dealing with family or marital issues.

But fasting can help you discover what you might be missing in recreation, hobbies, spiritual growth, and deeper intimacy with your spouse. Fast to improve your marriage. Remember, if we can't stay away from TV, we may be struggling with an addiction. We weren't called to be slaves. We were called to be free in Christ.

Auditing Life
Doesn't Work

Speak, for your servant is listening.
1 SAMUEL 1:10

What kind of regular exercise program do you have? Was that a bad question? For some it is nonexistent. But if you've ever been in one (or are now), there's a word associated with exercise—pain. Some even say, "No pain, no gain." When you first start an exercise program, expect pain. There's a good reason for it. You're using muscles that are not used to being stretched and challenged this way. There's a great remedy for eliminating the pain—use the muscles again and again. Your first inclination to get rid of the pain is to quit, to stop all that foolishness! But if you work your muscles more and make them hurt more, eventually you'll get into shape—you're stronger, you feel better, you have more energy, and your muscles don't ache.

But you have to be involved. You can't just watch an exercise video or "sit in" and observe. In college sometimes a student sits in on a class or "audits" it, instead of taking it for credit. Sometimes they even do the assignments, but they don't get credit for it.

Your marriage is the same way. Your Christian walk is the same way. You can't audit either one. You've got to be involved. For a marriage to improve, you have to contribute. You have to communicate. You have to hear what you sometimes don't want to hear from your spouse—especially if he or she is right. In your Christian life you have to take what you hear in church or read in the Bible and actually do it.

Ask yourself, "As a couple, are we sometimes auditing what we hear as believers or are we taking it for credit?" You've learned a lot already about your faith and about marriage. Why not put it into practice? Muscles grow that way. So will your life.[21]

Share It— Don't Keep It

Every man is a fool who gets rich on earth but not in heaven.
LUKE 12:21 TLB

Someone called from the crowd, "Sir, please tell my brother to divide my father's estate with me."

But Jesus replied, "Man, who made me a judge over you to decide such things as that? Beware! Don't always be wishing for what you don't have. For real life and real living are not related to how rich we are."

Then he gave an illustration: "A rich man had a fertile farm that produced fine crops. In fact, his barns were full to overflowing—he couldn't get everything in. He thought about his problem, and finally exclaimed, 'I know—I'll tear down my barns and build bigger ones! Then I'll have room enough. And I'll sit back and say, "Friend, you have enough stored away for years to come. Now take it easy! Wine, women, and song for you!" '

"But God said to him, 'Fool! Tonight you die. Then who will get it all?' " (Luke 12:13-19 TLB).

The man's request in verse 13 seems fair enough; his father has died, and his sibling is now refusing to share. But Jesus goes on to tell how the rich farmer portrays a man doing what seems to be wise. But God calls him a very strong epithet: fool. What's so bad about this man? His focus was on getting, not giving, on storing rather than sowing. Accumulation was his sole goal. All he wanted was a better life. In God's eyes, that's a dead-end street. The man's building project comes to a quick end—death. There would be no more harvests. Instead, the estate would be splintered.

Are rich couples happier? Not necessarily, as today's verse shows. The assets you accumulate may cause more problems. Possessions have a way of causing family headaches.

Ephesians 4:28 gives us one of the strangest reasons for a person to work hard and accumulate: "that he may have something to share with those in need" (TLB).

Accumulate something—but share it! Is there someone you could share with today?[22]

The Whole
Truth

Where is that happy spirit that we felt together then?
For in those days I know you would gladly have taken out your own
eyes and given them to replace mine if that would have helped me.
And now have I become your enemy because I tell you the truth?
GALATIANS 4:15,16 TLB

Couples joke about how starry-eyed they were in the beginning days, how blissfully blind was young love. And then they discovered the truth of the T-shirt sold in the tourist shops: "Pobody's nerfect."

It's more than just leaving dirty socks on the bedroom floor or neglecting to bring home the charge-card receipts. Those things are passed over easily enough. But what do you do when you're truly disappointed in your spouse, when the issue is significant (at least to you), and the more you try to talk about it, the more you seem like the "enemy" instead of a loving partner?

Everyone says about marriage, "You have to work at it." But what if your work seems only to aggravate the situation? Elisabeth Elliott once wrote to her daughter:

> Who is it you marry? You marry a sinner. There's nobody else to marry.
>
> So, remember that you did, in fact, marry only a sinner, but *so did he.*

It does no good to pretend otherwise, says the apostle John. "We are only fooling ourselves" (1 John 1:8 TLB). The truth that hurts, hurts either way. If buried and brushed over, it goes on hurting like a dull ache in the relationship. If brought to the surface and confronted, it stings for the moment, but then it evaporates in the warmth of resolution. Like a splinter being pulled from a fingertip, we can touch the spot with relief, knowing that healing can now begin.[23]

Husbands Encourage Your Wives

Therefore encourage one another
build each other up, just as in fact you are doing.
1 THESSALONIANS 5:11

And we urge you, brothers, warn those who are idle, encourage the
timid, help the weak, be patient with everyone.
1 THESSALONIANS 5:14

This is a message primarily to husbands (wives can read it, too). A husband speaks up about encouragement:

> As men, we have the ability to help produce the kind of wife we want simply by the words we say. If you shower your wife with compliments and encouragement, she will be happier. If you tell her how valuable she is to you on a regular basis, she will have a growing sense of self-confidence and productivity. If you point out her strengths and abilities, she will be much more willing to use those strengths to meet your needs.
>
> If on the other hand, you inundate her with insults and complaints, she will doubt her value to you. If you point out her shortcomings and run her down for being different from you, she will lose self-confidence. If you consistently criticize her and then ask her if she wants to get passionate, she will say, "Not with you!"
>
> When I practice giving positive feedback, it is as if I have a mirror on my chest that my loved ones are looking at and making positive conclusions about who they are. When I resort to criticism and negative feedback, it's like having a broken mirror on my chest, with lots of cracks and distortions. I am defying the ones I love to feel good about themselves despite my evaluation. The message I send out is my choice, and it takes a lot of determination to choose to be positive. The fact is, no one is perfect. Your wife will do things that disappoint you. She will do things that inconvenience your life and interrupt your plans. She will spend money differently than you, treat friendships differently than you, and do tasks differently than you. You will get discouraged with her, angry with her, disappointed with her, and irritated with her by the very things you love about her. It is your choice whether you will respond to her in the positive or the negative.[24]

Ambition

Again, it will be like a man going on a journey, who called his servants
and entrusted his property to them. To one he gave five talents of
money, to another two talents, and to another one talent, each
according to his ability. Then he went on his journey. The man who
had received the five talents went at once and put the money to work
and gained five more. So also, the one with the two talents gained two
more....."Well done, good and faithful servant! You have been faithful
with a few things: I will put you in charge of many things."
MATTHEW 25:14-17, 21

Would others call you an ambitious person? "Ambition" is
an interesting word. It comes from a Latin word that means to
"go around." It's movement around opportunities to reach a
goal.

The two men described in today's verses were ambitious for
their master. They made good investments. You need ambition
in order to be successful—to get ahead and make a mark in
this world. An ambitious person is someone who's on the
move, who's not standing still.

What direction are you moving in your marriage? Would
your partner say you're ambitious toward making your marriage stronger? In your personal life are you moving toward
God or the opposite way? Sometimes our ambition takes us
the wrong direction. Remember the apostle Paul? He very am-
bitiously persecuted the Christians. But God didn't put a
damper on his ambition; Paul was going the wrong way so
God changed his direction.

What about you? Are you making good investments for the
Lord? Do you see your faith and your walk with Him growing? Are you ambitious in your work, your family, and for the
kingdom of God? You may be a mover and a shaker. If so, God
can use you. He can direct you. He wants you to be ambitious
for Him and make an investment for Him. Think about this today: What's a new way you can be ambitious for the Lord? If
you want adventure in life, this is the way to get it.[1]

Enjoy One
Another's Bodies

*May your fountain be blessed,
and may you rejoice in the wife of your youth.*
PROVERBS 5:18

Doug Rosenau has some words of wisdom about sex. Consider his thoughts.

The Bible says you are to love your neighbor or your mate just as you love yourself. Fun sex depends on a husband and wife who have learned to love themselves. This means you take care of your health and exercise your body to keep it in shape. You should also enjoy and accept the body God gave you. Self-acceptance, self-esteem, and a good body image are healthy parts of sexiness and Christian self-love. Think of how difficult it is to sexually focus on your mate when you are embarrassed, inhibited, or self-conscious.

Psychological research has shown us that the people and things we are more familiar with, we tend to like more. People who live in the same apartment complex or go to church together seem to grow to like one another just by being in proximity with one another and sharing common things. As you get more comfortable with seeing your body and allowing it to be in your thoughts without negative criticism, you will start to like it more.

An important part of love is respecting and unconditionally accepting your mate. If you want to find and focus on flaws, you will put a damper on your partner's sexiness and the whole lovemaking process. First Corinthians tells us that true love protects, forgets, and doesn't keep a record of wrong (13:4-7).

You reap the benefit (or the destructiveness if you stay obsessive) of nurturing and helping your love revel in sexual appeal. Every time you affirm some particular aspect of masculinity or femininity that you admit and enjoy, you lovingly increase your mate's sex appeal. It's such a growth-producing process when you are unconditionally committed to accepting your own sexiness and affirming the sexiness of your partner. It creates an environment for a comfortable, safe, sexual greenhouse in which playfulness and risk-taking blossom. Unconditional love and acceptance and affirmation set the temperature for some fantastic sex.[2]

Justice

When justice is done, it brings joy
to the righteous but terror to evildoers.
PROVERBS 21:15

Is there justice in our world anymore? It's easy to think there isn't with some of the stuff that goes on today. Criminals caught in the act are released because of technicalities. Innocent people are sued and their lives ruined by those who lie on the witness stand. A wife or husband who works hard supporting his or her partner through medical school is dumped for someone else. In our nation's capital it seems the special interest groups with the most money end up with laws going their way.

In the Old West there was a different form of justice that emerged every now and then. Vigilantes engaged in frontier justice. When they caught a horse thief or cattle rustler, they found the nearest tree and hanged him on the spot. After all, who needed courts or judges when you had the thief with a branding iron in his hand!

We all want justice. Right should prevail, and wrong should be punished. But justice is easily hindered and sometimes destroyed by powerful and angry people. Politicians, lynch mobs, business owners, and even those in church have been known to prevent it. Even someone married can't keep it from happening in his or her own relationship. A marriage isn't just for the need fulfillment of one—that wouldn't be fair.

God wants justice to prevail, especially in our relationships. He wants us to be just and fair.

- To do what is right and just is more acceptable to the LORD than sacrifice (Proverbs 21:3).

- The violence of the wicked will drag them away, for they refuse to do what is right (Proverbs 21:7).

- By justice a king gives a country stability, but one who is greedy for bribes tears it down (Proverbs 29:4).

- Many seek an audience with a ruler, but it is from the LORD that man gets justice (Proverbs 29:26).

We honor God when we act in a just and fair way. Yes, it's tough to do sometimes, but it's possible. How could fairness be expressed more in your marriage?

The Sluggard

A lazy man sleeps soundly—and goes hungry.
PROVERBS 19:15 NLT

When you hear the word "sluggard" or "slothful," what image comes to mind? Maybe it's the same image I see—a slug. They don't seem to get anywhere, do much, or have purpose in life. The Hebrew word for this type of person is pretty much what I described—slow, hesitant, or sluggish. We would call him lazy and in low gear. Sometimes, unfortunately, one partner in a marriage behaves this way. This person seems to lack a Delco battery—or if he or she has one, it's dead. The person is not a self-starter. "Some men are so lazy, they won't even feed themselves!" (Proverbs 19:24, TLB). Maybe these people don't know what to do or they're low on fuel. You wonder if they can even take care of the basic necessities of life: "But you—all you do is sleep. When will you wake up?" (Proverbs 6:9 TLB). Lazy people rationalize and procrastinate: " 'Let me sleep a little longer!' Sure, just a little more!" (Proverbs 6:10 TLB).

This kind of person seems to just go downhill. He wants things but lacks the oomph to go after them. "The lazy man longs for many things but his hands refuse to work. He is greedy to get, while the godly love to give!" (Proverbs 21:25 TLB). And he's full of irrational fears. He thinks the worst of situations. "The lazy man is full of excuses. 'I can't go to work!' he says. 'If I go outside, I might meet a lion in the street and be killed!' " (Proverbs 22:13 TLB). He's his own worst enemy. "A lazy fellow has trouble all through life; the good man's path is easy!" (Proverbs 15:19 TLB). And he's got an inflated view of himself. He's a legend in his own mind. "He sticks to his bed like a door to its hinges! He is too tired even to lift his food from his dish to his mouth! Yet in his own opinion he is smarter than seven wise men" (Proverbs 26:14-16 TLB).

Not a pretty picture? No, it isn't. God has called us to a better way to live, and following its path will build your marriage.[3]

How Does God
Speak to You?

Then the LORD called Samuel. Samuel answered, "Here I am."
1 SAMUEL 3:4

Have you experienced a time when God spoke to you? If you're like most of us the answer is yes. But *how* did He speak to you? How did you know it was God? Have you ever discussed together as a couple how God has spoken to you individually? In what way has He spoken to you as a couple?

Questions! Questions! Questions! What about some answers? What does it mean when someone speaks to us? It's a way of directing or guiding our thoughts toward something. You're being led to think about something by someone else. As a married couple you influence the thoughts of one another. You do it by what you say or by your nonverbals—what you *don't* do or say or by written notes.

God can guide us through His Word, but He can also do it without our even being aware of it. We may not even know that it's happening or that it's God speaking. This happened to Samuel when he was a boy, and he needed the help of someone else to know it was God. C.S. Lewis talked about this idea:

> If your thoughts and passions were *directly present* to me, like my own, without any mark of externality or otherness, how should I distinguish them from mine?...You may reply, as a Christian, that God (and Satan) do, in fact, affect my consciousness in this direct way without signs of "externality." Yes, and the result is that most people remain ignorant of the existence of both.[4]

We want God's guidance for important decisions such as what job to take or what house to buy. But it's more than that. John Ortberg clarified the purpose of God speaking to us:

> God's purpose in guidance is not to get us to perform the right actions. His purpose is to help us become the right kind of people.[5]

I Don't Believe
in Prayer If...

The prayer of a righteous man is powerful and effective.
JAMES 5:16

I don't believe in prayer if
Prayer is *just* a magic charm.
But that's how some people pray. They pray
only so they'll be safe when they go on vacation, or
when someone they love goes on vacation.
only so their day will go smoothly.
only so their family will stay happy and healthy.
only so they will get the lucky breaks.
But I don't believe in that kind of prayer.

I don't believe in prayer if
Prayer is *just* a way to "place my order" with God.
But that's how some people pray. They pray
only because they'd like to have something they
   don't have.
only because they'd rather not have something they
   do have.
only because someone is bugging them
and they need to
have God straighten that person out.
only because they don't want to have to go through
   hard times.
But I don't believe in that kind of prayer.

I don't believe in prayer if
Prayer is *just* a tranquilizer.
But that's how some people pray. They pray
only because they feel so much better when they do.
only because they're more relaxed
and at peace with the world when they pray.
only because they're easier to be
around when they pray and they want
people to like being around them.
But I don't believe in that kind of prayer.

I don't believe in prayer if it's only a matter of what I
   can get from God.[6]

I Do Believe
in Prayer If...

The prayer of a righteous man is powerful and effective.
JAMES 5:16

I do believe in prayer if
Prayer is a conversation with someone I love.
And that's just how some people pray. They pray
because they want to show God how much they love
him (and spending time with him is a way
   to show him)....
because they want to let God know how they're
feeling and what they need him to do
for them and for others.
because they want to say thank you to God.
because they want to say, "I'm sorry."

I do believe in prayer if
Prayer is a window that lets me see into God's heart....
And that's just how some people pray. They pray
so they can listen to God.
so they can know what he wants them to do.

I do believe in prayer if prayer is a matter of what
   I can give to God—
my love, my admiration, my trust.
The chance of learning about myself,
of facing up to what I am.

Sometimes, Lord, often—
I don't know what to say to you.
But I still come, in quiet
for the comfort of two friends
sitting in silence.
And it's then, Lord, that I learn most from you.
When my mind slows down,
and my heart stops racing.
When I let go and wait in the quiet,
realizing that all the things I was going to ask for
you know already.
Then, Lord, without words,
in the stillness
you are there...
And I love you.
Lord, teach me to pray.[7]

Faithfulness—
God's Commandment

You shall not commit adultery.
EXODUS 20:14

This commandment is laughed at even by many Christians. They don't take it seriously—but God does. Otherwise it wouldn't be mentioned so much in His Word.

Adultery violates the sacredness of marriage, which is something God created. It breaks the marriage covenant. It's also a sin against one's own body. "Flee from sexual immorality. All other sins a man commits are outside his body, but he who sins sexually sins against his own body" (1 Corinthians 6:18).

A Christian's body is a member of Christ: "Do you not know that your bodies are members of Christ himself? Shall I then take the members of Christ and unite them with a prostitute? Never! Do you not know that he who unites himself with a prostitute is one with her in body? For it is said, 'The two shall become one flesh.' But he who unites himself with the Lord is one with him in spirit" (1 Corinthians 6:15-17).

Adultery is a sin against Christ himself, and it's definitely a sin against God. But, like other sins, it is forgivable. Repentance, which means "to change and commit, to never repeat the offense," makes it so. What I recommend next will not be popular. If someone has committed adultery, it's a sin that needs to be confessed to God, to his or her spouse, and to the church. And if the person who sinned is in any position of service in the church, he or she should resign and go through a time of healing and restoration until eligible to serve once again. Is this harsh? Not really because it's necessary for healing. Marriage *can survive* this violation, and can even grow and become stronger than ever.

There's just one more gentle nudge. Jesus said something else that cuts to the heart of the matter:

> You have heard that it was said, "Do not commit adultery." But I tell you that anyone who looks at a woman lustfully has already committed adultery with her in his heart (Matthew 5:27,28).

How's your heart and your thought life?

The First Team

Then God said, "Let us make man in our image, in our likeness."
GENESIS 1:26

We hear much today about teams. When the word is mentioned, naturally we think of sports (at least some do!). There are hockey teams, football teams, baseball teams, basketball teams, soccer teams—and they all have one thing in common. They all rely on teamwork to be successful.

The human race started out as a team. The first one had two members or two players—Adam and Eve. And they were *both* created in God's image. They had a calling and it was simple: to exercise dominion over everything alive on earth. They didn't get caught up in power struggles or who was in charge. They worked together.

As you look at the Scripture, you see the wife referred to as "help meet." This is not a term that we use today. In fact, it's often misunderstood. Unfortunately, a helper is someone we tend to think of as an assistant, one who has a lower status. That's *not* the meaning in the original language.

Help meet comes from two Hebrew words: *ezer* and *neged*. *Ezer* is the word for "help" or "helper," and it's used again and again in the Old Testament. God is referred to as a helper in Psalm 121:1-7. *Neged* means "corresponding to" or "fit for." A woman fits the man in a complementary manner. When we combine the words what do we have? A suitable partner for Adam. Eve wasn't a subordinate, she was a complement—an equal.

In marriage today, a husband and wife bring unique strengths and attributes to the team. In baseball a pitcher couldn't function without a catcher, and a catcher wouldn't be doing much without a pitcher. By themselves, they're incomplete and limited. Put them together and watch out.

So how's your teamwork?[8]

Do you
Implode or Build?

Let no unwholesome word proceed from your mouth,
but only such a word as is good for edification according to
the need of the moment, so that it will give grace to those who hear.
EPHESIANS 4:29 NASB

Do you want to know how to talk to each other? Tony and Lois Evans offer this advice:

> A few years ago, a historic building in downtown Dallas was imploded after all efforts to salvage it had failed. The implosion occurred early on a Sunday morning and was televised locally. It was an impressive sight watching this multistory building quiver and then collapse in a matter of seconds. All it took was for the workmen to weaken some key support beams and plant some charges in strategic places.
>
> In the same way, it's possible to "implode" a mate's spirit with a few well-chosen words spoken in anger or from a spirit of revenge. "Unwholesome" words can eat away a person's spirit and self-worth. The word "unwholesome" here means "rotten."
>
> Paul was saying that this kind of speech belongs in the garbage can with yesterday's leftovers.
>
> Another example of unwholesome words are the cuts and put-downs that are so popular today. A lot of people do this stuff in a joking way. But if you have ever been on the receiving end of one of these barbs, you know they're not always funny. Instead of tearing down your mate with your words, make it your commitment to build him or her up. We build people up when we speak appropriate, grace-producing words. Even when correction or rebuke is called for, we need to frame our words in a way that leaves the *person* standing while still handling the problem.
>
> The difference between the right word and the wrong word is the difference between lightning and a lightning bug—in other words, all the difference in the world! If you're wiring someone up for a verbal implosion today, better defuse those explosives![9]

A Prayer for
Your Marriage

There is a time for everything,
and a season for every activity under heaven.
ECCLESIASTES 3:1

Praying from Ecclesiastes 3:1-12.

Lord of time and eternity,

How much we need You in our marriage. Our lives bring so many changes day by day—and we keep changing too.

Help our precious love endure through every season of marriage. In fact, by Your redeeming love, work each season together for a good that's so good only You can imagine it (Romans 8:28, Ephesians 1:11).

In a time to be born, remind us that You make all things new—including us. You are the Lord of babies and beginnings (Ecclesiastes 3:2).

In a time to die, comfort us in our grief. Help us and those we love to reach in faith for eternity, our real home (verses 2,11).

In a time to plant, give us seeds of hope. Help us water our relationship with encouragement and perseverance and wait with joy for the good results (verse 2).

In a time to uproot, give us determination to pull up those weeds that are hindering our marriage—old habits, wrong attitudes, false assumptions (verse 2).

In a time to search—for truth or a solution to a nagging problem—give us perseverance (verse 6).

In a time to be silent, help us to listen with our whole beings and in a time to speak, grant us the wisdom to choose our words carefully and sensitively (verse 7).

In a time to love, help us to give ourselves to each other with glad abandon (verse 8).

Lord, no matter what kind of season or day we're having, help us to remember that all Your plans for us are good (Jeremiah 29:11).

Amen.[10]

Arguing by
God's Rules

Let your speech always be with grace, as though seasoned with salt,
so that you will know how you should respond to each person.
COLOSSIANS 4:6 NASB

Tony and Lois Evans offer some advice on how to argue:

> Here's a resolution for you to make today as a couple: Resolve that you won't waste your disagreements! What we mean by that is, agree together that you won't allow your arguments to simply deteriorate into hurtful words or accusations or name-calling. Promise each other that you won't argue unless each side presents at least one possible solution to the problem.
>
> You may be thinking, "That's a lot of work. I'd just rather get what I have to say off my chest." It may be a lot of work to bend over backward in an attempt to communicate fairly and avoid hurting your spouse. But one thing is certain. When you bend over backward, you never have to worry about falling on your face. Yes, it takes work to disagree agreeably with each other. But consider the possible alternatives: screaming and hollering, angry words and thoughts, put-downs, or frosty silences. These things don't have to happen if you follow God's rules for your speech, rules such as "Let no unwholesome word proceed from your mouth" and "Let all bitterness and wrath and anger...be put away from you" (Ephesians 4:29,31 NASB).
>
> Instead, the Bible advises us to season our words with salt. Salt is a preservative that keeps rottenness from setting in. If you'll salt down your words before you say them, you'll preserve your relationship and avoid the kind of words that can spoil a love relationship. Besides, rotten words grieve the Holy Spirit (see Ephesians 4:30), and a grieved Holy Spirit is like corrosion on a battery's terminals. When your battery gets corroded, you lose access to the power. The Holy Spirit is the power of the Christian life.
>
> Maybe you didn't know you could use God's rules for healthy communication even when you're disagreeing with one another. But the fact is, that's when you need God's rules the most![11]

The Power
Source

Yet I will rejoice in the LORD, I will be joyful in God my Savior.
The Sovereign LORD is my strength; he makes my feet
like the feet of a deer, he enables me to go on the heights.
HABAKKUK 3:18,19

You get in your car, put the key in the ignition, turn it, and... nothing. The battery is dead. There is not an ounce of electricity left to turn the engine over. You're not going anywhere. Some mornings you may feel like that battery—drained and dead. The alarm goes off and you're supposed to roll out of bed, but you never make it. You don't have what it takes. You're a depleted, disengaged, dead battery.

Why do batteries die? Sometimes they've simply lived out their life expectancy. They've given all they were meant to, and now there's nothing left in them capable of being recharged. Others die because people left the car lights or power on, draining the batteries of their strength.

We're a lot like a car battery. We keep running and running without stopping to rest and recharge. All too soon we can't function. We've run out of strength. Sometimes it's our marriage relationship that feels like a drained battery. We've taken from it, but we haven't kept it charged.

If you want strength, go to the power source—your Lord God. The phrase "I will rejoice in the Lord" really means "to leap for joy and spin around in exultation." Not too many of us do this literally, but perhaps it wouldn't be a bad idea.

Do you know the difference between the words "joy" and "happiness" as they're used here? The latter is based on having no problems or concerns. Joy means having faith in God, no matter what happens. When you trust in God rather than in your circumstances, you discover that God will give you the strength you need for yourself and for your marriage. And this strength will keep you moving ahead. Go to your power source—go to God.

Admit It

A man who refuses to admit his mistakes can never be successful.
But if he confesses and forsakes them, he gets another chance.
PROVERBS 28:13 TLB

Blame. We point our fingers at other people to get the focus off ourselves. And there's a lot to blame out there. Look at the people we have to deal with. Just look at the crazy drivers on the road. No wonder we lose our tempers. Blame is not a new response. It started in the garden.

> And he said, "Who told you that you were naked? Have you eaten from the tree that I commanded you not to eat from?" The man said, "The woman you put here with me—she gave me some fruit from the tree, and I ate it." Then the LORD God said to the woman, "What is this you have done?" The woman said, "The serpent deceived me, and I ate" (Genesis 3:11-13).

We blame our partners, circumstances, and even God. And most of the blaming statements aren't too original. Read through this list and note which ones you may have used.

1. Well, I didn't start this. It wasn't my fault. It's what you said.
2. What I did could have been worse. Besides, you provoked me.
3. If you hadn't said what you did, there wouldn't have been any problem.
4. Everybody at work was doing it, so I couldn't be the odd one.
5. I only spoke to you the way you spoke to me.
6. No one let me know that I was supposed to be there. You just think you did.

Blame neither builds relationships nor resolves differences. It pushes couples apart and sets up endless arguments. There is a better way to handle a mistake. Try saying,

1. You're right.
2. I am responsible.
3. I'm sorry.
4. I will be different the next time.

Love Is. . .

1 CORINTHIANS 13
Translation by Ronald Knox

I may speak with every tongue that men and angels use; yet, if I lack charity, I am no better than echoing bronze, or the clash of cymbals. I may have powers of prophecy, no secret hidden from me, no knowledge too deep for me; I may have utter faith, so that I can move mountains; yet if I lack charity, I count for nothing.

I may give away all that I have, to feed the poor; I may give myself up to be burnt at the stake; if I lack charity, it goes for nothing. Charity is patient, is kind; charity feels no envy; charity is never perverse or proud, never insolent; does not claim its right, cannot be provoked, does not brood over an injury; takes no pleasure in wrong-doing, but rejoices at the victory of truth; sustains, believes, hopes, endures, to the last....

Just so, when I was a child, I talked like a child, I had the intelligence, the thoughts of a child; since I became a man, I have outgrown childish ways. At present, we are looking at a confused reflection in a mirror; then, we shall see face to face; now I have only glimpses of knowledge; then, I shall recognize God as he has recognized me. Meanwhile, faith, hope and charity persist, all three; but the greatest of them all is charity.[12]

Imitate Me

Follow my example, as I follow the example of Christ.
1 CORINTHIANS 11:1

How would you respond if your spouse came up to you and said, "From this point on I want you to imitate me." After the laughter subsides, your comments could range from "Right!" to "Sure, in your dreams" to "How do you spell Fat Chance?" to "In your eating habits or what?"

After you get rid of all your reactionary responses, think about this request again. It's actually a command of Scripture. It's not simply a children's game of follow-the-leader, it's a statement to "do as I do." Paul told his readers this is what they are to do, but he went further. And he could get away with saying this because he was pointing people to Jesus. That's who we are to really imitate.

Paul was discipling others. We are called to disciple others as well. A disciple teaches others. Paul told people to follow him because he was following Jesus. "You then, my son, be strong in the grace that is in Christ Jesus. And the things you have heard me say in the presence of many witnesses entrust to reliable men who will also be qualified to teach others" (2 Timothy 2:1,2).

Can each of you stand before one another and say, "Honey, I want you to follow me because I am following Jesus"? It could be much easier to stand before your Sunday school class and make that statement. Your class doesn't know you the way your spouse does. He or she knows when you're living for Jesus and when you're not. But if this is what we're supposed to be doing, let's get with the program and live our lives in such a way that our spouses would say, "Yes, I want to learn from you what you've learned about Jesus." Wouldn't that be a blessing![13]

Joyful Couple

I have told you this so that my joy may be in you
and that your joy may be complete.
JOHN 15:11

Do you worship a joyful God? Think about it for a minute. Ask each other: "When you think of God, do you see Him as full of joy?" If we are to be full of joy, and we're created in the image of God, it follows that the God we worship is a joyful God.

How's the level of joy in your life? How's the level of joy in your marriage? God wants you as a couple to experience joy, to be joyful. Do you know who can really show us what joy is all about? A child. Children can be full of joy. Read this:

> Because children have abound [in] vitality, because they are in spirit fierce and free, therefore they want things repeated and unchanged. They always say, "Do it again"; and the grown-up person does it again until he is nearly dead. *For grown-up people are not strong enough to exult in monotony.* But perhaps God is strong enough to exult in monotony. It is possible that God says every morning, "Do it again" to the sun; and every evening, "Do it again" to the moon. It may not be automatic necessity that makes all daisies alike; it may be that God makes every daisy separately, but has never gotten tired of making them. It may be that He has the eternal appetite of infancy; *for we have sinned and grown old, and our Father is younger than we.*[14]

Isn't that last phrase different? Remember what God saw after each day of creation? "It was good." Can you imagine Him saying that in a monotone? It would be a shout of joy! He doesn't get bored with doing things over and over and over again. We lose the joy of being children, but God doesn't. And He doesn't want us to, either.

Our joy needs to reflect that Jesus is in our lives and our marriages. How could your life and marriage be more joyful?

Mine or Ours?

If you cling to your life, you will lose it;
but if you give it up for me, you will find it.
MATTHEW 10:39 NLT

What was one of the first words you learned as a child? If you're like the rest of us, it was "mine." Children become very possessive over what they think is theirs. And it's not just children. Have you ever seen possessive dogs? Their bones or toys are guarded with growls if there's any possibility that someone might take them. Dogs don't say "mine" verbally, but their actions shout it.

It's not easy to eliminate "mine" from our thoughts or vocabulary. We carry it with us into our marriages, even though the key word is now supposed to be "we."

Have you had difficulty translating the word "mine" to "ours" or "we"? Think about it for a minute. What if you're engrossed in a TV show and your spouse says, "I need your help"? What if your spouse gets sick the day you planned to go on a special outing? What if your spouse has other suggestions for the small stash of money you've been saving—or the IRS refund? There are some other "good" ways to use the word "mine" such as: "What about me? When do I ever get some time to myself?" "Hey, that belongs to me, and I don't want others using it. I don't want it worn out." "You get your way most of the time. I'd like to be happy, too." "Look at all I do for you. It's a two-way street you know." "Who took the last piece of pie? Everyone knows the last one always belongs to me!"

God's Word talks about clinging. When we say "mine," in a sense we're holding on, grabbing, or clinging. Jesus said there's a better way in our relationship with Him. And it's the best way in our relationship with one another as well.[15]

It's simple. It's called giving.

What's in
Your Sacks?

And my God will meet all your needs according
to his glorious riches in Christ Jesus.
PHILIPPIANS 4:19

There is an old legend about three men and their sacks. Each man had two sacks, one tied in front of his neck and the other tied around his back. When the first man was asked, "Hey, what's in the sacks?" he said, "Well, in the sack on my back are all the good things my friends and family have done. That way they're out of sight and hidden from view. In the front sack are all the bad things that have happened to me. Every now and then, I stop, open the sack, take the things out, examine them, and think about them."

Because he stopped so much to concentrate on all the bad stuff, he really didn't make much progress in life.

The second man was asked, "What have you got in those two sacks?" He replied, "In the front sack are all the good things I've done. I like them; I like to see them. So quite often I take them out to show them off to everyone around me. The sack in the back? I keep all my mistakes in there and carry them with me all the time. Sure, they're heavy. It's true that they slow me down. But you know, for some reason I can't put them down."

When the third man was asked about his two sacks, his answer was, "The sack in front is great. In this one I keep all the positive thoughts I have about people, all the blessings I've experienced, and all the great things other people have done for me.

"The sack on my back is empty. There's nothing in it. I cut a big hole in the bottom of it. So I can put all the bad things in there that I think about myself or hear about others. They go in one end and out the other so I'm not carrying around any extra weight at all."

What are you carrying around in your sacks? What is your spouse carrying? Which sack is full, the one of blessings or the one in back? How does this affect your marriage?[16]

Walls

"For this reason a man will leave his father and mother
and be united to his wife, and the two will become one flesh."
So they are no longer two, but one.
MARK 10:7-9

Wall *n.* 1. An upright structure serving to enclose, to divide. 2. A structure built as a defense. 3. Something virtually impenetrable.

Wall *vt.* 1. To enclose, surround, or fortify with or as if with a wall. 2. To divide or separate with or as if with a wall. 3. To enclose within a wall. 4. To block or close with or as if with a wall.

We live in a world of walls. Walls are everywhere. Brick walls, stone walls, wood walls. Graffiti-covered inner-city walls. Gated walls surrounding luxury developments.

Sterile prison walls, the granite walls of a high-rise building. High walls, low walls, wide walls. Walls with curls of barbed wire. Broken-down walls, impenetrable walls. Emotional walls. Walls of misunderstanding. Walls of routine. Walls of difference and indifference. Backs to the wall. Pushed to the wall. Up the wall. Off the wall.

A wall is simply an upright structure that encloses, protects, divides, or separates. People build walls for defense. Some walls keep people in, other walls keep people out.

Some walls are visible, many are not.

When walls go up in marriage, someone is hurting. Walls are defensive structures. Someone feels injured. Someone feels the pain of neglect. Someone can no longer bear to feel the sting of insult. Emotional wounds cut far more deeply than physical blows. So walls go up for defense.

Jesus Christ came to destroy the barrier that separates people. By His death and resurrection He has given us power to eliminate the walls we build between us, which are the fruit of living by our flesh. Any walls between us now are of our own making. The walls we construct in our marriages are built in the flesh, not the Spirit.

No matter how high or seemingly impenetrable the walls between us are, they are ready to come tumbling down like Jericho's walls, if we will use the Lord's power.[17]

Make the World a Better Place

And whatever you do, whether in word or deed, do it all in the name of the Lord Jesus, giving thanks to God the Father through him.
Colossians 3:17

How will you leave this world? A better place or the opposite?

- The world is a better place because Michelangelo didn't say, "I don't do ceilings."
- The world is a better place because Martin Luther didn't say, "I don't do doors."
- The world is a better place because Noah didn't say, "I don't do arks."
- The world is a better place because Jeremiah didn't say, "I don't do weeping."
- The world is a better place because Peter didn't say, "I don't do Gentiles."
- The world is a better place because Paul didn't say, "I don't do letters."
- The world is a better place because Mary didn't say, "I don't do virgin births."

What will be your legacy as a couple? What other couple are you mentoring? Will you discover and answer God's calling privately, publicly, individually, and as a couple?

Dwight L. Moody, the Billy Graham of the nineteenth century, one day heard these challenging words that marked the beginning of a new era in his life: "The world has yet to see what God will do, with and for, and through, and in, and by, the man who is fully and wholly consecrated in Him."

> He said "a man," thought Moody. He did not say a great man, nor a learned man, nor a rich man, nor a wise man, nor an eloquent man, nor a "smart" man, but simply "a man." I am a man, and it lies with the man himself whether he will, or will not, make that entire full consecration. I will try my utmost to be that man.[18]

Will you try your utmost to be that person, or better yet, that couple?

The world is a better place because Jesus didn't say, "I don't do crosses."[19]

God's Word for Your Marriage

Submit to one another out of reverence for Christ.
EPHESIANS 5:21

Guess what? You and your spouse are not 100-percent compatible. According to Webster's, "compatible" means "capable of existing together in harmony;" "designed to work with another...without modification." You may be becoming more compatible, but when first married the differences are quite apparent. That's all right. They enhance a marriage relationship. These differences can be resolved if you learn to listen, lighten up, and not withdraw or pull the silent treatment.

You will have conflicts. That's a given. And that's not the problem. Attacks and defensiveness win a war, but they are not good battle strategies for marriage. Consider your partner's point of view and learn to respond with, "That's a different way to look at this" or "Let me think about that for a minute." Here are some passages to consider from the Word of God. How could each one be applied to your marriage relationship?

> Correct, rebuke and encourage—with great patience and careful instruction (2 Timothy 4:2).

> Speaking the truth in love....Therefore, putting away lying, "Let each one of you speak truth with his neighbor."...Do not let the sun go down on your wrath (Ephesians 4:15,25,26 NKJV).

> ...Living as becomes you with complete lowliness of mind (humility) and meekness (unselfishness, gentleness, mildness), with patience, bearing with one another and making allowances because you love one another (Ephesians 4:2 AMP).

> Brothers, if someone is caught in a sin, you who are spiritual should restore him gently (Galatians 6:1).

> Exhort one another daily...lest any of you be hardened through the deceitfulness of sin (Hebrews 3:13 NKJV).

> Make straight paths for your feet, so that what is lame may not be dislocated, but rather healed....[Look] diligently lest anyone fall short of the grace of God; lest any root of bitterness springing up cause trouble, and by this many become defiled (Hebrews 12:13,15 NKJV).

Spend some time considering and talking about how you can apply these to your marriage.

Not Abandoned

For to us a child is born, to us a son is given,
and the government will be on his shoulders.
ISAIAH 9:6

A Christmas message from Steve Brown in his book *Jumping Hurdles, Hitting Glitches and Overcoming Setbacks:*

> While I was driving home the other day, I saw the ugliest car I have ever seen. This car wasn't just ugly—it was ugly on top of ugly. It had a large gash on its side; one of the doors was held together with baling wire; and several other body parts were almost completely rusted out. The car's muffler was so loose that with every bump, it hit the street, sending sparks in every direction. I couldn't tell the original color of the car. The rust had eaten away much of the paint, and so much of the car had been painted over with so many different colors that any one of them (or none of them) could have been the first coat. The most interesting thing about the car was the bumper sticker: "THIS IS NOT AN ABANDONED CAR."
>
> We live in a fallen world, and sometimes it looks as ugly as that car. Almost everywhere you turn, you can see tragedy and heartache.
>
> A long time ago, in a manger, a baby was born. He was a sign to us. His presence read, "THIS IS NOT AN ABANDONED WORLD."
>
> During every Christmas season, there's a break in the bleakness; a bit of beauty in the middle of the ugliness shines through. People will laugh and make merry. Most won't understand why they laugh. Many of them will make merry because that is what one is supposed to do during the holiday season. But there are some who will pause and remember, "For unto us a child is born."
>
> We have not been abandoned. Someday the Owner will return, then all the ugliness will be remedied. There won't be any more pain, and all the tears will be dried.[20]

Jesus' Birth

Jesus was born in Bethlehem in Judea.
MATTHEW 2:1

Christmas each year weaves its magic spell upon our hearts. Carols float on the air, and there is a surge of love and kindliness not felt at any other time of the year. Creches appear, reminding us of the miracle in the manger. In that feeding trough in lowly Bethlehem, a cry from that infant's throat broke the centuries of silence. For the first time God's voice could be heard coming from human vocal cords. C.S. Lewis called that event—the coming of Christ at Christmas—"the greatest rescue mission of history."

During each Christmas season the words of Micah resonate throughout the world. For he was inspired to give the prophecy that named the very birthplace of the Messiah: "But you, Bethlehem Ephrathah, though you are small among the clans of Judah, out of you will come for me one who will be ruler over Israel, whose origins are from of old, from ancient times" (5:2).

Micah was telling those who were proud and powerful and rich and self-righteous that God's great ruler would not come from their stately and royal environs. He would come forth from the nondescript hamlet of Bethlehem. When over 700 years later the wise men came searching for Him, the scribes had to brush off the dust from the book of Micah to direct them to the very location where he would be born.

The One who would come is One "whose origins are from of old, from ancient times." This literally means "from days of eternity." It speaks of the eternal existence of Christ. His providence and preeminence are also prophesied as one who "will stand and shepherd his flock...then his greatness will reach to the ends of the earth. And he will be their peace" (Micah 5:4,5). What beautiful and precious promises are ours from this plowman who became God's mighty penman.[21]

God's Awesome Provision

She gave birth to her firstborn, a son.
She wrapped him in cloths and placed him in a manger,
because there was no room for them in the inn.
LUKE 2:7

Here is a prayer for you as a couple to pray aloud today.

O God, our Father, we remember...how the eternal Word became flesh and dwelt among us.

We thank you that Jesus took our human body upon him, so that we can never again dare to despise or neglect or misuse the body, since you made it your dwelling-place.

We thank you that Jesus did a day's work like any working man, that he knew the problem of living together in a family, that he knew the frustration and irritation of serving the public, that he had to earn a living, and to face all the wearing routine of everyday work and life and living, and so clothed each common task with glory.

We thank you that he shared in all happy social occasions, that he was at home at weddings and at dinners and at festivals in the homes of simple ordinary people like ourselves. Grant that we may ever remember that in his unseen risen presence he is a guest in every home.

We thank you that he too had to bear unfair criticism, prejudiced opposition, malicious and deliberate misunderstanding.

We thank you that whatever happens to us, he has been there before, and that, because he himself has gone through things, he is able to help those who are going through them.

Help us never to forget that he knows life because he lived life and that he is with us at all times to enable us to live victoriously.

This we ask for your love's sake. Amen.[22]

Love Is a Choice

*Love the Lord your God with all your heart and
with all your soul and with all your mind and with all your strength.
The second is this: "Love your neighbor as yourself."
There is no commandment greater than these.*
MARK 12:30,31

Love is a choice. Yes, there may be feelings at times, but they come and go. It is a choice—especially *agape* love. This word is used in one form or another over 200 times in Scripture. It's the type of love that will make your marriage come alive. You can't do it on your own, though. It's difficult. You need God infusing you with this love and the strength to be consistent with it. If you want to know what it's like, look at Jesus. There are three ways that describe how Jesus loves us and how we're to love others.

He loves us unconditionally. He loves you with no conditions, no restrictions. No matter how wild you are, how bad you are, how mad you are, how vile you are, He loves you. Remember this: How you behave doesn't earn you any more of God's love. The man who murdered others? Jesus loves him as much as He loves you and me. That's unconditional love. How are you loving your partner?

He loves us willfully. Do you understand what this means? He loves you because He *wants* to love you. He wasn't forced to go to the cross for you, He chose to. He chose to touch lepers, He chose to heal the sick, He chose to die. How do we love others? By choosing to. And if that's difficult, as it will be sometimes, pray for a change of heart and attitude. It can happen.

He loves us sacrificially. Sacrificial love gives all expecting nothing in return. It's a costly love. It's not an easy love. It takes something from us. It takes us out of the comfort zone.

How could you love your spouse sacrificially today? When you've decided, go ahead and do it. In doing so, you become a bit more like Jesus.[23]

You're on a Pilgrimage

Let each of you esteem and look upon and be concerned for not
[merely] his own interests, but also each for the interests of others.
PHILIPPIANS 2:4 AMP

How's your pilgrimage going? You probably didn't realize it, but when you're a Christian and you're married, you're on a very special pilgrimage. You know what it is? It's learning to be a more mature Christian within a marriage relationship. And it's a challenge. In fact, living the Christian life toward your partner (who knows almost *everything* about you) is more difficult than responding toward others.

What's the key element of this pilgrimage? It's learning to *better serve one another*. That's what the Christian life is about. Serving others is our calling. And when you're married, who else is the main focus of serving others than one another?

So how are you doing on this journey of being a Christian in your marriage? Where are you at in your individual spiritual life? You both may be at the same place spiritually or you may be at different places. It's all right to be at a different level if you're willing to accept diversity in the expression of your faith. (If you're not, it may create some tension in your marriage.)

Do you ever talk about where you are in your personal relationship with God? Have you ever shared what you don't understand about Him? Knowing where each of you are, even if it's miles apart, isn't a cause for tension in a marriage. It can draw you closer together since you have a new level of understanding. In fact, you have to know where you are spiritually and what you believe in order to grow. It can help you minister better to one another as well.

Why not spend a few moments sharing your spiritual journey with one another? Enjoy this process.

The End of
Your Rope

When all kinds of trials and temptations crowd into your lives,
my brothers, don't resent them as intruders,
but welcome them as friends! Realize that they come
to test your faith and to produce in you the quality of endurance.
JAMES 1:2,3 PHILLIPS

I'm at the end of my rope." Have you ever said that? If you did, what did you really mean? Think about it. What does this phrase really mean? For some people it's a sign of exasperation. It may be the feeling that they have nothing more to give—whether it's their jobs, all the activities at home, or even to their marriages. Some people become quite desperate when they hit this low point in life.

Have you ever heard of the English poet William Cowper? At one point in his life he was at the end of his rope—literally. He tried to end it all by drinking poison. It didn't work; God led someone to find him. His stomach was pumped and he lived. But he still felt the same way. He hired a coach to take him to the Thames River where he intended to drown himself. But as he attempted to do so the driver grabbed him, got him back in the coach and drove him home. He failed again. He found a knife and as he attempted to fall on it, the blade broke. Can you believe it! So he got a rope, rigged it over a beam in the basement, put his neck in it and dropped. He was now at the end of his rope. Fortunately, someone found him before he strangled and took him down.

In desperation he turned to the Bible, turned to the book of Romans, and found a passage that led him to faith in Jesus Christ. When you're at the end of your rope, remember what James said in today's verses. William Cowper found a better way...so can you.

A Look...

Gray hair is a crown of splendor; it is attained by a righteous life.
PROVERBS 16:31

On the Eve of Their Golden Wedding Day
John C. Bonser

"Our Golden Wedding Day draws near,"
   the husband said.
The elderly woman, smiling, raised her head,
"Will you write me a poem as you used to do?
That's the gift I'd like most from you!"

The old man, agreeing, limped from the room,
Went out on the porch in the twilight's gloom,
Leaned on the railing and reminisced:
Often we sat here, shared hopes, and kissed.

"Dear Lord, how the years have hurried by—
Those memories of youth make an old man sigh!
Now we grow weary and bent and gray,
What clever words can I possibly say

"To show that I love her just as much
As I did when her cheeks were soft to my touch,
When her eyes were bright and her lips were warm,
And we happily walked with her hand on my arm!"

So the husband stood while the evening breeze
Echoed his sigh through the nearby trees
Till the joys they had shared in days long past
Merged into thoughts he could voice at last,

...into the Future

And he went inside and got paper and pen;
Sat down at the kitchen table and then
Carefully wrote what his wife had desired:
A gift as "golden" as a love inspired.

Sweetheart, dear wife, my closest friend,
With you my days begin and end.
Though time has stolen strength and youth,
It cannot change this shining truth:

Our love has lasted all these years
While hardships came and sorrow's tears.
We've met each test and gotten by,
And I will love you till I die!

We are not rich in worldly wealth
But we own nothing gained by stealth,
And you remain my greatest treasure,
My source of pride and quiet pleasure.

I wish you all the happiness
With which two loving hearts are blessed;
You were, and are, my choice for life,
My girl, my lady, my sweet wife!
The poem finished, the husband arose,
Went into the room where his good wife dozed
And tenderly kissing her nodding head,
"Wake up, 'sleeping beauty,' and come to bed!"[24]

What Makes
a Marriage Last?

Love never fails [never fades out].
1 CORINTHIANS 13:8 AMP

A couple shares:

> We've been married 47 years. Our most positive experience has been that we have had a mutual love, devotion, and commitment to each other, and to Jesus Christ, as well as for our four children and nine grandchildren.
>
> The three things I have done that have helped our marriage have been being completely devoted to my husband, eagerly and joyfully assuming the responsibilities of a homemaker, and I have always tried to keep myself attractive at all times so my husband would be proud of me.
>
> For me [the husband], I have never given her cause to worry about my whereabouts or my association with the opposite sex. I worked diligently to be a good provider, but not at the expense of neglecting time with my family. I've also continually expressed my devotion and loyalty to my wife, our children, and our parents as being second only to my Lord and God. My career and church responsibilities followed after them, but I have [since my conversion two years after we were married] been a faithful spiritual leader in our home.
>
> Our greatest adjustments were [in the area of] financial responsibility. In the earlier years of our marriage we did not always agree upon major expenditures and investments. However, over the years confidence was established that the husband had the responsibility, and most of the time profit was realized.

A couple married for 58 years shared:

> If we had any advice to give to couples, it would be just be true to each other. Love each other. I remember one thing I told my wife, "If I did anything wrong, and you want to correct me, don't tell anybody else. Tell me first." And I think she's always done that. Again, we're not perfect. I'm not trying to play it up.

What will you say to others when you've been married a long time?

NOTES

Pages 1–30

1. Patrick Morley, *Two-Part Harmony* (Nashville: Thomas Nelson, 1995), pp. 4-5, adapted. (Republished by Zondervan as *Devotions for Couples*. Used by permission of Zondervan Publishing House.)
2. Ibid., pp. 98-99.
3. Dennis and Barbara Rainey, *Moments Together for Couples* (Ventura, CA: Regal Books, 1995), March 21, adapted. Used by permission.
4. Ibid.
5. Hannah Hurnard, *Kingdom of Love* (Wheaton, IL: Tyndale House Publishers, Inc., 1975), preface.
6. Ibid.
7. See Proverbs 24:14.
8. Rainey and Rainey, *Moments Together*, September 13, adapted.
9. Les and Leslie Parrott, *Becoming Soul Mates* (Grand Rapids, MI: Zondervan, 1995), p. 144, adapted. Used by permission.
10. Rainey and Rainey, *Moments Together,* September 11, adapted.
11. Ibid., March 16, adapted.
12. Charles Swindoll, *Hope Again* (Dallas: Word, 1996), p. 71, adapted. Used by permission. All rights reserved.
13. William Barclay, *A Barclay Prayer Book* (London: SCM Press Ltd., 1963), pp. 8-9.
14. Tom Marshall, *Right Relationships* (Kent, England: Sovereign World, 1992), pp. 43-46, adapted.
15. Ibid., pp. 47-50, adapted.
16. Rainey and Rainey, *Moments Together*, September 30, adapted.
17. Bill and Pam Farrel, *Love to Love You* (Eugene, OR: Harvest House, 1997), pp. 123, 126, 129, 131. Used by permission.
18. Rainey and Rainey, *Moments Together*, January 31, adapted.
19. Cited in Ken Gire, *Reflections on the Word* (Colorado Springs: Chariot Victor, 1998), pp. 132-33. Used by permission of Cook Communications Ministries. May not be further reproduced. All rights reserved. Poem originally in *Prayers from the Heart*.
20. Jeanette C. Laves and Robert H. Laves. *'Til Death Do Us Part* (Harrington, NY: Park Press, 1986), p. 179, adapted.
21. Bernard I. Morstein, *Paths to Marriage* (San Mateo, CA: Sage Publications, 1986), p. 110, original source unknown.
22. Rainey and Rainey, *Moments Together,* December 13.
23. Warren Wiersbe, *Be Hopeful* (Wheaton, IL: SP Publications, Victor Books, 1982), p. 57. Used by permission of Cook Communications Ministries. All rights reserved; see also Swindoll, *Hope Again*, pp. 73-75, adapted.
24. Rainey and Rainey, *Moments Together,* May 9, adapted.
25. Morley, *Two-Part Harmony*, pp. 38-39, adapted.
26. Swindoll, *Hope Again*, pp. 119-27, adapted.
27. Gordon MacDonald, *Restoring Your Spiritual Passion* (Nashville: Thomas Nelson, 1986), pp. 96-104, adapted.
28. Rainey and Rainey, *Moments Together,* January 15, adapted.
29. Ibid., March 2.

Pages 31–57

1. Cliff and Joyce Penner, *Men and Sex* (Nashville: Thomas Nelson, 1997), selections from pp. 1-50.
2. Larry Crabb, *Men and Women* (Grand Rapids, MI: Zondervan, 1991), pp. 299, 211, 212. Used by permission.
3. David and Heather Kopp, *Unquenchable Love* (Eugene, OR: Harvest House, 1999), pp. 172-73, adapted. Used by permission.

NOTES

4. Fawn Parish, *Honor—What Love Looks Like* (Ventura, CA: Renew, 1999), p. 27, adapted. Used by permission of Regal Books, Ventura, CA.

5. Charles R. Swindoll, *The Finishing Touch* (Dallas: Word, Inc., 1994), p. 281, all caps changed to italics. Used by permission. All rights reserved.

6. Dr. Richard Matteson and Janis Long Harris, *What If I Married the Wrong Person?* (Minneapolis: Bethany House Publishers, 1997), pp. 236-38, adapted. Used by permission.

7. Cited in Fritz Ridenour, *The Marriage Collection* (Grand Rapids, MI: Zondervan Publishers, 1989), pp. 442-43, from *How to Start and Keep It Going* by Charlie and Martha Shedd, "Praying Together." *Marriage Collection* material used by permission of Zondervan Publishing House.

8. Matteson and Harris, *What If I Married,* pp. 240-43, adapted.

9. Charles Stanley, *The Source of My Strength* (Nashville: Thomas Nelson, 1994), p. 103.

10. Bill and Pam Farrel, *Love to Love You* (Eugene, OR: Harvest House, 1997), pp. 72-73. Used by permission.

11. Swindoll, *Finishing Touch,* pp. 58-59.

12. Taken from Kenneth S. Wuest, *The New Testament: An Expanded Translation,* 9th ed. (Grand Rapids, MI: William B. Eerdmans Publishing Co., 1997), 1 Corinthians 13:1-7,11-13.

13. Ronnie W. Floyd, *Choices* (Nashville: Broadman & Holman, 1994), pp. 112-14, adapted.

14. William Mitchell, *Winning in the Land of Giants* (Nashville: Thomas Nelson, 1995), pp. 27-28.

15. Stanley, *The Source,* pp. 163, 165.

16. Joe E. Brown, *Battle Fatigue* (Nashville: Broadman & Holman, 1995), pp. 14-15, adapted. Used by permission.

17. Swindoll, *Finishing Touch,* pp. 108-09, "all caps" changed to italics.

18. John F. MacArthur, *Drawing Near* (Wheaton, IL: Crossway Books, 1993), January 22, adapted. Used by permission.

19. David and Claudia Arp, *The Second Half of Marriage* (Grand Rapids, MI: Zondervan, 1996), pp. 104-06, adapted.

Pages 58–87

1. Les and Leslie Parrott, *Becoming Soul Mates* (Grand Rapids, MI: Zondervan, 1995), p. 25. Used by permission.

2. Wellington Boone, "Breaking Through, " in Nick Harrison, *Promises to Keep—Devotions for Men Seeking Integrity* (New York: Harper Collins, 1996), pp. 170-71, adapted.

3. David and Heather Kopp, *Praying the Bible for Your Marriage* (Colorado Springs, CO: Waterbrook Press, 1998), p. 101, adapted. Used by permission.

4. Joe B. Brown, *Battle Fatigue* (Nashville: Broadman & Holman, 1994), pp. 11-15, adapted. Used by permission.

5. Ibid., pp. 19-20.

6. Dennis and Ruth Gibson, *The Sandwich Years* (Grand Rapids, MI: Baker Book House, 1991), pp. 162-63.

7. Fawn Parish, *Honor—What Love Looks Like* (Ventura, CA: Renew, 1999), pp. 190-91. Used by permission of Regal Books, Ventura, CA.

8. Quoted in Charles Swindoll, *The Finishing Touch* (Nashville: Word, Inc., 1994), pp. 124-25. Used by permission. All rights reserved.

9. Quoted in Jon Johnston, *Walls or Bridges* (Grand Rapids, MI: Baker Book House, 1988), pp. 176-77, taken from W.T. Purkiser, "Five Ways to Have a Nervous Breakdown," *Herald of Holiness,* Oct. 9, 1974.

10. James Patterson and Peter Kim, *The Day America Told the Truth* (New York: Prentice Hall, 1991), pp. 45, 49, adapted.

11. Angela McCord, student paper, quoted in Parrott and Parrott, *Becoming Soul Mates,* pp. 36-37.

12. William L. Coleman, *Before I Give You Away* (Minneapolis: Bethany House Publishers, 1995), pp. 25-28.

13. Ken Gire, *Reflections on the Word* (Colorado Springs: Chariot Victor, 1998), pp. 138-39, adapted. Used by permission.

14. Tim Riter, *Deep Down* (Wheaton, IL: Tyndale House, 1995), p. 52, adapted. Used by permission.

15. Dr. Richard Matteson and Janis Long Harris, *What If I Married the Wrong Person?* (Minneapolis: Bethany House Publishers, 1997), pp. 178-79, italics in original. Used by permission.

16. Richard Swenson, *The Overload Syndrome* (Colorado Springs: NavPress, 1998), pp. 35-36.

17. Ibid., pp. 36-37.

18. Ibid., pp. 68-70.

19. C.S. Lewis, *The Problem of Pain* (London: Collins, 1962), p. 93.

20. Rudolph F. Norden, *Each Day with Jesus* (St. Louis: Concordia Publishing House, 1994), p. 304, adapted.

21. Parrott and Parrott, *Becoming Soul Mates*, p. 17.

22. Thomas F. Jones, *Sex and Love When You're Single Again* (Nashville: Thomas Nelson Publishers, 1990), pp. 93-96, adapted.

23. Taken from *Finding the Love of Your Life* by Dr. Neil Clark Warren, published by Focus on the Family. Copyright (c) 1992, Neil Clark Warren, pp. 81, 82. All rights reserved. International copyright secured. Used by permission.

24. Lloyd John Ogilvie, *Silent Strength* (Eugene, OR: Harvest House, 1990), p. 321, adapted. Used by permission.

Pages 88–116

1. Fawn Parish, *Honor—What Love Looks Like* (Ventura, CA: Renew, 1999), pp. 126-28. Used by permission of Regal Books, Ventura, CA.

2. Lee Roberts, *Praying God's Will for My Marriage* (Nashville: Thomas Nelson, 1994), pp. 1, 9, 19, 28, 102, 115, 227, 267.

3. Clifford Notarius and Howard Markman, *We Can Work It Out* (New York: G.P. Putnam's Sons, 1993), pp. 70-73, adapted.

4. Charles Swindoll, *Hope Again* (Dallas: Word, 1996), pp. 45-46, adapted. Used by permission. All rights reserved.

5. Tony and Lois Evans, *Seasons of Life* (Nashville: Word, 1998), p. 1, adapted. Used by permission. All rights reserved.

6. Charles Swindoll, *Moses* (Nashville: Word, 1999), p. 219. Used by permission. All rights reserved.

7. Joe B. Brown, *Battle Fatigue* (Nashville: Broadman & Holman, 1994), pp. 31-32, adapted. Used by permission.

8. Carol Kent, *Tame Your Fears* (Colorado Springs: Navpress, 1993), pp. 28-29.

9. Bill McCartney, ed., *What Makes a Man* (Colorado Springs: NavPress, 1992), adapted from an article by Steve Farrar, pp. 58-59. Used by permission of Steve Farrar.

10. Douglas E. Rosenau, *A Celebration of Sex* (Nashville: Thomas Nelson, 1994), p. 21.

11. William L. Coleman. *Before I Give You Away* (Minneapolis: Bethany House Publishers, 1995), pp. 19-21.

12. J. Oswald Sanders, as quoted in Les and Leslie Parrott, *Becoming Soul Mates* (Grand Rapids, MI: Zondervan, 1995), pp. 41-42. Used by permission.

13. Richard Exley, *Straight from the Heart for Couples* (Tulsa: Honor Books, 1993), pp. 21, 22, 57, 69, 72.

14. Max Lucado, *A Gentle Thunder* (Dallas: Word, Inc., 1995), pp. 68-69, adapted.

15. Tim Hansel, *When I Relax I Feel Guilty* (Elgin, IL: David C. Cook, 1979), pp. 146-47. Used by permission of author.

16. Lloyd John Ogilvie, *Enjoying God* (Dallas: Word, Inc, 1989), pp. 198-201, adapted.

17. Kent Hughes, *Disciplines of a Godly Man* (Wheaton, IL: Crossway, 1991), pp. 172-81, adapted. Used by permission of author.

18. Richard Swenson, *The Overload Syndrome* (Colorado Springs: NavPress, 1998), pp. 73, 88-89, adapted.

19. David Stoop, *Seeking God Together* (formerly *Experiencing God Together*) (Wheaton, IL: Tyndale House, 1996), pp. 11-12. Used by permission. All rights reserved.

20. Original source unknown.

21. Steve and Valerie Bell, *Made to Be Loved* (Chicago: Moody Press, 1999), pp. 53-55, adapted.
22. Ann McGee-Cooper, *You Don't Have to Come Home from Work Exhausted* (New York: Bantam Books, 1990), pp. 18-32, adapted.
23. David Morris, *Lifestyle of Worship* (Ventura, CA: Renew, 1998), pp. 18-19, adapted.

Pages 117–146

1. Dennis and Barbara Rainey, *Moments Together for Couples* (Ventura, CA: Regal Books, 1995), Dec. 4. Used by permission.
2. Fawn Parish, *Honor—What Love Looks Like* (Ventura, CA: Renew, 1999), pp. 45-46, adapted. Used by permission of Regal Books, Ventura, CA.
3. Gary Rosberg, *Guard Your Heart* (Sisters, OR: Multnomah, 1994), pp. 105-11, adapted.
4. Steve Farrar, *If I'm Not Tarzan and My Wife Isn't Jane, Then What Are We Doing in the Jungle?* (Portland, OR: Multnomah, 1991), pp. 193-94, adapted. Used by permission of Men's Leadership Ministries, Bryan, TX 77802.
5. Joe B. Brown, *Battle Fatigue* (Nashville: Broadman & Holman, 1994), p. 97. Used by permission.
6. David Stoop, *Seeking God Together* (formerly *Experiencing God Together*) (Wheaton, IL: Tyndale House, 1996), pp. 57-61. Used by permission. All rights reserved.
7. Ibid.
8. Phillip Keller, *Strength of Soul* (Grand Rapids, MI: Kregel Publications, 1993), pp. 172-77, adapted. Used by permission.
9. Ibid., pp. 178.
10. The Modern Language Bible, The New Berkeley Version in Modern English, revised edition, copyright 1969 by Henderson Publishers, Inc., Peabody, Massachusetts.
11. Lloyd John Ogilvie, *Silent Strength* (Eugene, OR: Harvest House, 1990), p. 233, adapted. Used by permission.
12. Henry Gariepy, *100 Portraits of Christ* (Wheaton, IL: Victor Books, 1987), pp. 95-96, adapted. Used by permission of author.
13. Ibid., p. 96.
14. Ogilvie, *Silent Strength*, p. 222.
15. Bill Bright, *God, Discover His Character* (Orlando: New Life Publishers, 1999), pp. 251-53, adapted.
16. Bob and Cheryl Moeller, *Marriage Minutes* (Chicago: Moody Press, 1998), Aug. 21, adapted.
17. Bright, *God,* pp. 190-191, 196, adapted.
18. Rainey and Rainey, *Moments Together,* Feb. 10, adapted.
19. Patrick Morley, *Two-Part Harmony* (Nashville: Thomas Nelson, 1994), pp. 60-61, adapted. (Republished by Zondervan as *Devotions for Couples.* Used by permission of Zondervan Publishing House.)
20. Ibid., pp. 62-63, adapted.
21. Keller, *Strength of Soul,* p. 29.
22. Kent Hughes, *Disciplines of Grace* (Wheaton, IL: Crossway, 1993), pp. 93-94. Used by permission of author.
23. S. Craig Glickman, *A Song for Lovers,* quoted in Ken Gire, *Reflections on the Word* (Colorado Springs: Chariot Victor, 1998), pp. 56-57.

Pages 147–175

1. David Keirsey and Marilyn Bates, *Please Understand Me* (Del Mar, CA: Prometheus Nemesis Books, 1978), p. 1.
2. Tony and Lois Evans, *Seasons of Life* (Nashville: Word, 1998), p. 52, adapted. Used by permission. All rights reserved.
3. Dennis and Ruth Gibson, *The Sandwich Years* (Grand Rapids, MI: Baker Book House, 1991), pp. 163-65, adapted.
4. Gibson, p. 153, adapted.
5. Gary Rosberg, *Guard Your Heart* (Sisters, OR: Multnomah, 1994), pp. 47-52, adapted.
6. Evans and Evans, *Seasons,* p. 260, adapted.

7. Charles Stanley, *The Source of My Strength* (Nashville: Thomas Nelson, 1994), pp. 97-99.

8. Evans and Evans, *Seasons*, p. 195, adapted.

9. Les and Leslie Parrott, *Becoming Soul Mates* (Grand Rapids, MI: Zondervan, 1995), p. 92. Used by permission.

10. Cotton Patch Version of Paul's Epistles by Clarence Jordan (1968). Brackets in original.

11. E. Stanley Jones, *Christian Maturity* (Nashville: Abingdon Press), adapted.

12. Henry Gariepy, *A Light in a Dark Place* (Wheaton, IL: Victor Books, 1995), pp. 72-73, adapted. Used by permission of author.

13. Bob and Cheryl Moeller, *Marriage Minutes* (Chicago: Moody Press, 1998), March 15, adapted.

14. Ibid., June 11, adapted.

15. Ibid., May 9, adapted.

16. Frederick Buechner, *The Magnificent Defeat*, as quoted in Ken Gire, *Reflections on the Word* (Colorado Springs, CO: Chariot Victor, 1998), pp. 98-99.

17. A.W. Tozer, *The Pursuit of God*, as quoted in Gire, *Reflections*, pp. 98-99.

18. Harold Myra, "An Ode to Marriage," *Moody* magazine, May 1979, pp. 60-62.

19. Ibid.

20. Taken from Charles M. Sell, *Transitions* (Chicago: Moody Press, 1985), p. xi. Used by permission.

21. Jim Smoke, *Facing 50* (Nashville: Thomas Nelson, 1994), pp. 40, 41. Used by permission.

22. Paul Pearsall, *The Ten Laws of Lasting Love* (New York: Simon & Schuster, 1993), pp. 298-99, adapted.

Pages 176–205

1. Taken from Gary Rosberg, *Guard Your Heart* (Sisters, OR: Multnomah, 1994), pp. 39, 40, adapted.

2. Ibid., pp. 24-27, adapted.

3. William Barclay, *A Barclay Prayer Book* (London: SCM Press Ltd., 1963), pp. 254-55, adapted.

4. David W. Smith, *Men Without Friends* (Nashville: Thomas Nelson, 1990), pp. 79-80, adapted.

5. Steve Farrar, *If I'm Not Tarzan and My Wife Isn't Jane, Then What Are We Doing in the Jungle?* (Portland, OR: Multnomah, 1991), pp. 65-66, adapted. Used by permission of author.

6. Walter Martin and Jill Martin Rische, *Through the Windows of Heaven* (Nashville: Broadman & Holman, 1999), p. 174, adapted.

7. Joseph Aldrich, *Secrets to Inner Beauty* (Santa Barbara, CA: Vision House, 1977), pp. 87-88.

8. Philip Yancey, *I Was Just Wondering* (Grand Rapids, MI: Eerdmans, 1989), pp. 174-75. Used by permission.

9. Charles Swindoll, *Hope Again* (Dallas: Word, 1996), pp. 99-100. Used by permission. All rights reserved.

10. Eric Liddell, *Disciplines of the Christian Life*, cited in Nick Harrison, *Promises to Keep—Devotions for Men Seeking Integrity* (New York: Harper Collins, 1996), pp. 317-18. *Disciplines of the Christian Life* used by permission of Abingdon Press, Nashville, TN.

11. Lloyd John Ogilvie, *The Loose Ends* (Dallas: Word, Inc., 1991), pp. 43-47, adapted.

12. Patrick Morley, *Two-Part Harmony* (Nashville: Thomas Nelson, 1994), pp. 146-47. (Republished by Zondervan as *Devotions for Couples*. Used by permission of Zondervan Publishing House.)

13. Twentieth Century New Testament (New York: Sheed and Ward, 1944).

14. G. Campbell Morgan, *The Ten Commandments* (New York: Revell, 1901), pp. 18-19.

15. Kent Hughes, *Disciplines of Grace* (Wheaton, IL: Crossway, 1993), pp. 34-39, adapted. Used by permission of author.

16. Ibid., pp. 98-104, adapted.

17. Ibid., pp. 116-20, adapted.

18. Douglas Rosenau, *A Celebration of Sex* (Nashville: Thomas Nelson, 1994), pp. 8-9.

19. James Patterson and Peter Kim, *The Day America Told the Truth* (New York: Prentice Hall, 1991), p. 155.

20. Hughes, *Disciplines of a Godly Man* (Wheaton, IL: Crossway, 1991), pp. 142-47, adapted. Used by permission of Crossway Books, a division of Good News Publishers, Wheaton, IL.
21. H. Norman Wright, *How to Encourage the Man in Your Life* (Nashville: Word, 1998), pp. 2-3. Used by permission. All rights reserved.
22. Bill Bright, *God, Discover His Character* (Orlando: New Life Publishers, 1999), p. 149, adapted.
23. Bob and Cheryl Moeller, *Marriage Minutes* (Chicago: Moody Press, 1998), Oct. 14-16, adapted.
24. Donald Harvey, *The Drifting Marriage* (Grand Rapids, MI: Revell, 1988), p. 213. Used by permission of Baker Book House.
25. Neil Clark Warren, *Finding the Love of Your Life*, p. 171. Copyright (c) 1992, Neil Clark Warren, Ph.D. All rights reserved. International copyright secured. Used by permission of Focus on the Family.
26. Taken from Charles R. Swindoll, *Growing Strong in the Seasons of Life,* (Grand Rapids, MI: Zondervan, 1983), pp. 66, 67. Used by permission.

Pages 206–235

1. Dennis and Barbara Rainey, *Moments Together for Couples* (Ventura, CA: Regal Books, 1995), Sep. 12. Used by permission.
2. Ken Gire, comp. and ed., *Between Heaven and Earth* (San Francisco: HarperCollins, 1997), pp. 10-15, adapted. Used by permission.
3. As quoted in Dean Merrill, *Wait Quietly* (Wheaton, IL: Tyndale, 1994), p. 63.
4. Ibid., pp. 62-63, adapted.
5. Taken from Charles Swindoll, *Growing Strong in the Seasons of Life* (Grand Rapids, MI: Zondervan, 1983) in Nick Harrison, *Promises to Keep—Devotions for Men Seeking Integrity* (New York: Harper Collins, 1996), pp. 55-57. Used by permission of Zondervan Publishing House.
6. Frank Minirth, "How to Beat Burnout" in ibid., pp. 130-31. Used by permission of Moody Press, Chicago, IL.
7. Patrick Morley, *Two-Part Harmony* (Nashville: Thomas Nelson, 1994), pp. 182-83. (Republished by Zondervan as *Devotions for Couples.* Used by permission of Zondervan Publishing House.)
8. William Barclay, *A Barclay Prayer Book* (London: SCM Press Ltd., 1963), pp. 248-49, adapted.
9. Chris Thurman, *If Christ Were Your Counselor* (Nashville: Thomas Nelson, 1993), p. 134.
10. Larry Crabb, *Men and Women* (Grand Rapids, MI: Zondervan, 1991), pp. 140-43, adapted. Used by permission.
11. Walter Martin and Jill Martin Rische, *Through the Windows of Heaven* (Nashville: Broadman & Holman, 1999), p. 174, adapted.
12. Shawn Craig, *Between Sundays* (West Monroe, LA: Howard Publishing, 1998), p. 263, adapted.
13. Tom Marshall, *Right Relationships* (Kent, England: Sovereign Word, 1992), pp. 28-29, adapted.
14. John Ortberg, *The Life You've Always Wanted* (Grand Rapids, MI: Zondervan, 1997), pp. 153-56, adapted. Used by permission.
15. New International Reader's Version (Confraternity of Christian Doctrine, 1970), as quoted in Les and Leslie Parrott, *Becoming Soul Mates* (Grand Rapids, MI: Zondervan, 1999), pp. 72, 73.
16. Ortberg, *The Life*, pp. 22-23, adapted.
17. The Good News Bible in Today's English version, 2d ed., Copyright 1992 by American Bible Society. Used by permission.
18. Taken from Harrison, *Promises to Keep,* pp. 266-67.
19. Charles Stanley, "A Man's Touch," in ibid., p. 225. Used by permission of Donald Black, In Touch Ministries, Atlanta, GA.
20. Tim Stafford, "Knowing the Face of God," in ibid., pp. 214-15, adapted.
21. S.D. Gordon, "Quiet Talks on Power," in ibid., pp. 183-84, adapted.

NOTES

22. Marshall, *Right Relationships*, pp. 52-54, adapted.
23. Ibid., pp. 34-39, adapted.
24. Crabb, *Men and Women*, pp. 45-46, adapted.
25. Walter Wangerin, Jr., "The Manger Is Empty" in Harrison, *Promises to Keep*, p. 362.
26. Rainey and Rainey, *Moments Together*, April 24, adapted.
27. John Mark Templeton, *Discovering the Laws of Life* (New York: Continuum, 1994) pp. 74, 75, adapted.

Pages 236–264

1. William Barclay, *One Prayer at a Time*, quoted in Ken Gire, *Reflections on the Word* (Colorado Springs: Chariot Victor, 1998), pp. 84-85, adapted.
2. Shawn Craig, *Between Sundays* (West Monroe, LA: Howard Publishing, 1998), p. 7, adapted.
3. Bill Bright, *God, Discover His Character* (Orlando: New Life Publishers, 1999), pp. 142-47, adapted.
4. Henri Nouwen, *Seeds of Hope*, Robert Durback, ed. (New York: Doubleday, 1997), original source not cited.
5. Richard A. Swenson, M.D., *Margin: How to Create the Emotional, Physical, and Time Reserves You Need* (Colorado Springs: NavPress, 1992), p. 147, adapted.
6. Ronald E. Hawkins, *Marital Intimacy* (Grand Rapids, MI: Baker Book House, 1991), pp. 135-37.
7. Ibid., pp. 35-36, adapted.
8. Dean Merrill, *Wait Quietly* (Wheaton, IL: Tyndale House, 1991), pp. 4-5.
9. Charles R. Swindoll, *The Finishing Touch* (Dallas: Word, Inc., 1994), pp. 60-61, adapted. Used by permission. All rights reserved.
10. William Barclay, *A Barclay Prayer Book* (London: SCM Press Ltd., 1963), pp. 28,29, adapted.
11. Charles Stanley, *The Source of My Strength* (Nashville: Thomas Nelson, 1994), pp. 182-83, adapted.
12. W. Bingham Hunter, *The God Who Hears* (Downer's Grove, IL: InterVarsity Press, 1986), pp. 18-29, adapted.
13. Tony and Lois Evans, *Seasons of Life* (Nashville: Word, 1998), p. 210, adapted. Used by permission. All rights reserved.
14. Hunter, *The God Who Hears*, pp. 76-80, adapted.
15. Evans and Evans, *Seasons*, p. 123, adapted.
16. Ibid., p. 128, adapted.
17. Jim Ryun, "In Quest of God," in Nick Harrison, *Promises to Keep—Devotions for Men Seeking Integrity* (New York: Harper Collins, 1996), pp. 174-75.
18. Eric Liddell, *Disciplines of the Christian Life*, taken from ibid., pp. 181-82. *Disciplines of the Christian Life* used by permission of Abingdon Press, Nashville, TN.
19. Taken from Harrison, *Promises*, pp. 122-24.
20. Fred Littauer, "Wake Up, Men!" taken from ibid., pp. 25-26.

Pages 265–294

1. William Kirk Kilpatrick, *Psychological Seduction*, quoted in Nick Harrison, *Promises to Keep—Devotions for Men Seeking Integrity* (New York: Harper Collins, 1996).
2. Henry Gariepy, *100 Portraits of Christ* (Wheaton, IL: SP Publications, 1987), pp. 78-79. Used by permission of author.
3. As quoted in Dean Merrill, *Wait Quietly* (Wheaton, IL: Tyndale, 1994), p. 49.
4. Willard Harley, *His Needs, Her Needs*, quoted in Harrison, *Promises*, pp. 40-41.
5. Ann McGee-Cooper with Duane Trammell, *Time Management for Unmanageable People* (New York: Bantam Books, 1993), p. xvii, adapted.
6. Alec Mackenzie, *The Time Trap* (New York: American Management Association, 1990), p. 65, adapted.
7. David and Heather Kopp, *Praying the Bible for Your Marriage* (Colorado Springs: Waterbrook Press, 1998), pp. 52-53. Used by permission. All rights reserved.

361

8. Webster's II New Riverside Dictionary, 2d ed. (Boston: Houghton Mifflin, 1996), s.v. "failure."

9. Basic Bible Translation (F.P. Dutton Co., Inc., 1950), developed by G.K. Ogden of the Orthological Institute, England.

10. Shawn Craig, *Between Sundays* (West Monroe, LA: Howard Publishing, 1998), p. 37, adapted.

11. Tony and Lois Evans, *Seasons of Life* (Nashville: Word, 1998), p. 156, adapted. Used by permission. All rights reserved.

12. Archibald Hart, *Healing for Hidden Addictions*, taken from Harrison, *Promises*, pp. 153-54, adapted.

13. Ron Auch, *The Heart of the King*, taken from ibid., pp. 149-50.

14. Fred Hartley, *Men and Marriage* (Minneapolis: Bethany House, 1994), taken from ibid., pp. 100-01. Used by permission of Bethany House.

15. Dino Kartsonakis, *Dino*, taken from ibid., p. 73.

16. Gary Rosberg, *Guard Your Heart* (Portland, OR: Multnomah, 1994), pp. 15-17, adapted.

17. Merrill, *Wait Quietly*, pp. 100-01, adapted.

18. Ibid., pp. 8-9, adapted.

19. Ibid., pp. 16-18.

20. Ibid., pp. 78-80, adapted.

21. Kopp and Kopp, *Praying the Bible*, p. 27.

22. Charles Swindoll, *The Finishing Touch* (Dallas: Word, Inc., 1994), pp. 64-65, adapted. Used by permission. All rights reserved.

23. Elton Trueblood, as quoted in ibid., p. 65.

Pages 295–323

1. Bill Farrel, *Let Her Know You Love Her* (Eugene, OR: Harvest House, 1998), pp. 9-11. Used by permission.

2. Jonathan Edwards in Nick Harrison, *Promises to Keep—Devotions for Men Seeking Integrity* (New York: HarperCollins, 1996), pp. 14-15.

3. John Baillie, *A Diary of Private Prayer* (Toronto: Oxford University Press, 1979), p. 47, adapted.

4. Patrick Morley, *Seven Seasons of a Man's Life* (Nashville: Thomas Nelson, 1990), pp. 90-91, adapted.

5. Don Aslett, *How to Have a 48-Hour Day* (Cincinnati: Marsh Creek Press, 1996), p. 39, adapted.

6. John C. Maxwell, *Developing the Leader Within You* (Nashville: Thomas Nelson, 1993), p. 32, adapted.

7. H. Norman Wright, *Secrets of a Lasting Marriage* (Ventura, CA: Regal Books, 1995), p. 87, adapted.

8. Charles Stanley, *The Source of My Strength* (Nashville: Thomas Nelson, 1994), pp. 128-29, adapted.

9. Steve and Valerie Bell, *Made to Be Loved* (Chicago: Moody Press, 1999), pp. 128-29, adapted.

10. Paul Stephens, *Marriage Spirituality* (Downer's Grove, IL: InterVarsity Press, 1989), p. 50, adapted.

11. Bill Bright, *God, Discover His Character* (Orlando: New Life Publishers, 1999), pp. 128-29, adapted.

12. David and Heather Kopp, *Unquenchable Love* (Eugene, OR: Harvest House, 1999), pp. 111-12. Used by permission.

13. Ibid., pp. 130-31.

14. Tony Evans in Tony and Lois Evans, *Seasons of Life* (Nashville: Word, 1998), p. 20. Used by permission. All rights reserved.

15. Max Lucado in Harrison, *Promises*, pp. 2-3.

16. Charles Swindoll, *The Finishing Touch* (Nashville: Word, Inc., 1994), p. 69, adapted. Used by permission. All rights reserved.

NOTES

17. David and Heather Kopp, *Praying the Bible for Your Marriage* (Colorado Springs: Waterbrook Press, 1998), pp. 8-9. Used by permission. All rights reserved.

18. Dean Merrill, *Wait Quietly* (Wheaton, IL: Tyndale House, 1991), pp. 186-87, adapted.

19. Roberta Bondi, *To Pray and Love* (Minneapolis: Augsburg Fortress, 1991), pp. 54-55, as found in Ken Gire, *Between Heaven and Earth* (San Francisco: HarperCollins, 1997), pp. 11-12.

20. Lloyd John Ogilvie, *Silent Strength* (Eugene, OR: Harvest House, 1990), pp. 345-46, adapted. Used by permission.

21. Evans and Evans, *Seasons*, p. 84, adapted.

22. Merrill, *Wait*, pp. 111-13, adapted.

23. Ibid., pp. 192-94.

24. Farrel, *Let Her Know*, pp. 26-27

Pages 324–353

1. Lloyd John Ogilvie, *The Heart of God* (Ventura, CA: Regal Books, 1994), pp. 240-43, adapted.

2. Douglas Rosenau, *A Celebration of Sex* (Nashville: Thomas Nelson, 1994), pp. 26-27.

3. Robert Hicks, *In Search of Wisdom* (Colorado Springs: NavPress, 1995), pp. 45-54, adapted.

4. C.S. Lewis, *The Problem with Pain* (New York: Macmillan, 1962), p. 30, as quoted in John Ortberg, *The Life You've Always Wanted* (Grand Rapids, MI: Zondervan, 1997), p. 139.

5. This entire devotion is based on John Ortberg, *The Life You've Always Wanted* (Grand Rapids, MI: Zondervan, 1997), pp. 139-43, adapted. Used by permission.

6. Ruth Sender, "I Don't Believe in Prayer If..." *Campus Life* magazine, Carol Stream, IL: Christianity Today, 1995, as quoted in Ken Gire, *Between Heaven and Earth* (San Francisco: HarperCollins, 1997), pp. 18-19.

7. Ibid., pp. 19-20.

8. Ronald E. Hawkins, *Marital Intimacy* (Grand Rapids, MI: Baker Book House, 1991), pp. 14, 15, adapted. Used by permission.

9. Tony and Lois Evans, *Seasons of Life* (Nashville: Word, 1998), p. 42. Used by permission. All rights reserved.

10. David and Heather Kopp, *Praying the Bible for Your Marriage* (Colorado Springs: Waterbrook Press, 1998), pp. 31-32, adapted. Used by permission. All rights reserved.

11. Evans and Evans, *Seasons*, p. 54.

12. Ronald Knox (New York: Sheed and Ward, Inc., 1944).

13. Evans and Evans, *Seasons*, p. 61, adapted.

14. As quoted in John Ortberg, *The Life You've Always Wanted*, (Grand Rapids, MI: Zondervan, 1997), p. 65. Used by permission.

15 Shawn Craig, *Beyond Sundays* (West Monroe, LA: Howard Publishing, 1998), p. 38, adapted.

16. John Mark Templeton, *Discovering the Laws of Life* (New York: Continuum, 1994), pp. 247-48, adapted.

17. Patrick Morley, *Two-Part Harmony* (Nashville: Thomas Nelson, 1994), pp. 24-25. (Republished by Zondervan as *Devotions for Couples*. Used by permission of Zondervan Publishing House.)

18. W.P. Moody, *The Life of Dwight L. Moody* (Westwood: Barbour & Co., 1985), p. 122.

19. Patrick Morley, *Seven Seasons of a Man's Life* (Nashville: Thomas Nelson, 1990), pp. 274-75, adapted.

20. Steve Brown, *Jumping Hurdles, Hitting Glitches and Overcoming Setbacks*, quoted in Harrison, *Promises*, pp. 403-04.

21. Henry Gariepy, *Light in a Dark Place* (Wheaton, IL: Victor, 1995), pp. 250-51, adapted. Used by permission of author.

22. William Barclay, *A Barclay Prayer Book* (London: SCM Press Ltd., 1963), pp. 8-9.

23. Ronnie W. Floyd, *Choices* (Nashville: Broadman and Holman, 1994), pp. 38-41, adapted.

24. Used by permission of John C. Bonser, Florissant, Missouri.

Other Good
Harvest House Reading

Quiet Times for Couples
by *H. Norman Wright*

This classic bestseller has helped hundreds of thousands of couples develop healthy, lifelong marriages. Designed to stimulate open communication, *Quiet Times for Couples* helps you and your spouse share your deepest thoughts and feelings so you can experience the joys of having a growing, vital relationship.

Quiet Times for Parents
by *H. Norman Wright*

Whether your children are just born or have moved out on their own, *Quiet Times for Parents* was written for you. Through one-page devotions and quotations, you will find encouragement, inspiration, and suggestions for raising children in the Lord.

Winning Over Your Emotions
by *H. Norman Wright*

In today's fast-paced world, everyone struggles with worry, anxiety, anger, and stress. But these emotions don't have to defeat or overwhelm you! Through practical suggestions and step-by-step guidance, Christian counselor Norm Wright helps you break free of worry and transform stress into positive action.

Creative Romance
by *Doug Fields*

From dinner at a classy restaurant to an at-home outdoor theater night, Doug Fields reveals fun, flirtatious, fabulous ways you can tell your spouse that romance is still alive and well in your heart. Packed with zany and lighthearted ideas, *Creative Romance* provides just the right touch of humor, sensitivity, and thoughtfulness for many memorable times together.

The Power of a Praying Parent
by *Stormie Omartian*

In 30 short, uplifting chapters, Stormie shares how you can pray through the stages of your child's life—including safety, friends, and hunger for God—and release every detail of parenting into God's loving and capable hands.